Naked at Gender Gap

Naked at Gender Gap

A Man's View of the War Between the Sexes

Asa Baber

A Birch Lane Press Book
Published by Carol Publishing Group

A Birch Lane Press Book
Published by Carol Publishing Group
Birch Lane Press is a registered trademark of Carol
    Communications, Inc.

Editorial Offices: 600 Madison Avenue, New York, N.Y. 10022
Sales & Distribution Offices: 120 Enterprise Avenue, Secaucus,
    N.J. 07094

In Canada: Canadian Manda Group, P.O. Box 920, Station U,
    Toronto, Ontario M8Z 5P9

Queries regarding rights and permissions should be addressed to
Carol Publishing Group, 600 Madison Avenue, New York, N.Y. 10022

Carol Publishing Group books are available at special discounts
for bulk purchases, for sales promotions, fund raising, or
educational purposes. Special editions can be created to specifications.
For details, contact: Special Sales Department, Carol Publishing
Group, 120 Enterprise Avenue, Secaucus, N.J. 07094

Manufactured in the United States of America
10 9 8 7 6 5 4 3 2 1

Library of Congress Cataloging-in-Publication Data

Baber, Asa.
    Naked at gender gap : a man's view of the war between the sexes /
by Asa Baber.
        p. cm.
    "A Birch Lane Press Book."
    ISBN 1–55972–114–6
    1. Men—Psychology. 2. Masculinity (Psychology) 3. Sex role.
    I. Title.
    BF692.5.B35 1992
    155.6'32—dc20
                                                        92–9355
                                                         CIP

To Jim and Brendan

Contents

Part Two: Men and Women

Acknowledgments⎯⎯⎯⎯⎯⎯⎯⎯

Special thanks to Sherri Stubbs for her love and laughter, to Jonathan Black for his editing and advice, to all my new Warrior brothers, to Marci Enos for her wisdom and support, and to the many kind people at *Playboy*—especially Walter Lowe, Barbara Wellis, Harriet Pease, and the folks in the mail room (the late Carl Grant, Jr., included). My literary agent, Candice Fuhrman, and my editor for this book, Gail Kinn, have my deepest gratitude.

Gender Gap: The territory where we all live in a naked and vulnerable condition. The male and the female of the species are situated on separate sides of Gender Gap, each man and each woman yearning to close the distance between the sexes.

None of us is sure of how to do that.

Life at Gender Gap is hard for men and hard for women. As much as we might wish for it, there is no escape. Its landscape stretches to infinity. It is a place of great temperature extremes where the wind doesn't blow, it sucks.

Here's hoping we learn how to live together in Gender Gap with more tolerance and respect for one another.

*Walking Point*_____

Cut to a fall day in Chicago, 1981:

Bigfoot strolls into my office at *Playboy.* He puts his big foot up on my desk and looks at me for a minute. "Ace," he says, "why don't you write a 'Men' column for this magazine?"

"Okay," I say.

"You find the voice for it. You find the subjects. Let the 'Men' column speak about what men are going through today."

"Okay," I say.

That is about it. Bigfoot and I do not talk a lot. It is not our style. A proposal for a "Men" column has been made, and now it is up to me to deliver. I begin to write, and now, more than ten years later, I am still at it.

Bigfoot is also known as Arthur Kretchmer. For the past twenty years Arthur has been the editorial director of *Playboy* magazine. Giving me first crack at the "Men" column was Arthur's idea, and standing by me, as opposition to the column reached a very high level of intensity, was also his idea. So before I say anything else, I want to express my gratitude to Arthur for his editorial guidance and protection. Arthur is, quite simply, the finest editor I have ever worked with.

The "Men" column grew out of an article I published in *Playboy* in

1978. It was titled "Who Gets Screwed in a Divorce? I Do!" and it talked about men and masculinity in a new way.

In it I described the problems men encounter during and after the process of divorce. I examined how self-destructive and despairing men can become when their marriages fall apart and they lose custody of their children. I talked about the vulnerability of the male psyche in a system that seemed to be prejudiced against men. I went on to ask a fundamental question that was not being asked much in print in 1978: "How can we find identity and pride and self-worth as men?" That simple but revolutionary question was really the foundation for the "Men" column.

"*Men* must begin making a case for themselves," I wrote in 1978. "Manhood is an honorable condition. It seems clear that men need help today in perceiving themselves as men, and such help can come only from themselves."

Toward the end of that article, I wrote about some of the finer aspects of manhood, aspects that a man going through the agony of a divorce might want to remember from time to time. I outlined certain male qualities that are not always appreciated in this strange age—qualities such as courage, generosity, sensitivity, intellect, wit and humor. I encouraged us, as men, to focus on the gifts that we bring the world, and to remember them when we are in trouble. "Men have a job to do redefining our roles and reaching out for health and identity," I said.

Arthur Kretchmer responded very positively to that article. He called me one evening at home as the December issue was hitting the newsstands in the late fall of 1978. "You're onto something in that divorce article, Ace," Arthur said to me. "I don't know what it is exactly, but we should think about it."

We thought about it. We exchanged ideas and traded a few memos for a couple of years, and then we made the leap. It was quite a gamble, but I took it without hesitation.

Back in 1981 there were no role models for a "Men" column. Writing about sexual politics from a male point of view was simply not done. While the publishing industry was ignoring men's issues, it was making billions of dollars from books glorifying feminism. The feminist writing of those turbulent years offered no guidelines for me for conducting a meaningful discussion of gender issues. Generally speaking, feminist rhetoric of that era was poisonous, humorless and blind. I did not want my work to follow that example.

Arthur's offer was both an opportunity and a challenge. The challenge required me to write something original which also gave me the opportunity of falling flat on my face in front of millions of readers.

I wonder if Arthur knew back then how tough the road ahead was going to be for the "Men" column. Did he know that for many years I would be writing what I called "postcards from Siberia?" That I would become a cultural exile because of my point of view? Did he know that I would be under fire from both men and women? Did he know that just about everyone at *Playboy* would be howling for my scalp? If Arthur knew all of this before I started writing the column, I'm going to fine him for damages. A big bill, itemized. Because I soon thought of myself as a man walking point on patrol in dangerous territory.

The first "Men" column was called "Role Models." It was published in April, 1982. It is a piece about the men who served as mentors for me in my younger years, men as diverse as a college English professor, a Marine Corps drill instructor and a boxing coach at a summer camp. Even more importantly, it discusses how we learn to be men as we grow into manhood.

"Role Models" suggests that men learn how to be men by imitation, that this universal male need to imitate the men we admire is a simple and primitive transaction, as basic to us as breathing. While growing up, we watch our elders carefully—first and foremost, our fathers and the other men in our lives.

When a young man grows up without valid mentors, when he is deserted and misled and abandoned, he is then placed in a terrible psychological limbo. He is basically left without definition as a man. He remains uninitiated, uninformed, and lost in confusion, sometimes for his entire life. He also remains angry and embittered, feeling that he has been cheated by the men he depended on.

One would think that such a column as "Role Models" would have been a welcome addition to the gender debate and to the pages of the magazine. The column was moderate in tone, it focused on the weighty problems of male identity and did not take on feminist issues. It stated simple (and not so simple) truths about masculinity.

The reception "Role Models" received at *Playboy* was chilling. The first "Men" column was mocked and resented by most of the editors and staff at the magazine, as were the subsequent "Men" columns over the next couple of years.

This chilling effect was brought home to me at that time when a young new editorial assistant, who had eagerly agreed to have lunch with me, cancelled our appointment within twenty-four hours. She cut off communications with me entirely. Just like that.

After a meeting in 1984 of the entire *Playboy* editorial staff, I was told by another editor friend: "Ace, I'm not supposed to tell you this but I think you should know. Most of the magazine staff wants you fired. The women really hate the 'Men' column, and a lot of the men agree with them. At one point, Arthur stopped the discussion and said, 'You're asking me to fire Asa?' and most of the people in the room said 'Yes!'"

What saved the "Men" column? Two things: (1) the stubbornness and courage of Arthur Kretchmer, who felt that the column met a real need and was therefore willing to ride out the firestorm, and (2) the endorsement of the "Men" column by many of the *Playboy* readers. Talk about the democracy of the marketplace! The mail, the calls, and the feedback from the readers in favor of the column have saved it from extinction.

Even at that disastrous meeting in 1984 it was reported that the column was getting good mail. Today, the mail is even better, often surpassing other sections including the centerfold! It turns out that the old joke, "I just buy *Playboy* for the articles," has some truth to it.

Over the years, though, the climate at the magazine has definitely warmed to the "Men" column. It is now received with tolerance and humor and enthusiasm in most quarters.

That's the real lowdown. I have had a great time and have learned a few things about the power of sexual politics. I also had the opportunity to write early on about the gender gap that exists between men and women. I was able to explain some things to myself and to my readers. And I even got paid for it!

The "Men" columns that follow represent one man's search through the mine field of our current cultural debate as it relates to gender issues. Some of them are serious, some are humorous, and all of them were written in the hope that they would enlighten and encourage us. They are no longer postcards from Siberia but rather postcards from home.

So here they are. From me to you.

Enjoy.

Part One————————————————————

MEN

Still Counting _____

This all began with Epictetus. That probably sounds fancy, but it's the truth. The year was 1977, and I was sitting in a farmhouse in central Illinois. It was snowing, many days and nights of snow, huge drifts, no communication with the outside world, telephone lines down, roads closed.

I felt like a stranded astronaut. It was not a good feeling for me, because I did not like facing myself. I was not proud of my life. I was particularly worried about my two sons, children I'd lost in a truncated custody case. The snow paralyzed me, cut off my chances to lose myself in busywork and be blind to my own weaknesses and failure. I couldn't call people or fix a fence or drive to town for coffee.

So I read whatever I could get my hands on, and as the wind roared and the house rattled and the fire glowed in the wood stove, I came across some lines from a Stoic philosopher that changed my life.

"There is only one thing I can say to you," wrote Epictetus, "that the man who does not know who he is, and what he was born for, and what sort of world this is that he exists in...and is unable to follow either reason or demonstration, or what is true and what is false, and cannot distinguish one from the other—such a man, to sum it all up, will go about deaf and blind, thinking that he is somebody when he

3

really is nobody.... And do you think that this is something new? Has it not been true from the time when the human race began, that every mistake and every misfortune has been due to this kind of ignorance?"

I copied those words on a card and pinned it above my desk. They summarized the major questions of my life. Who was I? A father? How could I be a father when my children did not live with me? A husband? I had failed in one marriage and could easily see how my second marriage might collapse, too. A fighter? Too much of one; I'd been raised with aggression as my middle name and it didn't fit in polite society, not the form I knew. A lover? Too much of one; like so many men's, my sexuality was sometimes enormous, and when it was in full force, I had a hard time following either the reason or the demonstration recommended by Epictetus.

I was suffering, in short, from a lack of identity. But that was not the only point. What I saw that winter night was that I was not alone.

What I saw was that many men were undergoing the same things I was. Male identity was becoming more difficult to define for all of us. The culture in which we lived was not necessarily friendly to men. It was neither supportive nor respectful. Indeed, the feminist revolution was moving into a rather mean place, self-indulgent, hypercritical, propagandistic. That revolution captured a large body of thought, and it was affecting almost everyone I knew, male and female alike.

What sort of world did we men exist in? It was a question we never asked one another and rarely asked ourselves. We put our heads in the snow and hoped the storm would pass. It didn't.

In the winter of 1977, I decided to commit myself to writing about the American male. *Playboy* gave me room to do that. I wrote an article called "*Who Gets Screwed in a Divorce? I Do!*" In it, I quoted Epictetus. I talked frankly about the challenges and difficulties for the male in divorce court. I quoted studies that showed that men had incredible problems after divorce. And I closed the article not with a detraction of manhood but with a discussion of its virtues. I suggested that men had sensitivity, generosity, courage, intellect, wit and humor. And I went on to argue that divorce was not the end of the world, that it could even be a good thing, for the divorced male was not likely to romanticize women or be a fool about them.

I still get mail asking for reprints of that article, and the questions raised in it seemed to strike a familiar chord in many men. It was clear to me that the spirit of Epictetus moved in us and that we had many questions about ourselves, especially in this age of feminism. I tried to address those issues in both my fiction and my nonfiction over the next years.

Then, in April 1982 I published my first "Men" column. It was called "Role Models." More than anything else, it was a tribute to the late Sergeant Danny Gross, my Marine Corps drill instructor, a man who taught me things that later saved my life. My thesis in that column was that men learn how to be men by imitating other men, that good role models are vital to us if we are to grow up with a strong sense of self. That led to a succession of columns that will continue, I hope, as long as it seems to be working well.

I had two goals when I started: (1) to keep the admonition of Epictetus in mind at all times and (2) to approach the subject of manhood differently from the way that feminists dealt with womanhood.

As I read their work, the feminists attacked men much more than they examined themselves. And when they did look at themselves, it seemed to me that their focus was a soft and self-deceptive one.

I thought that men could do better than that, and so some of my columns were tough on the male animal. I wanted to discuss our tendencies toward aggression—why were we trained that way? What did it to do us? And our fight against emasculation—how did the modern world and the modern woman threaten us, and how could we overcome those threats? And our struggles to love—why were we so often seen as unloving when that was not the case, and how could we learn to communicate better with the people we loved?

I'd give myself about a B plus. Some people would say that's incredibly generous of me—to which I would say that it's taken a long time for this male to learn to be generous to himself, so get off my case.

(1986)

Tomorrow's Headlines Today!_____

Extra! Extra! Read all about it! Your *Playboy* "Men" columnist has seen the future. It came to him in a dream. There they were, in bold letters—the newspaper headlines of the future! Guys, you probably won't believe me when I tell you what they are and summarize the stories behind them. But great happiness is ahead for us, incredible bliss, unbounded joy!

The following are the most significant headlines I saw in my clairvoyant dream. Read 'em and smile:

"OPRAH MARRIES THE DICEMAN!!!" (December 12, 1991). Wow, what a scoop! In a small wedding in a chapel in the moonlight in Nevada, Oprah Winfrey and Andrew Dice Clay were married by the Reverend Roone Arledge. "I was attracted to Dicey-poo's emotional honesty," Winfrey said after the wedding vows. "You know, in my own way, I am as much of a sexist as he is. I'm just more slick about it," she continued. According to the article, The Diceman was not available for comment. He was puking his guts out in the parking lot after imbibing too much cake and champagne.

"NOW DISBANDS, ADMITS THAT MEN ARE THE SUPERIOR SEX AND WOMEN ARE HOPELESS SLUTS" (March 6, 1992). "We renounce feminism and all its pomp," chanted 3,000 women in unison at the

6

latest National Organization for Women convention. *"Playgirl, Playgirl,* all we read is *Playgirl,"* they sang while clapping their hands and whistling at the men in the visitors' gallery. "Hunks, hunks!" they yelled.

A NOW spokesperson said the organization is officially disbanding. "We were wrong and we know it," she said. "Men are goddamn jewels, aren't they? Makes my thighs tingle thinking about it. Our new slogan? *Penis power in perpetuity!"*

"STARTING TODAY, SELECTIVE SERVICE APPLIES ONLY TO WOMEN" (June 19, 1994). In a startling reversal of legal and historical precedent, the all-female Supreme Court reversed the methods and goals of the Selective Service System and military draft obligations. As of today, men are absolved from military duty (unless they choose to volunteer), whereas young women are required to register with the Federal Government at the age of 18. If women do not fulfill this requirement, they will be subject to a fine and imprisonment. Chief Justice Sofia Coppola commented after the decision, "For centuries, only men have been subjected to such a deadly and controlling situation as the military draft. Now it's our turn in the barrel. I mean, if women want equal rights, how about our accepting equal responsibilities, too?"

"WOODY ALLEN RECANTS ALL HIS MOVIES AT HIS BAPTISM" (August 8, 1995). In a touching baptismal ceremony in a river in the hills of Kentucky, the Reverend Jimmy Swaggart held Woody Allen under water for ten minutes and then pronounced him spiritually reborn. When he revived, Allen was grateful. "I've lived my life assuming I should be punished, waiting to be punished, almost hoping for it, really," he said through his oxygen mask, "and now I've learned my lesson. I will never make another movie that stars me as a wimpy little whiner whom all women secretly yearn to cuddle. That's an obnoxious image of the American male that mocks masculinity, and I am through with that kind of pro-feminist propaganda."

"PHIL DONAHUE ADMITS HE WANTS MEN TO LIKE HIM, TOO" (September 8, 1997). "OK," Donahue said on his television show today, "I confess: I did drive male bashing into the ground, along with all the other talk-show hosts for the past twenty years. But I didn't know you guys would ever tune in and find out what the girls and I have been saying about you schmucks. Now that I know some of you men watch my show, I'm going to be the best damned Uncle Phil you ever had. I promise that from now on, some of the guys I choose as my guests will be literate, rational and capable of logical thought. Not many, but some. Why, I wouldn't ever stack the deck against men on my show, would I? Hey, I'm one of you. Now that it pays, that is."

"MEN AWARDED CHILD CUSTODY AS FREQUENTLY AS WOMEN" (October 23, 1999). A new statistical study of contested child-custody cases shows that for the first time in history, fathers are being awarded custody of their children as frequently as mothers after a divorce. Dr. Willard Scott, executive director of The Bureau of Weather and Statistics, put it this way: "I think the antimale sexism that clearly existed in the divorce system is finally coming to an end. What a revolution! It used to be that the father was considered an unnecessary appendage to the family structure. Why, we even had an epidemic of unmarried women choosing to have children without fathers, as if the father were an obstruction to a child's development. But not anymore. Men are back as vigorous role models and strong father figures!" Dr. Scott spoke from the front porch of his home in Puerto Rico. He looked darling in a bright floral-print dress and a Carmen Miranda bonnet of fresh fruit and flowers.

"MALE CIRCUMCISION OUTLAWED IN ALL HOSPITALS" (January 1, 2001). This New Year's Day sees the start of the 21st century—and the cessation of the painful practice of penis pinching that has been used on most male babies at birth. "We did computer studies that deciphered what the baby boys were *really* saying as their little weenies were cut," Dr. George Gallup V said, "and you never heard such foul language from infants in your life! 'Let go my joy toy, you dickhead' was the most common reaction from just-born males. 'If this is sex, then fuck it' was the second most common reaction. Those kids are doing more than crying, let me tell you. They are trying to tell us something!"

If I see any more headlines, I'll let you know. Good news travels fast, but this is ridiculous!

(1991)

*Calling All Blysters*_____

When Bill Moyers interviewed Robert Bly on PBS a few years ago, no one expected the public reaction that followed. Bly's artful use of image and myth (as well as his perceptions about the contemporary American male and what ails him) traveled like wildfire into a certain segment of this culture's consciousness.

It is not that Bly's words were totally original. Other men and women had been writing about Jungian thought and archetypes for years—specifically, Robert Moore and his colleague, Douglas Gillette, had been mapping much of the territory that Bly commandeered—but Bly got the national coverage. He had the easily accessible image of the grandfather-guru as well as a certain aptitude for self-promotion. He avoided certain controversies while appearing to be controversial, and he brought a sense of style and grace to his message that no one else could match.

Above all else, Bly was polite and nonconfrontational on the subject of feminism and feminists. He usually praised women, even those women who were bashing the very men he was talking to, and his language (for example, his use of the term "male mother" to describe the nurturing man) was conciliatory in the extreme. That approach was one of the reasons he was so marketable.

The thorny issues of sexual politics—Who gets the job? Who goes to war? What happens to fathers and kids in a divorce? What is sexual harassment and who will be fired for it?—did not concern Bly. He was, he and his loyal acolytes have always insisted, doing much more fundamental work than that. He was saving souls and psyches.

(The deadly tinge of intellectual snobbery floats like a ghost around Bly's poetic musings, and he and his mesmerized followers often seem to present themselves as an intellectually privileged elite. This elitism could be their undoing, especially in the general population of men. We are not crazy about snobs.)

Iron John, Bly's best-selling book, set the publishing industry on its ear. For 25 years, the publishers of America turned out books that basically praised women and bashed men. Now, suddenly, here was a book that examined men from a masculine perspective, and it sold big-time. Even the most feminist of editors and publishers took notice of that. *Iron John* broke the publishing logjam that blocked men from being able to find male-friendly literature. That will eventually be seen as Bly's greatest contribution to our era.

But it is now time to send a challenge to the Blysters, as I call those more rabid followers of Robert Bly who seem totally entranced with him and his approach to men's work. Many are steadfastly ignoring some of the tougher obligations of manhood. So to those Blysters I say: I honor your work, but let's get on with it, gentlemen. There are boys and men who could use your help but will never feel comfortable with your exotic rituals and Jungian vocabulary. Please reach out to more men and make yourselves available for a greater variety of work.

For example, here are some practical things you might consider doing:

- *Join and support a father's rights/divorce reform group.* At the present time, the father in America is an expendable item. The father is excluded on questions of abortion, ignored during a child's younger years, exiled to a noncustodial role in case of divorce, and classified as either evil or clumsy in most of the media. If this treatment of fathers continues, we are doomed as a culture. The fatherless family is *not* the ideal family. It is not just economics that is destroying the family; it is politics as well. If you won't organize and vote and campaign for honorable fatherhood, what will you fight for?

- *Choose to mentor one or more fatherless boys in your neighborhood.* There are organizations like the Boy Scouts and Big Brothers that do this kind of work. Join them as a financial and spiritual supporter. Give of your time and your money. And if that kind of organized effort does not appeal to you, do your own private thing. Look around you. See all those boys without fathers in their homes? Take a kid to lunch, take him to the ball game, teach him how to hit a baseball or cast a fishing line or shoot a basketball. Remember your days of loneliness as a boy? Remember wondering why few older men seemed to take an interest in you or your growth? We can change that sense of isolation so many boys have. We can change that today.

If you have the money and the time, allow yourself to experience the great variety of men's work that now exists in this culture, but do not stop there. Over the past few years, and without great fanfare or public recognition, many different kinds of men's weekends and seminars and retreats have sprung up. You can learn tracking in the desert or whitewater rafting in the canyon or meditation in a monastery. You can examine your relationships with women or your struggles with your father or your fears for your children. You can go through a process of male initiation that brings you some sense of what the tribal male receives from his elders. All of this work is useful and valid. But it usually costs money and is not available to the majority of men. So please come back from those experiences with a willingness to confront the real world and its tough questions about gender and politics.

I am not suggesting that Robert Bly and the Blysters are irrelevant or unimportant. But as I have watched the Bly phenomenon develop, I have been very much aware that Bly's need to be liked by women, not to offend them, means that once again the American male is being led into a state of political passivity. And you know and I know that the man who is primarily passive is a dangerous man. Better that he should speak his anger when politically abused than to ignore it and suppress it while he chokes on it.

Come back, Blysters. We need you.

(1992)

My Day With Hans and Franz_____

I could not believe my luck. There they were, pumping iron as I walked into the weight room for my workout—Hans and Franz, the heroes of *Saturday Night Live*.

"Wow!" I said. "Hans and Franz! Good to meet you guys. I'm Asa Baber."

"Go away, girly-man," they said sharply. Hans was spotting Franz on the bench press.

"Me? A girly-man?" I asked. "Hey, I write the 'Men' column for *Playboy*. You can't get any more macho than that."

"Go away, girly-man, before we hurt you bad and hurt you worse," Hans said.

"*Ja*," Franz said, grunting hard, "go away, girly-curly-man, before we rip out your inner vitals and make them your outer vitals in a furious instant."

"What's going on here?" I asked. "You guys sent me some fan mail not long ago. You said you liked my 'Men' column. Why this sudden change in attitude?"

"I have never known such a girly-whirly-man as you," Hans said. "Hear me now and hear me later and remember from your past that you have heard me now in case you forget to hear me later."

"*Ja!*" Franz said.

"Because you are not doing your job as the 'Men' columnist, girly-man. You are letting real men like us be given stinky bad names. Suddenly, all these girly-man reporters are saying there is no men's movement. They are trashing us!"

"*Ja!*" Franz said, "you have really let us down, schnitzel face. Where are your muscles? Where is your manly power?"

Hans shook his head. "Just after we got used to the feminists insulting us, the media send *girly-men* after us! It stinks like a barrel of rotten herring!"

"It sucks the sausage," Franz said.

"Franz and I, we are doing all the right things," said Hans. "We are reading *Iron John* and going to a new warrior weekend and buying a drum."

"A big drum that only real men can carry," Franz said, "weighing many kilos."

"And we are running around naked in the woods at night."

"In the snow and the cold with our enormous pretzels slowly turning blue."

"And now we are reading other men saying that it is wrong to do those things, that we are fools and stupid dunces."

"Sorry about that," I said, "but this backlash had to happen. Why are you so surprised by it?"

Hans held up the October issue of *Esquire.* "Hear me now and hear me later, girly-'Men' columnist. There is an article by a girly-man in this *Esquire* magazine that makes fun of the new warrior training you wrote about in *Playboy.*"

"*Ja,*" Franz said, "*Esquire* is showing us no respect here. They are making us look like wimpy noodles and puny pancakes."

"So, what else is new?" I asked.

Hans and Franz looked shocked, absolutely shocked. "What?" they asked.

"It's par for the course," I said. "*Esquire* hires a so-called journalist to go to a new warrior weekend without revealing that he's on assignment. The reporter signs a pledge promising that he will not reveal what goes on. He refuses to participate fully in the weekend, but he watches other men do their work. Then he breaks his word and writes a cynical article and makes money off the venture. It's just another day in Mediaville."

"He is paid by *Esquire* to laugh at the men he went through the training with?" Franz said. "What kind of a schnitzel would do a thing like that?"

"'Journalistic ethics' is often a contradiction in terms," I said, laughing.

"But it should not be like this," Franz said. "We must punish him, *ja*? We must teach that *Esquire* girly-man a lesson."

"It's a free country," I said. "He can write whatever he wants to write, even if he was a little shit in the way he went about it."

"We must stop these men!" Hans said. He was holding this issue of *Playboy* and pointing at the "Media" column by my colleague Stephen Randall. "Look, another traitor! He calls our work 'a movement with virtually no followers.' I will take care of this Stevie-Weevie-Randall-man."

"Look," I said, "you can't go around bullying reporters whenever they piss you off, Hans."

"We can do anything we want!" Franz said. "With our biceps and triceps and quads, the world is at our command." He flexed and got red in the face.

"Great thinking—for Nazis, that is," I said.

"You call us Nazis?" Franz asked with a glower. "Why?"

"Because of your dumb ideas," I said. "Hear me now and hear me later, Hans and Franz. We've just been through twenty-five years of feminists saying that they had the only politically correct answers to everything. As men, are we going to follow their act? Are we that weak?"

"I don't want other men making fun of me!" Hans cried. "I can't stand it!"

"Hans," I said, "some men are *always* going to make fun of you. And me. And all the guys who do any of this work. We're talking about basic male identity here. It's a touchy subject. So let's just do our work and shut up. No new orthodoxies, no new gurus. Just good work.

"I have many muscles!" Hans bellowed.

"Yeah, great," I said.

"No one can mock my huge and manly muscles! I am invincible!"

"You guys may pump a lot of iron," I said, "but think about my situation, would you? I have had to carry people like Steevie-Weevie-

Randall-man around for years. And most of the feminists in America. They are always taking potshots at me. Now *that's* heavy."

"*Mein Führer!*" Hans and Franz cried as they unrolled a poster of Robert Bly. "We worship you! And our great male god, Iron John! *Sieg Heil!*" they shouted.

I took off for a sauna and steam. Later, as I left the club, I could hear Hans and Franz singing *Robert, Robert, Über Alles* in the weight room.

Some guys never learn.

(1992)

The Chickenshit Factor _____

Gentlemen, some women would pay a lot to learn the secret that I am going to reveal about us in this column. So let's agree to keep it confidential—just between us chickens, you might say.

You know our secret. As men, we wrestle with the perpetual fear of being rejected by women. For most men, being snubbed by women is a major nightmare.

I call this fearful male attitude the Chickenshit Factor, and I happen to own my fair share of it. It lies like a sleeping terrorist at the center of my male heart, and it can kick into action at any moment— especially when I see a woman I would like to meet and date. I am usually very shy and awkward then. Indeed, I usually feel like a fool. And I am not proud of that.

I can hear you howling. "Why are you telling women the truth about us, Baber? Go back to the party line. You know the drill: 'As men, we are not chickenshit. We are not shy or bumbling or afraid to meet women. We are red-blooded, all-American studs, each and every one of us.'"

OK, Macho Man, I often make the same claims of boldness and I often swagger to hide my fear. As I said, I can cluck with the best of them. But this, too, is true: I frequently stand tongue-tied and frozen

16

in embarrassment before a woman who appeals to me, and, yes, those are definitely chicken feathers you then see growing out of my shoulder blades. The Chickenshit Factor has dominated my life, and the women who entice me also tend to paralyze me. Isn't that true for you, too?

Let me ask you another question, Macho Man: In the past few weeks, has there not been a female to whom you failed to introduce yourself because you chickened out? Was there not at least one woman who passed through your life (no matter how fleetingly) who fascinated you, excited you—but who also mesmerized you, stunned you and left you speechless?

You yearned to talk to her, to let her know that your little chicken heart was going pumpety-pump and your little chicken brain felt like lightning had ripped it apart, but nothing happened. You said nary an intelligible word, you sat on your thumbs—excuse me, your chicken claws—and your quarry faded into the mist of another lost opportunity in the barnyard of sexuality: At that moment, the *Chickenshit Factor struck again!*

Take heart. This is not just your imagination. You're not a congenital wimp. Because, while meeting and greeting the women who intrigue us can be hell, the social conventions of our society still demand that we, as men, initiate the overtures. It is not an equal burden, it is not fair to us as men, but that is the way it is.

Given this, I've come up with some specific strategies to counter the Chickenshit Factor when it kicks loose in our hearts. I list these suggestions here to help us break away from the shyness that binds us as men, a shyness that may occasionally seem charming to others but that often leaves us with a sense of frustration and impotence.

1. *Remember that she is probably just as lonely as you are.* It is called the human condition. The lives of both men and women are not easy or simple, and a certain kind of loneliness seems to be a constant in all human hearts. Do not assume that anyone is totally unapproachable. What you see is often *not* what you get. She may seem aloof, but you will never know her true status until you ask her.

2. *Stop griping, start acting.* Sure, you've been rejected about 6,000 times and it hurts. Sure, you're tired of the social rule that mandates that you, as the male, are the one who is obliged to run the first risk of rejection. And, sure, some women can be vicious in their put-downs of men who attempt to talk to them. But so what? You've

got work to do, Macho Man, if you're going to meet the women who appeal to you. You know the rules. Now play according to them. That is how men handle life.

3. *You are not as lecherous as she may make you feel.* The subject of lechery in this puritanical society is a complicated one, but suffice it to say that your attempt to meet a woman who is attractive to you is not a sin. As a man, your motives for socializing will often be questioned, and it might be claimed that there will always be a tinge of the sexual about them. Guess what? Your sexuality is no crime. You are reacting as a man to the presence of a woman who interests you. But here's a news flash: You were programmed to respond sexually. It's called nature, and a lot of people have tried to legislate against it. To put their efforts into historical perspective, they might as well legislate against glaciers and gravity. Sex is here to stay. Let's hope somebody tells the puritans someday.

4. *At all times, take no for an answer.* This has got to be your one unbreakable rule. After you have conquered the Chickenshit Factor, and after you have made your move, if she says no to your introduction, she means *no*. Do not debate, do not hang around, do not harass. Make yourself scarce and live to fight another day. And please understand that I do not say this simply out of a misguided sense of chivalry. Because the fact is that if you set limits on yourself, if you put a governor on how much flirtation you will attempt and how much rejection you will absorb, your shyness will gradually fade and the simple act of meeting a woman will become much easier. Your self-limitation will provide you with self-protection, and difficult moments will lessen in number. If you honor her turndown, you will have continued to play by the rules. Once again, that is what men do. And, believe it or not, she will respect you as a man for your self-control.

So remember: The Chickenshit Factor can reign in our hearts and minds. It can oppress us and concern us. But not always, not necessarily and, I hope, not now.

(1991)

*The 10,000-Pound Hat*_____

It happened one evening in November, 1989. I was sitting in the Grand Ballroom of the Chicago Hilton Hotel on Michigan Avenue, attending a dinner. The food was excellent, the company grand, and I even managed to be sociable, not always an easy task for me. But I was engaged in more than small talk. Something private and very powerful was taking place: Although he had died in 1960, my father's presence surrounded me there in that ballroom that evening. It was as if he were there in person.

The fact that I was sitting in the Chicago Hilton had a lot to do with it: Jim Baber, a small-town boy from Paris, Illinois, was an employee of that very hotel back in the Thirties. It was known as The Stevens then. My dad began work as a mailboy there when he was 20 years old, a college dropout whose father and mother had almost been ruined in the Great Depression. My dad worked very hard at The Stevens and eventually rose to the position of assistant manager. He met celebrities, calmed angry hotel guests, coordinated security. He also helped supervise banquets in the Grand Ballroom on occasion.

It was strange for me to be sitting there in a room that had been so familiar to my father. It was also enlightening. For the first time in my life, and through a process of ghostly osmosis, I was gaining a clearer understanding of who my father had been before I knew him.

That evening, I could envision him as a young man at his best—handsome, lively, dapper, full of fun, primed for risk and reward. I saw him as energetic and refreshed as he stood there under the stylish arch of the entryway, dressed in black tie and tails, hair slicked back, smoking his perpetual cigarette, the proximate image of Humphrey Bogart, a charming rogue of enormous potential whose laughter was so wired and vibrant that it made other people amused just by the sound of it. I saw him sneaking a glass of champagne, eying a beautiful woman in red, pouring some wine for a guest, charting the ebb and flow of the banquet hall.

In my mind's eye, I smiled at my father and toasted him. He smiled and raised his glass to me. I was thinking that it was an honor to have this eerie glimpse of him in his springtime. And I was saddened that he had not been able to hold on to that lively, happy side of himself in the years I spent with him. My father's days at The Stevens, I suddenly knew, were the last truly happy days of his life, his final liberated season in the sun without the burdensome weight of family and children.

On that evening last November, I understood that once I was born, something deadly happened to Jim Baber: He became overwhelmed with his new responsibilities as father and breadwinner, and the prospect of supporting a family frightened him so much that he tried to rein in his happier and more audacious instincts. He attempted to sit on his massive energy and smother it, to suppress his grandest dreams. He tried to make himself into a harmless drudge.

It didn't work, of course. He became angry with his choices and, eventually, he imploded. Beautiful man that he was in his youth, he exiled himself into passive captivity—only to be crushed by the rage he felt at the weight of that decision.

And it was all symbolized in his hat.

Ah, yes, his hat. It was a battered fedora, cheaply made, brown, stained with house paint and cigarette burns, the front brim turned up, sweat marks on the band. Whenever my father came home from work (he left the hotel business in the late Thirties and went through several phases of employment), he would take off his suit, climb into his work clothes and put on his hat.

With a fatigued sigh, he would then turn to the unending domestic chores at hand. Angry, trapped, resentful, my father sweat and slaved, but he also often punished me for the frustrations he felt. His work literally never stopped, and neither did his temper tantrums. He walked on the razor's edge of violence, and when he slipped, I sometimes bled.

In the earliest picture I have of the two of us together, my father is wearing his hat (and smoking a cigarette) as he stares at the camera. We are in a park somewhere in Illinois. He holds me by my hands as I, probably two years old, stand at his feet and squint toward the camera. Even in this early picture, my father's face is tired and he slouches. His hat weighs on him.

As I study that photo today, I want to rip his hat off his head. I want him to be unencumbered, to sail like an eagle, explore, take chances, live. I want him out from under the weight of that hat, no matter what the risks.

You cannot believe how much I still want today for my long-dead father. If I could control time, I would have him come back to me. I would give him a chance to live a more complete life, and I would show him how to do that. I would make him stop smoking. I would take him to the club for a workout. I would tell him that he had to allow his male energy a lot of room in which to flourish. I would tell him that even as a child, I wanted him to be true to himself, to set an example for me, to live vigorously and not passively, to love me and not resent me.

"Look, old man," I would say to him, "you are my father. I love you and I always will. I want you to be free and fulfilled. I want you to read and write and whistle and tinker and love and laugh. I am not here to weigh you down. I'm here for you to enjoy. Let's celebrate who we are. Let's party and roar and argue and wrestle and laugh. Let's be men together. That's all I ever wanted from you. We will romp with my two wonderful sons, your grandsons, young men you've never met. The four of us will have a ball. Come on, Dad, how about it?"

And sometime during his first evening back with us, after I have given him a good hug, I will snatch my father's hat from his head and toss it into the fireplace. As he and I and my sons watch it burn, we will sit, arm in arm, around the fire. Then, at our own pace, in our own seasons, we will tell jokes and stories and histories and lies. Forever, I hope.

(1989)

*The Roots of Aggression, Part One*_____

One of my earliest childhood memories is of boxing with my father. I was about five years old when we started doing that. I remember that the gloves were brown and smelled like new leather. They were too large for my hands, and they were hot and heavy to tote around the living room. "Come on, Ace," my father would say as we circled each other. Jab, jab, jab, light punches into my face, nose-stinging, scary. There was no way I could reach him, but I tried. "That-a-boy, come on."

Understand that I loved my father and I honor him. But that image of the two of us sparring fits our history perfectly. In my heart, I am sure my father wanted to be my friend, but the role he assigned himself was that of master. Because I was the boy of the house, he often unleashed his aggression and anger directly at me, achieving obedience, yes, and possibly easing the frustration he felt from his failing career. But he set a way of being that was damaging to me. The first lesson I learned was that to be male, you must be angry. The second was that my fellow males were as likely to hurt me as they were to help me.

I wasn't alone in receiving those messages. At home, my childhood colleagues and I were whipped and spanked and hit, and then we went out into the street to do the same to one another. Fighting was a male rite of passage. Like all rites, it set a tone and left scars.

When I was eight, a kid named Jamie Hodkins used to beat the shit out of me every day before school. Jamie smelled like a garbage can and lived in a tenement. He was a couple of years older than me and seemed huge. I tried running and ducking, I tried hiding. I tried every dodge I could think of, but Jamie always caught me before I could get to the school door.

I took about a week of that crap. Then, on a morning I still clearly remember, something in me snapped. I didn't know it at the time, but what was breaking inside me was my last hope for innocence. Jamie had me pinned to the playground and was doing a tattoo on my face. The other kids were cheering the morning's entertainment. The teachers were looking the other way. "I don't like this," I told myself, "and if I don't do something about it, I'm going to end up with a busted skull."

That was the morning I discovered that I have very quick hands and no physical fear in certain situations. I rose up and smote Jamie with a number of well-placed punches. The sight of his nose splashed all over his face was not peaceful or wonderful to me, but better his nose than mine, I decided. And to keep the momentum, I turned the tables and ambushed him every day of the following week as he went to school. I even enjoyed my new status as bully. I hadn't yet learned that those whom the gods of aggression will destroy they first make victorious.

I can chart my youth in the Forties and Fifties by referring to specific fights. The culture itself reinforced the idea that aggression was OK. Movies and television taught me that you could kill Indians, Germans, Japanese and anybody else you defined as bad guys, and that was perfectly all right. As a matter of fact, it was rewarded.

Dying seemed to be mostly a male preoccupation. Friends of mine died in the street, in the military, in prison. "Live fast, die young and have a good-looking corpse!" Willard Motley wrote. Most of us bought that concept, not because we weren't inwardly frightened but because we wanted approval. Aggression begat approval, especially from the men on whom we modeled ourselves.

I am saying that the male world is a unique world. The male

consciousness is exposed to excessive violence as it is forming, and it is no accident that most men can give you a list of rumbles, collisions and punishments from their youth that they remember vividly to this day. Aggression is drilled into us. In most cases, it is the *only* consistent standard of behavior held up to us as acceptable. At home, in school, in sports, in the culture, we learn that if we don't stay aggressive, terrible things may happen to us. Aggression is made central to our lives, and I submit that—whether tapped or not—it runs through us like a river. We spend much of each day trying to determine when to use it, when to react to it, when to control it.

So what's the problem?

It depends on whom you talk with, I guess, but I see major complications: (1) I believe that continuous aggression is taught to us, that it is not natural; (2) the river that runs through us wears on us and destroys us prematurely; (3) aggression as a pattern of behavior is essentially a loser's pattern, not a winner's (and, as a corollary to that, men who buy aggression as the way to function are buying the scam of the century).

I grew up in the house of a man who was extremely aggressive. A handsome man, always well groomed, graceful and compact, my father could lose his sense of humanity in a flash. Yet his anger never served him well. It hurt him with his family and it hurt him at work. His aggressiveness destroyed him. And still he held it out as one of the only things he could teach me. Much to my sorrow, I learned his lesson well, and controlling my temper has always been one of my basic struggles. I believe I have many brothers in that inherited struggle. It is primarily male. But I maintain that the river that runs through us men is channeled there; it is not solely born in us.

Women, for example, handle aggression much differently from men, and for my money, they handle it better. Why is that? Because they are raised in another world and the signals they receive about aggression and anger are completely different from the ones we receive.

That's what I want to talk about next: anger and aggression as learned emotions. And the fact that what is learned can be unlearned if we're willing to think clearly.

Those of us caught in aggression's trap can use our wits and our intelligence to get out of it, and we would be wise to be about it.

(1984)

Ball-Bustin' Blues, Part One____

One evening last spring, I arrived home to find a concerned younger son. "I got called down to the lobby this afternoon," Brendan said. "There was a man there. He showed me his I.D. and gave me this paper to give to you. He didn't say much. What's going on, Dad?"

What had been delivered was a notice from the Internal Revenue Service. I laughed at first. It seemed the IRS could always find me when it wanted to.

"They think we owe them money," I explained, "but we don't agree."

"So what's going to happen?"

"Well, I don't know," I said. "We send them information. They never respond. Sometimes, we send the same stuff five or six times. They ignore us. Now they show up at the door, like the police."

"Will you pay them?"

"Not until we get it straightened out," I said. Little did I know how soon I would eat those words.

"Was that guy a sheriff?"

"No," I said, "he was an IRS agent."

"Weird."

25

"Very," I said. And it was. My wife and I had written to and called the IRS on numerous occasions. We had sent information, copies of correspondence and tax returns, queries, all to no avail. The situation was right out of Kafka. There was no particular person in charge of our case, no appointments could be made, the IRS lost almost everything except the checks we sent and now had shown up at our front door. How do you explain that form of Government to a 14-year-old?

Worse, how do you explain what happened next? In a very few weeks—and in spite of the fact that we had promptly replied to the summons—there was a call from an officer at our bank. "The IRS is going to take what it thinks it's owed out of your account," he said. "We'll try to wait a week. See what you can do."

We called and wrote to the IRS again. Again, no response. And, sure enough, the IRS raided our account the next week, took what it thought it was owed and continued to ignore any questions or proof we had that it owed us a similar sum.

"What's the difference between that and robbery?" Brendan asked.

I did not have an immediate or witty answer. But I recognized the empty, angry feelings I was having. They were similar to the emotions I had experienced in 1972 when a judge ordered that I could not visit my home or my children when I was going through a divorce. I felt emasculated, disenfranchised, helpless, impotent (though the IRS action was far less painful than the loss of child custody). I came to the conclusion that I lived in a totalitarian superstate that could take what it wanted from me at will, without fair proceedings.

The trouble is that men are raised on the wrong images, images of independence and freedom and self-determination: the lone sheriff in the Western movie who sticks to his guns and cleans up the town, the brave soldier who takes matters into his own hands and wins the battle, the graceful athlete who scores the winning goal. The male as proud, independent protector; that's the diet on which most of us are raised.

It turns out, of course, that our diet is poisonous to us. The images we carry with us have placed us in direct conflict with our bureaucratic, technocratic society. The male's pipe dream that he should be provider and protector is frequently obliterated by the superstate. Face it: Shane can't ride out of town until he has paid his taxes, and Superman can't go faster than a speeding bullet without permission from the EPA. Big Brother has grown into Big Father, and the superstate has taken over most of the functions that men were raised to believe were their responsibility. As a result, we see our ideal selves disappearing before our very eyes—and, as with my involuntary surrender to the IRS, before the eyes of our families.

None of this is to say that women have it easy. But I think that men are raised with more rigid role models, more heroic standards, and the transition into life in the superstate is probably a longer and more painful journey for us.

"The great majority of men were, and still are, educated according to codes which are almost impossible to put into practice in our society," writes Karl Bednarik in his book *The Male in Crisis*. "Our world does not want the rebellious man who thinks and acts for himself at any risk. Even though it may officially proclaim the opposite for the sake of public relations, the workaday world actually wants the adjustable, adaptable man who can take orders and carry them out. . . . The old male role . . . is diminished; indeed, it seems to have become completely obsolete, with nothing new to take its place and furnish a guiding code of the same reliability and self-certainty. We have no serviceable, universally recognized image for the passive man. We have no image for the man in retreat . . . for the man who is expected to display the one characteristic most contrary to his nature: submission."

I don't know about you, but to me, Bednarik seems right on target when he writes about the male problem. "The majority of men suffer from a central disturbance in their masculine life," he writes. And I agree. The cause of that disturbance? In major part, the loss of power and control over our lives, lives truncated by the superstate.

Is there a way out of the prison in which we men are trapped? I think so. I'm working on it, and I'll try to share what I'm learning. It involves a revolution in male thought. I think we all have to go through that revolution if we are to survive.

Tune in next month.

Oh, yes, I almost forgot: What odds will you give me on my getting audited by the IRS again?

(1983)

Ball-Bustin' Blues, Part Two

We were living in Honolulu, near Kahala Beach, in 1972. The marriage was in final convulsion. Life in paradise had not been able to cover up the enormous fault line running down the center of our relationship. It was a mess, and as discontent rumbled through the house, I knew nothing was going to put Humpty Dumpty together again.

We were two adults who had made a bad choice; by that time, I didn't care. We could go our separate ways. But about the two children of that marriage, I cared desperately. I was a creature common on the American scene: a cavalier husband who was nevertheless a good father.

I knew two contradictory things: (1) If I didn't get out of the marriage, I would lose all sense of self-respect; (2) if I did get out of the marriage, I would be ordered to give up custody of the two people in the world most important to me.

When my two sons were born, some three years apart, I was there. I held them early and I held them often. I spent a lot of time with them and loved it: and, yes, I gave up some career possibilities, but I gained much more. We wrestled just about every day. We joked and laughed. I got to know them and they got to know me. I set limits; they challenged them. I was tough with them when I had to be, but because we had built a web of mutual trust, I don't believe there was ever a time when my sternness was taken as rejection. I don't say I was (or am) the perfect father; I'm just saying that I gave fatherhood my best shot, gave more to it than to anything else in my life. What I was doing, though I probably would not have called it this at the time, was learning to love. It's safe to say that not until I became a father did I know the meaning of love. And it is precisely that—learning to love—that is the revolution in male thought to which I referred in my September column.

In case you haven't noticed, divorce as a system is skewed against fathers. They don't usually get custody of their kids (this may be changing gradually, but back in 1972, it almost never happened). I was no exception to the rule, and as the divorce came down, I experienced an emasculation that is hard to describe. I was barred from my home, limited in contact with my children, stripped of finances, portrayed as unworthy and dispensable.

Nothing in my training had prepared me for that disaster. The images on which I had been raised were typically male—images from the street, the boxing ring, boot camp, sports, movies. I had been raised to win—or to die trying. Yet there I was, in pain, confused, losing that which I held most dear.

Frankly, I was in mourning. Yes, men do mourn, though they may not show it often. Our grief is subterranean, like a fire in a peat bog that burns deeply and springs out in surprising places. I was in mourning not for the marriage but for the truncated chance at fatherhood.

I feared for my sons. What role models would they have? Would they accept the image of the father as a throwaway item? Would they come to see themselves as equally dispensable? I feared for myself. How could I rebuild a sense of self-worth after the trauma of divorce?

I am convinced that those days will always stand in my mind as the darkest time of my life. I think a lot of men know what I'm talking about. In divorce the superstate comes in and socks it to men, both fathers and sons. They are almost always split apart, and it is my belief that until that splitting stops—until same-sex custody is more seriously considered and more frequently awarded—we will have no chance for a truly healthy society. If you banish good role models and ignore the struggle to establish personal and sexual identity, what you decree is what you'll get: generations of lost sons and disappearing fathers.

In the months right after the divorce, before my sons were to move away from Hawaii, I set my face like a bulldog's and held to one idea: that love could not be neutralized by a person or a power. I can't tell you how hard it was for me to believe that sometimes.

I took my kids to the beach, to the zoo, to concerts in the park, and I died inside. It was painful in the extreme to be with them, knowing that soon I would be able to see them only a few days a year. Their confusion was evident, too, and I knew that they had their own kind of pain to deal with: Why had I left them if I loved them? Were the things they were hearing about me true? Were fathers unfaithful by definition?

"In the midst of winter, I finally learned that there was in me an invincible summer," Camus wrote. Slowly, I learned what he meant. I refused to be a nonperson, and I stayed in touch with my sons through thick and thin after they were moved away from me, even when it seemed that the pressure on them to forget me was tremendous. I paid more than my share of child support, saw them whenever possible, called them to joke and kid and talk. I let them know I loved them.

Humor kept us in contact more than anything else, I think. Male humor. Vaudeville, bawdy, noisy, cornball, the kind so often seen as immature. "What's new?" I'd always ask first whenever I called. "New York, New Jersey, New Hampshire," they would Groucho Marx back; and then one of them would say "Rhode Island" or something like that, and I'd ask, "What's new about Rhode Island?" and they'd yell back in unison, "Not a damn thing." We thought that was funny for years. I was, simply, myself—a man—with them. They understood what I was doing, and they had the guts to love me for it.

Something happens to young men about the age of 12. If their fathers have kept the lines of communication open, there comes a time when that relationship can no longer be broken, when the search for identity is paramount and growth cannot be stopped. It was at that age that both of my sons came to live with me. We had to check one another out. It was as simple as that.

I call it the Zen of manhood, this revolution I'm talking about. We men find ourselves by losing ourselves. As our needy egos are broken, so can they be more solidly restructured. As we learn to love, we turn into more worthy role models and better companions.

To put it bluntly, one of these days, I think the superstate is going to learn not to fuck with the father-son relationship. There's something too vital there.

It is a day most men wish for mightily.

(1983)

*Real Men Don't Eat Credit*_____

This is my lucky day. I've just received a letter from Citibank in Sioux Falls, South Dakota. I hadn't realized I was so well known in South Dakota, but evidently James L. Bailey has heard of me. He wants me to apply for the Citibank Preferred VISA Card. As a senior vice-president of Citibank, Bailey is offering me an initial $5,000 line of credit that is expandable to $50,000. He writes that this offer is "for a very select group of people. People like you, who handle credit very responsibly and will find its unique advantages most useful."

Isn't that something? And I didn't even have to ask for an introduction!

Could I use $50,000? Absolutely. I've always wanted to take my family to France, for example: cruise the canals in a fancy barge, visit the wine country, stay near the Champs E´lyse´es in Paris, travel to Arles and Van Gogh country, lie on the nude beaches of the Riviera. Sure, I could use $50,000. It would last me several months on a family vacation. Or a week if I went alone.

Am I going to snort the Citibank line of credit? No, I'm not. Why not? Well, for one thing, if I piled all the credit I've been offered into one sum, it would come to more than I'll make in a lifetime. I'm distinctly uncomfortable with that.

For another, we're a society of credit junkies, myself included, and I want to withdraw from the drug before it's too late. As a nation and as individuals, we're in debt up to our noses. Credit is the cocaine of this culture, the artificial stimulant that flutters the heart and brightens the brain—but at what expense? We double our national deficit in a few years, expand consumer debt, put the nation into hock, and toward what end? Nobody seems to be asking that question today. But that doesn't mean it shouldn't be asked.

If I were allowed only one piece of advice for my own kids, it would take me no time at all to decide what it would be. "Cover your debts as soon as you can," I would tell them. "Don't get so deeply in debt that somebody else owns you."

Yes, that's stodgy advice from a cantankerous man, but chances are it will sound pretty good in a few years. And I know this: (1) There is something very unmanly about being deeply in debt; (2) the financial gurus may lead you to think that the cocaine of credit is the only way to fly, but *every* economy crashes from time to time, and when this one bottoms out, indebtedness will be a disastrous place to inhabit. Better to practice controlled withdrawal now than to have to go cold turkey without warning.

The link between economic structures and masculinity is central to our lives. It is emasculating in the extreme to be owned by someone else, whether it is a person or an institution. Live by the loan, die by the loan call? How many men are truly comfortable with that?

I can't prove it, but I maintain that we men have certain ideas ingrained in our collective consciousness. It is not generally acknowledged these days, but we really are very fine people in our deepest selves. Concepts of loyalty, community, stability, humor, self-discipline and health are central to our makeup. I do not claim that we always live up to this sense of manhood, but it is embedded in us. The fact that we are led away from it does not mean it has disappeared.

Genetic truth, you might call it. You can measure our tension by the degree to which we depart from it. We may pretend that it's easy to do away with genetic truth, but that is not the case. We are deeply scarred when we violate our sense of manhood. Snorting too much credit cuts close to the male heart, because in losing our financial independence, we lose an important part of ourselves.

I come by my cantankerousness naturally. I'm the descendant of a long line of farmers, generations of people from Kentucky and Indiana and Illinois. I'm the first male in my family to get a college degree. My forebears were tough people who mistrusted high finance and fancy arguments for indebtedness. When the Great Depression arrived, my grandfather had already been battling bankruptcy for several years. The farmers of America got caught early in the Depression's squeeze. They were hurting in the Twenties. The bankers with the big cigars didn't get trounced until the Thirties.

If that pattern sounds familiar, it should. The same thing is happening to America's farmers today, but the illusion being offered us is that our current agricultural difficulties won't drag the rest of the economy down. I'm no expert, but the bet in this corner is that history is going to repeat itself and that the times ahead are going to be rocky, indeed.

I'm writing this in the summer of 1986. Anything can happen, of course. We are faced with the prospect of an economic sea change. What's next? Inflation or depression? How will it reveal itself, this new trend? Will gold take off or crash? Will interest rates continue to decline? Place your bets, ladies and gentlemen; place your bets.

By the time you read this, the Dow may bet at 3000 and the boom may be on again. If so, more power to it; but you'll find me working hard to get out of as much debt as possible. Because as I see it, this economy—and the banking system that fuels it and underlies it—is a house of cards. I don't trust the system or the people running it.

Take a look around. We live in a culture that punishes savings and rewards indebtedness. Tax structures have prodded people into taking on maximum debt to receive maximum tax write-offs. Credit is held out to consumers and advertised on TV and sent through the mails and called in over the phone. I once had a banker tell me I was a disloyal American because I wouldn't take the loan he offered me. "You're not playing the game," he said in a bewildered voice.

That's right. I'm not playing the game. Not the one where they have the ball and the bat and the gloves and the diamond—and if I sign my life away, I get to play, too. For a while.

It's time to hunker down and hang tough and be a man. "Man" as in "solvent," that is.

(1986)

The Roots of Aggression, Part Two ——————————————

"The colonel wants the shields off, Lieutenant," Gunny Door yelled to me from the fire-direction center. It was almost dusk. I was standing in a ravine in the Mojave desert, trying to line up eight 105 howitzers in the proper firing direction. "We've got to strip 'em. The colonel wants them ready for chopper transport." The gunny looked at me with his chiseled face and crooked grin. His eyes glinted the way they always did when he heard an order that he thought was crazy.

Gunnery Sergeant Door had been in the Marine Corps for almost thirty years. From the things he had told me after I gained his confidence, he had encountered some strange commanding officers in his time. But the gentleman who ran the battalion now seemed especially aggressive. The colonel had taken command with an efficiency that bordered on vengeance, and although he was not an artillery officer, he had proceeded to revamp our procedures in the field and in garrison. I am sure he thought he was putting the stamp of leadership on his troops. The gunny and I thought he didn't know what he was doing.

It is never really peacetime in the artillery because you are always firing live ammunition. Hanging around high explosives has a way of focusing your energies on the job at hand, and the idea that we were being ordered to cut safety put me in a strange position. Taking the protective shields off a howitzer exposed the gun crew to much more danger.

"What's he up to, Gunny?" I asked. "There's not a chopper near here." This was in the early Sixties and we were moving howitzers by trucks, not helicopters. "We've had some bad ammo. If we get a muzzle burst and we don't have our shields, we lose some people."

A lot of thoughts went through my mind. I was a young man in conflict, no question about that. Not too long before, I had been as aggressive and mean and as tough as anybody I worked with. But I was going through a quantum change in my thinking about life and manhood. Originally gung ho, I now found myself trying to save lives, not take them. I had become a very independent Marine, indeed. Caution, stealth, safety, a cold look at the odds in each situation, a refusal to do anything blindly, life, not death, as a goal—those had become my methods.

Two things had happened to me between boot camp and my final months in the Marine Corps. First, I had been sent overseas before most of the world knew we were overseas, and I had been unnerved by the casual way politicians had committed military men to tasks that were unachievable. That experience on the edges of a secret war affected me deeply. Even in those early days, friends of mine were killed in the jungles of Southeast Asia. War was not a theoretical issue for me anymore. War cost.

I know now that my instincts at the time—instincts that made me uncomfortable, because I felt it must be unmanly to be opposed to war—were the right ones, and I will always believe that if the thousands of men who died in the Vietnam war could speak today, most of them would speak against such aggression.

But another event in my life had an even greater impact on my thinking as I wrestled with my urge to disobey the order I'd been given: Shortly before he died, my father and I had made our peace with each other. As we shook hands for the last time, my father had smiled and said, "Well, I hope you make it, kid." I remember that I felt very sad at that moment but that I did not show my sadness. I remember also that I knew then that my father and I loved each other and had traveled beyond aggression. Such traveling is hard for men to do, but unless we learn how to do it, the role of the male in this culture will not improve.

I had been raised in a tense and aggressive atmosphere at home, schooled in a peculiarly polite brand of aggression in the Ivy League, trained as a Marine to attack and destroy. Yet one brief moment of genuine love between my father and me had shown me that I was not just a killer and a competitor. Warm and kind relationships between me and my fellow men had been few and far apart until then. Once that happened—and I admit that it happened at an awkward time for the aggressive Marine I was supposed to be—it was impossible for me to look on men as disposable cannon fodder.

As men, we are taught from an early age that male-on-male aggression is natural and acceptable. We see it in cartoons, news reports, movies, TV shows, boxing matches, football games. We are raised on a steady diet of male killings and maimings. Indeed, one of the tests of manhood can be to demonstrate how fully we subscribe to the cheapness of male life. The fuller, the manlier—so the thinking goes.

Sooner or later, men are going to come to the understanding that it is as foul for us to hurt and kill one another as it is to hurt and kill women and children. The aggression that has been primed in us by the barrage of signals from our society will be seen as dangerous. And we will set about learning to unlearn aggression.

My father's spirit moved in me. "Leave the shields on, Gunny," I said.

"Yes, sir," he saluted.

We fired our howitzers on through the night: high explosives, white phosphorus, illumination rounds. The battalion commander never came into our position and my act of rebellion was not discovered. But I was not at ease. After all, I had disobeyed an order.

About three in the morning, word came on the radio that there had been a muzzle burst in a nearby battery. They hadn't had their shields on. Several men had been killed. We were to put our shields back on and not to fire until then.

In the twenty-four years since his death, my father has come to stand for kindness and love. He may have knocked me around, but that's because he was trapped inside a male myth. I know now that he wanted out. He just didn't know the way. I don't either—not completely. But I am damn well looking for it, and I believe many other men are, too.

Let's think for ourselves and not undervalue male life and health. Let's not be so afraid of genuine friendship. Above all else, when there's a choice and we can either sacrifice men or shield them, let's do the latter.

Who knows? The lives we save may be our own.

(1984)

Hitler's Dream _____

I traveled through Germany a decade after World War Two. The countryside was scarred and the cities were full of rubble. In those days, as Germany crawled out from its ashes, even a very young American was tolerated as he asked questions about Hitler and fascism. "How did it happen?" I continually inquired.

No one with whom I talked would accept personal responsibility for the Third Reich. Evidently, no one had voted for Hitler, no one had wanted him in power, no one had ever cheered for him at rallies and no one understood how a culture that had produced Beethoven and Bernkasteler Doktor had also produced a vengeful, hysterical *Führer.*

Where had the spirit of tolerance and mutual respect gone? Hitler had turned dreams into nightmares; but how? People seemed mystified by their own history, almost speechless. But one conversation sticks in my mind to this day, a talk with a former SS officer who ran a café in Berlin. "Hitler divided us and then offered to save us," he said. "That's how fascism works."

If Hitler were alive today, he would have an ideal vehicle for a new fascism—the specter of AIDS. He would convert the problem into a panic. He would orchestrate men against one another, straight against gay, and he would drape the mantle of health and purity over his own strange persona.

Homophobia was an elemental part of Hitler's political code. Homosexuals were thrown into concentration camps and suffered terrible deaths. Hitler's major nightmare was saved for the Jews, a Holocaust that set up the hypersensitive climate in which all nations now live.

The flaw in Hitler's dream had to do with the nature of his scapegoats. They were ordinary people, human beings who were living and letting live, who tended gardens and hiked in the countryside and listened to concerts. Which Jew was the greatest threat? The man playing the violin? The mother in the park? And which homosexual? The man carrying beer kegs? The banker in the fedora?

It doesn't take a lot of imagination to understand how the AIDS problem could be molded into political dynamite. It would require three things: (1) a lack of sufficient education about the disease, so that casual contact could be construed as a cause of infection and homosexuals targeted as the sole cause and carriers, (2) calls for quarantining AIDS cases, as Jesse Helms and others have already done, (3) a fanning of the flames of intolerance between straight and gay males, an intolerance that can exist on both sides.

That's a simple outline for disaster. A modern Hitler could have a ball with it. Gays would become the new scapegoats. They would be packed into camps, along with others who might possibly have the virus.

We can make sure this never comes to pass. We can campaign for strong AIDS educational measures to take the mystery out of the disease. We can work to defeat at the polls those politicians who propose fascist solutions to human problems.

Finally, we can work to moderate the divisions that exist between straight and gay men. We can take a tough look at our own intolerance, whether directed toward heterosexuals or toward homosexuals. Gay bashing is a Nazi tactic. But straight snubbing is also chilling and divisive. We can ask a basic question: Who are we to judge one another's sexuality? Straight or gay, who is totally pure and sexually pristine?

It is not encouraging in the midst of this burgeoning crisis to encounter the kind of snubbing Congressman Barney Frank used against this magazine. From the *New York Times* after Frank came out of the closet and announced that he was a homosexual: "Mr. Frank...received many interview requests...and turned many down, including one from *Playboy* magazine. 'I said I didn't want to be in *Playboy* and they said, "Oh, but we also want your views on the issues." I said, "Why didn't you ask me for my views on the issues last week?"'

Excuse the term, Barney, but I think you blew it. This is a magazine read mostly by straight males, and there is a need for some open dialogue between gays and straights. I'm sorry you chose to ice us out. It's our loss; but it's yours, too.

There are a lot of questions I have for the Congressman. I'd like to know more about his life in the closet and how that affected him. I'd like to hear about his history, his struggles, the reactions he received from his electorate after he made his announcement. When did he first know he was a homosexual, how many of his friends tolerated him, who rejected him? What proposals does he have to keep the AIDS crisis free from fascist manipulation?

How can communications between straight and gay males be improved? Is the Congressman really opposed to talking to *Playboy*? Why? Is it snobbery, defensiveness, disgust, moral superiority, fear? Is he in touch with the fact that homosexual men sometimes snub straight males, acting as if those who are not gay are somehow inferior, cowardly, dumb? Does Barney Frank have an Ed Meese inside him secretly struggling to get out? I'd like to talk with Frank, man to man, and demystify the myth of homosexuality. He could educate us from his perspective. We could listen. It wouldn't hurt us.

I ran some pretty dumb risks when I was in Germany back in the Fifties. I drove through East Germany, for example, going off the autobahn illegally, dodging Russian troops and East German security police, checking out places that were off limits to Americans: Eisenach and Leipzig and Magdeburg and other cities and towns. I was 19 years old, an adventurous college kid who was checking out a Communist superstate and loving every minute of it.

A lot of people were afraid to talk with me, but among those who would, the refrain was the same: We don't know how it happened, we weren't prepared for Hitler, he surprised us.

Let's make a deal, men. This next time, no surprises. We talk with each other, accept each other's lifestyles, live and let live. We choose our dream.

(1987)

The Mr. Fixit Virus _____

Tim Allen, star of the TV show *Home Improvements*, has got it right. For most guys, life is filled with various home repair projects that run amuck. "IF IT AIN'T BROKE, FIX IT" is our motto. "EVERY JOB A FUCKUP" is our pledge.

My father planted the deadly habit of home improvements in my mind at a relatively early age. It all began when we left our rented apartment in the inner city and moved to a Chicago suburb. We were overmortgaged, overextended and overwrought, and it showed.

The house on Oak Street drove my father crazy. In his opinion, everything was wrong with it. You name it, he had to repair it. From inefficient plumbing to rotting eaves to a lawn that he saw as filled with crabgrass and dandelions, nothing pleased the restless and hyperactive Jim Baber. He would walk into the house after a day's work at the office, and within minutes he would be dressed in his work clothes and strapped into his tool belt.

My father carried a hammer the way a grunt carries an M-16. He injected me with the paranoia that only a homeowner can know, and he turned me into a regular Mr. Fixit. When it rains, you do not see April showers; instead, you check for leaks in the roof and you buy a new sump pump for the basement. When it snows, you do not see

Nature's glory; instead, you feel every cold draft as a personal insult to the insulation you installed the previous summer.

There is no peace in the world of home improvements. It is like life on the West Bank. The best you can hope for is a temporary accommodation with the place in which you live, and disaster is always lurking out there like a terrorist.

Do not misunderstand me: I am very proud of all the projects my Dad and I undertook. Only our special awkwardness could have made them the screwups they truly were. The lawn died, the eaves crumbled, the plumbing jammed, the fuse box exploded. In every case, my Dad and I snatched defeat from the jaws of victory, and that's home improvement talent!

What I did not realize until later was that the instinct to be a Mr. Fixit is like a computer virus. The Mr. Fixit Virus starts in one section of the male brain, but soon it takes over the entire system, every synapse, every neural impulse. It is addictive in the extreme, and there is no twelve-step program to help you through it.

I found out that I was doomed forever to be a Mr. Fixit with the first car I ever owned. It was a 1967 Plymouth Barracuda. I bought it used, and if I'd left that car alone, it would still be running today.

But what is the point of buying a car and never fixing it? Where's the fun? Even more important, how do I put my mark on it if I don't fix it when it doesn't need fixing?

Marking is what the Mr. Fixit Virus is all about, of course. Home improvements, car improvements, whatever. It's territorial and it's male. We spray our personal property like tomcats because we need to mark it to prove it is ours. Thus the first and only rule of the Mr. Fixit Virus: *If I have not fucked with it, it is not mine.*

My Plymouth Barracuda was bright yellow. To my mind, it clearly needed racing stipes, so I painted some on. They might have looked more like drips than stripes, but so what? They were *mine.*

Tires? No Mr. Fixit worth his salt stays with factory tires. Get wider tires, better tires, racing tires—or die a cuckold and a putz. The choice is simple.

New tires require new wheels. Alloy wheels. Racing wheels. Shock absorbers? How can you call yourself a man if you don't get new shocks? And of course you need a new steering wheel that is covered in leather and easy to grip. A real man's steering wheel, that is.

(Please note: It is at this point that the woman in your life will ask, "Honey, isn't all this stuff costing too much? You're doubling the price of the car, aren't you?" When this happens, do not argue with her. Do not say a word. Just smirk once, grunt, and go back to the garage. Remember: She does not have the Mr. Fixit Virus, so she cannot understand your addiction.)

What else did I do to my Barracuda? You name it, I tried it. New suspension, new battery, new sunroof, and a lot of fucking with the engine. OK, I admit it. A new engine with an overhead cam and many more horses, the special Chrysler Hemi engine with an air intake in the hood and a great sound composed of many dBA's... the sound of anger and power... the sound of victory.

Throw in a B-pillar and an antisway bar, chop it and channel it, change the camber, replace the slushbox, add a limited-slip differential, adjust for wheel hop and tuck in a jounce bumper and monitor the fuel injection, and you'll have some sense of how I messed with my personal Barracuda.

I loved that car, and it loved me back. It understood me. It went where I told it to go, and it never argued, it never fussed.

I loved that car so much that when I got a job in Hawaii, I drove my Barracuda from Iowa to California and had it shipped by ocean freight to Honolulu. Sure, it would have been cheaper to sell it and buy another car over there. But this car was mine.

I treated it like a baby. I washed it and waxed it and vacuumed it and serviced it. I adjusted the rpm's and corrected the oversteer and relined the brakes. I upgraded the tape deck and installed four speakers in the doors and two on the back shelf.

Then I rewired it.

To this day, I think I did it right. And if I had to make the choice again, I would do what I did. But something happened. I'll never know what it was exactly. I just hope that my Barracuda is up in Car Heaven, and that it forgives me for killing it.

I remember the moment clearly. I turned the key in the ignition and poof, like that, there was a big billow of smoke, then flames. The whole chassis was ablaze in two minutes.

I watched my beautiful Barracuda burn like a magnesium flare, and I felt great sadness. I was losing a friend.

But I am a man with the Mr. Fixit Virus, so I also felt great pride and accomplishment. After all, I had created that car. It had my stamp, my mark, my signature. *And now no other man in the world would ever be able to fuck with it.*

Like I said: Victory. Sort of.

(1992)

Don't Play It Again, Sam _____

Sam Donaldson refers only once to the impact of feminism on his life in his autobiography, *Hold On, Mr. President!* It's just after he brags about his tenacious questioning of any and all guests who appear on ABC-TVs Sunday-morning *This Week With David Brinkley.* "Because of me," he writes, "no one gets a free ride."

Sam soon eats those words:

> All right, *one* time I gave a free ride: I failed to ask a single challenging, provocative question of leaders of feminist organizations on a program about the New Bedford rape case... I'd gotten burned when it comes to women's issues once in Idaho, when, covering Jimmy Carter's raft trip down the Salmon River, I interviewed a young park ranger named Judy Fink. On the air, I labeled her a "rangerette." Switchboards at ABC affiliates all over America were swamped with protests. The next day, I did another interview with Ms. Fink and she saved me by indignantly insisting that rangerette was her proper title and she resented the complaints. But ever since, I've been very careful about offending women.... I'll challenge Presidents any day, but taking on half the world is asking too much.

46

I am here to invite you, whenever you get the balls, to join me in challenging the excesses of feminism, Sam. The next time you're confronted on *This Week With David Brinkley* by feminists whose presence seems to stop you from asking a "single challenging, provocative question," I hope you'll go ahead and ask it anyway. Men need all the help we can get, and we could use your pugnaciousness.

And Sam, since you're in Washington and have great political contacts, would you let the Democratic leadership know that it has been as chickenshit in this area as you admit to having been? It, too, has crumbled before the feminist onslaught.

What a miserable record! Who among the Democratic Presidential candidates of the past two decades has spoken boldly about men's rights? Who has even used that phrase? Who has represented us on the Presidential stump in the areas of divorce, child custody, abortion, military-draft registration, false accusations of rape, high unemployment for both young and old men, male longevity and health, discrimination against men in the workplace and in the culture?

Not a word have any of the Democratic candidates spoken about any of this, Sam. The leaders of the party that claims to represent the common man have gone out of their way to ignore the common man.

Since 1968, the Democrats have had a habit of choosing men for national leadership who seem more like choirboys than like regular guys, and they've done it deliberately to woo women, not men. It is no accident that for the past 20 years, the Democratic Party—once the home of such rough-and-tumble politicians as Franklin Delano Roosevelt, Harry S. Truman and John Fitzgerald Kennedy—has handed its Presidential nomination to the likes of Messrs. Humphrey, McGovern, Carter, Mondale and Dukakis. Five sweet and gentle souls, I am sure, but role models for me, men I'd choose as friends, guys I'd trust with my life, men who care about men's rights, effective Presidents of the United States? Doubtful, Sam, doubtful.

I have yet to vote for a Republican for President, Sam, but I'm getting awfully close to doing so. I can't take this much longer. So here's what I want you to tell the Democrats to consider—assuming they'd like to appeal to men again—the next time they choose a candidate for President.

I call it the High School Yearbook Test. It is very simple: When choosing the next Democratic nominee, picture the potential candidate as he would fit into a typical high school graduating class. Because, for us, choosing a President is a tribal, intuitive thing. We check out the whole man, not just his words. Privately, we categorize every Presidential candidate according to who they remind us of from our high school graduating class.

Example? Jimmy Carter was the teacher's pet you wanted to beat up; Mike Dukakis was the grind who played the trumpet in the band; Walter Mondale never left the library and wore three-piece suits every Friday; Hubert Humphrey always cut his fingers in shop and then cried about it; George McGovern never invited anybody home and was rumored to live in his basement.

As for the early crop of possible Democratic candidates, here's how they run: Lloyd Bentsen is the high school principal who speaks softly but carries a big belt; Bill Bradley is the basketball captain who does everything right but is still a little dull to talk to; Mario Cuomo is the all-state linebacker who makes his own wine at home and drives a 1956 Chevy he repaired himself; Paul Simon heads the debating team and has no friends; Richard Gephardt is president of the 4-H club and dreams of opening a McDonald's franchise one day; Al Gore plays squash at his father's country club and dates all the girls you're in love with; Gary Hart speaks to everybody but doesn't remember anyone's name; Jesse Jackson never answers a question in class with less than a ten-minute sermon; Bruce Babbit serves ice cream in the cafeteria every lunch hour and placed third in the regional cross-country meet; Sam Nunn studies very hard and is liked by everyone but seems remote.

That's a partial early line on what we think of the men who might run for the next Democratic nomination, Sam. Whoever wins, may he have the courage to talk about men's rights in the next election campaign.

Then again, it just might be in our interests to have a woman nominated for President. Think about it. By definition, she would have to talk honestly to us, to ease our fears and address our needs. *She* would not be able to take our vote for granted the way the choirboys have.

Gentlemen, get out your yearbooks! And Sam—don't chicken out next time.

(1989)

Equal Rights for Men, 1983 _____

The new year is not a bad time for us men to take stock of our situation, to ask ourselves where we've been and where we're going and how we'll get there. For 15 to 20 years, we've moved to the sidelines while we've watched a necessary and revolutionary change in our society: the renewed fight for women's rights. That's where the action has been; that's where the sea change is occurring. So one of the questions we confront today is whether or not we have anything to offer ourselves, our mates, our children, one another. Or are we essentially footnotes in the history of this time, unmindful of another struggle to which we have not attended: equal rights for men?

The phrase equal rights for men provokes quite an argument in some circles. Some people believe that men have been spoiled, protected and promoted beyond all logic and that it is foolish to suggest that they have been treated unfairly. Men, the argument goes, have tyrannized and oppressed: Why talk about equal rights for dictators? some people ask. I believe that that position took men by surprise, educated us to some of our blindness, hurt us and still echoes in our culture.

That one-sided view of the male came home to me a few weeks ago when a friend of mine tried to apply to a foundation for a grant. He heads an organization in Washington, D.C., called Free Men. He and I had discussed the possibility of organizing a conference on men in the Eighties, a meeting that would bring together the fledgling divorce-reform and men's-rights groups that are struggling to give some voice to the problems of American males. The foundation in question seemed reasonable to approach because of its work in women's rights and sex-law reform. But the woman who serves as its executive director did not encourage an application for aid. "We're not interested in your issues," she said bluntly.

Sexism, in short, takes many forms, and men are victims of it today, just as women are victims of it. If this society is after equal rights—not just women's rights or men's rights but equal rights for all—then there's work to be done on both sides. That is the significance of this new year: Men are beginning to recognize more clearly the job to be done.

One of the best examples of the unequal treatment of American men is the singular requirement for military service. I believe that there will never be equal rights for all in this country until that burden is shared by men and women. If women are raised with the specter of rape as a terrorizing factor from their early years, men are raised with the specter of death in combat. How many millions of men have been killed or wounded in service to this country over the past 200 years? How many millions more have run that risk, survived it with some damage and then watched their sons prepare to go through the same traumatic cycle? No other single social respon- sibility causes such internal conflict for men as the fact that for a period of years, the state can own their lives.

It is inexcusable, I think, for some women to argue that they should not be equally subject to the call to defend their country. Until the time that women are as vulnerable as men to the military draft, I am afraid that inside the male psyche, there will be the perception that women are pampered, that society's contract is corrupt, that equality for men is a myth.

In much the same spirit, if you listen to men talk about the way divorce is granted in our legal system, you will hear mostly cynical discussion. Child custody, property settlements, legal fees, court costs, child support—all of those elements have been historically skewed against the male. There is a great deal of work to be done before the divorce court becomes an equitable place for men. Fortunately, we are starting to do it (witness the progress of such divorce-reform groups as the Joint Custody Association in Los Angeles; they are putting together the legislative packages needed to equalize divorce law). In divorce and child-custody decisions, men are still considered the bad guys. Surely, men deserve child custody more of the time than they get it. Surely, financial obligations can be fairly divided between the couple.

Our systems of draft registration and divorce are just two of many unequal pressures on men. But what is really maddening for men today, I think, is the belief that women are trying to have it both ways. On the one hand, they are claiming their equal rights to jobs, liberated sex roles, social opportunities. On the other, many of them are willing to hide behind the fog of sexist definitions when it suits them, as it does when the draft board calls or the divorce judge sits. (It should not go unnoticed that women *and men* support E.R.A. in virtually equal numbers.)

Both men and women have logical reasons to believe they are victims of unfair laws and practices. Equality is not served up to either sex, and the tasks of reaching a compromise, of giving and gaining and communicating, are not easy for male or female. We live in a time of double signals, of national schizophrenia. There's only one way we're going to get it together as a people, and I think that at last, *both* men and women are doing it: Each sex has to form a solid sense of identity. Women have been doing so for a number of years. Now it's our turn.

"I think," writes Betty Friedan in *The Second Stage,* "that the women's movement has come just about as far as it can in terms of women alone." She goes on to say that "men may be at the cutting edge of the second stage" of that struggle for human liberation. Friedan is sending us a signal: It is our responsibility to define ourselves instead of letting others do that. If men do the thinking and reading and writing that women have done for themselves, we will soon have a better sense of who we are. Then, perhaps, men and women will be able to turn to one another and behave fairly toward one another. Utopian? Probably. But worth working for.

(1983)

Role Models

I didn't really learn to swear until Sergeant Danny Gross, my Marine Corps drill instructor, taught me. He could surely use the language. He said I was a pinheaded, no-brained, foreskin-chewing, pogey-bait maggot, lower than worm life, and if I ever got out of boot camp it would be either in a hearse or in skirts, because I certainly didn't have the makings of a Marine.

Sergeant Gross taught me a lot of other things, too—things that later saved my life. He had a list of don'ts that he entitled "Don't Fuck with Watashi." According to Sergeant Gross, "Watashi" was his name for death. You don't fuck with Watashi by opening a 105 howitzer breechblock immediately after a misfire. You don't stick your head up on top of a hill, because that's where the snipers will be looking. You don't stay on the low ground, because that means somebody might have the high ground. Watashi is sneaky and mean, and you have to think if you want to stay out of his way.

I heard that—through no fault of his own—Sergeant Gross met Watashi a few years later, but the good sergeant's tough spirit and humorous way with language are still with me. As a matter of fact, it's my belief that men like Sergeant Gross serve as examples for the rest of us because men look for role models as we grow and try to mature.

We don't always find the right models, but that doesn't mean we aren't looking.

"No man is an island," John Donne wrote, and it fits in its less universal sense, too. Men are by nature collegiate. We are convivial scavengers, patching our personalities together with chewing gum and baling wire. We collect traits from a million different sources, taking what we can use wherever we find it. We work by improvisation, watching other men, learning by example, not by talk. For most of us, talking a lot about ourselves would be like talking about a jailbreak. We'd rather be filing through the bars and lowering the ropes and getting the hell out of there. We see talk as cheap and misleading. Action reveals a man's true nature. Better yet, action can be learned from and imitated.

I had one English professor in many years of education who understood that. His name was R. P. Blackmur. He was a poet and a critic, one of the only professors at Princeton without an advanced degree. Blackmur was generally snubbed by the bright and aggressive scholars of the English department, but he was the best teacher I ever had. Like Sergeant Gross, he made language come alive. Blackmur was short, a heavy man with a magnificent voice, and when he toddled into the lecture hall with his green book bag in tow, he looked like a koala bear. His routine never varied. He would dump a pile of books onto the lectern, look around like an amused owl and proceed to read poetry—read it, not just talk about it. He read Yeats, Pound, Stevens, Shakespeare, Wyatt, Chaucer and a host of other wordsmiths. It was not theoretical or academic discussion. It was incantation and invocation, and it set a premium on the words themselves.

I collected many things from Blackmur. For example, I read everything I write today aloud, and until the words sound right, I do not share them with anyone else. Blackmur taught me that and sparked in me a love of uncorrupted language.

Like other men, I am composed of pieces of a puzzle, made up of disparate parts borrowed from the men I tried to mold myself after. Dan Sakal, a boxing coach, listened to me whining between rounds in a tough fight and said, "Kid, you lose in your head, not out there in the ring." I repeat that message to myself with every rejection slip and failure. My father taught me how to be dapper and smiling in the face of hardship: He wore a salesman's grin and a trim bow tie every day as he headed toward a job that was, by definition, a dead end for him because he had never finished college.

Like a squirrel, like a pack rat, I collected bits and pieces of personality from all of these men. They showed me how to live by living.

There were public models, too—political figures, sports heroes, movie stars. President Kennedy was one. His rhetoric was catching. In a way, I owe him my life. People say he was ready to start a great big war in Asia, but I don't think so. I was one of a special group of Marines sent overseas in 1961, and you can say what you want to about J.F.K., but I am here to tell you that he tried to keep things under control, and he chose *not* to go to total war in Laos. That took more guts and common sense than barging in there with everything we had, and I admired that.

Interestingly enough, there's a twist, a curve ball, a fateful thing that happens to the role-model idea. Stay alive, age a little, have kids, friends, associates, and before you know it, you'll find younger men watching you, taking what they can use and rejecting the rest. It's an eerie, vital process that I think is intuitively, genetically understood by men.

Fathers and sons, that's what it's really all about. We men adopt one another. We challenge, set standards, approve and disapprove, all without articulating it, really. It's no big deal; it's just how we are. And the fun of it is that the lines are never that clear-cut. My sons have helped me mature as much as I have helped them. My fathers have given me approaches to life that have made life bearable.

On the last night of boot camp, Sergeant Gross came into the barracks about three A.M. and dumped me out of my bunk and told me to report to the obstacle course on the double, which I did. He made me give him 50 push-ups, and then he told me to stand easy. He uncovered a case of beer, put it between us, shook my hand and allowed as how I might make a good Marine after all. He was giving me his seal of approval, and it meant a lot to me. We drank the beer and he told me war stories and we laughed a lot about the summer's history. It was a moment of mutual respect and affection, although we never would have labeled it as such. The last thing Danny Gross said to me was, "Remember, don't fuck with Watashi."

I haven't, and I won't, not even when he comes for me. Sergeant Gross taught me that.

(1982)

*Taps for a Career*_____

"I understood why they were stealing," Swanee said. "Korea was poor as hell and the country had been occupied for years by different armies. But that didn't make my job any easier. We called the Korean men who stole for a living 'slicky boys.' It was an unwritten policy that it was our responsibility to stop them from robbing us blind."

There was a lot of tension in Korea in 1962. Swanee—his name is Dave Swanson, but I usually call him Swanee—was a rifle-company commander there, a recent graduate of West Point and a career military officer. One day, his men caught a Korean slicky boy inside their compound. In the process of capturing him, they roughed him up. Swanee was involved in that incident, rubbing dirt in the man's face and spanking him with a light stick.

"He had some bruises and a sprained finger," Swanee said. "Then, two days after we arrested him, somebody filed charges against us. It was a politically sensitive time, and somebody decided to make an issue of it. I was charged with unlawful arrest, assault and battery and making a false official statement. I did make a false statement: I said at first that I had been the only person involved."

Swanee paid high dues for his actions. He was reprimanded, fined, relieved of command. Although senior officers spoke well of him—his battle-group commander called him the best company commander he had—charges were still pressed. Swanee finally cut a deal. "I made a pretrial agreement to plead guilty if they'd agree not to kick me out of the Army. I wanted to stay for a full career."

Well, he came close. But that incident in Korea was a blot that no amount of courage could erase.

By 1966, Swanee was a rifle-company commander again: Alpha Company, First Battalion, Seventh Cavalry. He and his troops had been ordered into the An Lao Valley in South Vietnam. While South Vietnamese marines swept up the valley, Alpha company and other American units set up ambushes and blocked the avenues of exit out of the valley. Alpha Company made considerable contact, and in one ambush they killed a man who appeared to be a fully equipped North Vietnamese officer.

When word reached battalion headquarters that Alpha Company had killed a North Vietnamese, it was decided that a photographer should be sent out to get a photograph of the corpse.

By that time, of course, Swanee had pulled his men away from the ambush site. As shrewd and tough and competent as they come, Swanee knew that once an ambush had been sprung, it was time to get out of the area and avoid probable counterattack. He refused to go back to the site. Division G-2 insisted. "We will go and see how the area looks," Swanee radioed, committing himself to as little as possible.

The unit of Alpha Company that went back to search for the body was badly hit. The battalion commander picked up Swanee in a helicopter and they flew over the combat zone, calling in gunfire. Swanee ordered the chopper to put him down on the ground so he could join his men.

Under intense fire, Swanee saw three of his men killed in succession: first a wounded trooper, then a medic who tried to rescue him, then a third man who had run out to try to help the two others. Later that afternoon, Swanee and his first sergeant reached those bodies. As they lifted one to carry it back to their own lines, they were hit. The first sergeant suffered a serious chest wound. Swanee took a round through his helmet that hit the back of his head and knocked him out. When he came to, he saw that two fingers of his left hand had been shot off and he had also been hit in the left arm. He gave first aid to the sergeant and ordered him evacuated. Then he took his own first-aid pouch, stuck what remained of his fingers back on his hand and continued to call in supporting fire. He refused to leave the position until the situation was under control. He stayed there for several hours, then accepted evacuation to spend thirty days in the hospital. He lost both fingers, by the way.

Those wounds were not the only ones Swanee incurred in Vietnam. He was also in a helicopter accident in 1967, ten days before his tour of duty was to be over. He was flying with a new and eager battalion commander who twice ordered the helicopter pilot to fly lower. Against his better judgment, the pilot did so, only to find his tail rotor sheared off by tall trees. The chopper crashed. Swanee dragged himself and another man out and then collapsed, paralyzed with a broken back, broken leg, broken ribs. This time, he spent about twenty days in a hospital in Japan, then a month in a hospital in the U.S.A.

Swanee had not seen the last of Vietnam. He returned there in 1969 for a tour of duty with U.S. Army Headquarters in Long Binh. He was involved in staff work in that area.

If you looked at this man's career, you would find quite a record. He seems to have done it all. He certainly has proved his courage in combat. And the list of his credentials aside from Vietnam reads well: after West Point, service with the 101st Airborne; thirteen months in Korea with the First Cavalry; two years at Fort Benning, Georgia; a tour as an aide to a two-star general; a graduate degree (an M.A. in speech communication and human relations) from the University of Kansas; plus assignments to the right staff colleges, headquarters and bases. In addition to all that, Swanee is the man who started the R.O.T.C. program on Guam. But none of that has been enough.

A lieutenant colonel now, Swanee has been passed over twice for promotion to full bird colonel. In the Army, it's up or out, so Swanee will be leaving soon. The Korean incident has come back to haunt him.

The funny thing is that compared with much of the aggression and violence in his life, that incident is typical. I mean, this is a man who at the age of fourteen was ordered to beat the shit out of one of his best friends.

That friend was me. I was fourteen, too, and I was under orders to beat the shit out of Swanee. Like most young men, we followed orders, more or less. But the situation confused us, and in my mind, at least, it set off a chain reaction that still troubles me.

(1984)

Taps for a Career, Part Two_____

"You've got to fight Dave Swanson," the coach said. He was a short, tough Chicago Pole who had been a pro boxer himself. "You guys are two of the best in your weight class."

The year was 1950. I had just turned 14. The summer camp was a military one, and it took its boxing very seriously. We trained daily and fought weekly. We also marched in formation to meals and classes, hiked and paraded, canoed and competed. We wore uniforms, held rank, shouted orders, obeyed them.

"I'm not going to fight him," I objected. It took some courage to say that. The boxing coach held the rank of captain. "Swanee's my best friend."

That was true. I didn't have a lot of friends as a kid, but the ones I had I really cared about.

I was something of a punk from Chicago's South Side. Swanee was an all-American boy from Galesburg, Illinois. Evar Swanson, his father, had once played professional baseball with the Chicago White Sox. Evar was fast in his day. He had been timed circling the bases in 13.2 seconds in 1932, a record that still stands.

Swanee and I were both good athletes. I was leaner and faster; Swanee was shorter and more powerful. Dave had an open disposition, a friendly face and gentle humor. He was a perfect foil for my intensity and city wit. We got along famously, trusted each other and agreed to be tentmates for that summer of our 14th year.

"Coach says we've got to box," Swanee said to me.

"Yeah, he told me that, too."

"He says it's an order."

"Right," I nodded.

We left the subject hanging in the air, but we were both uncomfortable. It was a double bind, something that men know a lot about.

I never saw Swanee box that way before or after. He put his head down and windmill punched. I stepped aside and tapped him on the forehead. I won the fight on points, though Swanee could have taken me out whenever he wanted to.

Our friendship was based on the unspoken pledge that we would never fight seriously. To the best of our ability, we upheld that pledge in the ring. But the situation confused us, and what we went through is symbolic of the mixed and mean signals young men receive from their culture.

If it is all right for us to beat up our friends, what space of safety and peace is left for us? If the line between those whom we can hit and those whom we cannot is obliterated, what limits and governors remain in our thinking?

I am going to say something here that could get me into trouble and could be misinterpreted, but it is the nub of male stress: To this day, I still fantasize about coldcocking someone who's being threatening or obnoxious to me. I control myself, and I do not go around hitting people; but often, under pressure, I want to. If a car almost runs me over, if somebody screws me professionally, if the mockery and contempt I have to eat as a writer are served up in too big a dish, I do not always want to talk about the situation, I might also want to throw hands.

The point is not that I am a walking time bomb who will soon strike out in all directions. I have chosen never to do that. The point is that my sometimes violent fantasies are very expensive to my system.

I do not think I am alone in this. I believe I am describing the struggle of many males. Raised to explode, we eventually implode. We sit on our programmed rage and our anger; we feel isolated and inhuman as we do; and, sooner or later, the raging river that runs through us carries us away. We see our voluntary implosion as a service and sacrifice to our society and, given the alternative, it is. But ours is a hell of a choice, and it would be nice if we didn't have to make it.

If I read his life correctly, Swanee suffered just as much as I did from the confusion we were put through. The only difference between us is that once, he struck out at somebody and got caught at it. It was a mistake, one that limited his career, but I understand why he did what he did, and I know that he would take back his decision if he could, no matter how extenuating the circumstances.

"I was young and zealous," Dave said. "If I had it to do over again, I wouldn't do it, even if I thought I was following orders—which I did."

He was speaking of the incident in 1962 that eventually came back to hurt him. A young lieutenant at the time, he had helped rough up a Korean civilian who had been caught stealing from a U.S. Army base. Swanee was court-marshaled for being involved in the physical punishment of that prisoner. Twenty-two years later, he found himself passed over twice for promotion to colonel, in spite of an outstanding combat record. The message was clear: One slip in a career is enough to end that career. Dave Swanee, man of action, had acted once too often.

"I was something of a pawn in that Korean incident," Swanee said. "We had a new battle-group commander. He told us that the policies of the preceding group commander were in effect unless he changed them. Well, the former commander had told us to beat the Devil out of those Korean 'slicky boys' when we caught them stealing. As a matter of fact, he said we should bring them in not standing. An enlisted man got an automatic promotion if he caught a thief, and it was expected that there'd be some rough stuff.

"There were political pressures, too. Chung Hee Park, acting president of Korea at the time, wanted the U.S. Army to turn over to him all Servicemen charged with crimes against Koreans. The Army wasn't about to relinquish its people to the Korean criminal-justice system, but it had to show that it took such charges seriously. I got caught in the middle of all that.

"I thought I was doing what I was supposed to do," Swanee said, "but if I had it to do over again, I never would do it."

It has been a privilege knowing Lieutenant Colonel David Swanson. Personally, I think the Army has missed a bet. Swanee is an outstanding officer and a stand-up guy, a winner of the Silver Star, two Bronze Stars, the Purple Heart and numerous other awards. It is a waste to put him out to pasture.

Then again, we men know a lot about waste. It figures, doesn't it? After all, we're programmed for obsolescence. Ain't that a shame? And won't it be something if, together, we reprogram ourselves?

It's time.

(1985)

Coming to Terms With 'Nam——————

It's been a decade since America's commitment to Vietnam ended. Now that the hype surrounding the tenth anniversary of our withdrawal from Saigon is over, maybe we can talk rationally about the Vietnam war and the haunting memories it evoked this past spring.

Vietnam is a subject many men still think about: More than 58,000 men (and eight women) are listed on the Vietnam Veterans Memorial, and questions about that war—the nature of it, its meaning, who went and who didn't, how it was fought, how it was concluded—are alive and kicking in the male consciousness.

Mostly, we are confused about Vietnam. That may sound like a simple sentence, but it's not. Confusion is something men are not supposed to admit to, at least not for very long. Confusion is considered unmanly, unintelligent, inconvenient. "What's the matter, can't you make up your mind?" is an internal taunt with which men often torment themselves.

I suggest that with a subject as complex as Vietnam, confusion is as natural as the wind, and we should not be so afraid of it. As a matter of fact, it will be a good day when men can say to one another, "Vietnam? I think we were right and I think we were wrong. I think we killed and I think we created. I think we were brave and I think we were cowardly."

When I came back from a brief assignment to the Far East in the early sixties, I was a confused young man who had seen the beginnings of a secret war shaping up. I had no one to talk with about it, no role models in life or literature; and, to be blunt, no one wanted to listen to the tales I had to tell. Places like Vietnam and Laos were as distant as the moon to most Americans in those years, and they could not have cared less about what went on there.

Later, after our involvement was over, it became clear that America wanted to forget the Vietnam War as fast as possible, and those of us who wrote and talked about it were an embarrassment. Worse, we spoke in divisive tongues, some of us against the war in all its forms, others for it. What was to be gained by listening to such disharmony? In this culture, confused men who send conflicting signals are considered useless, bothersome, foolish.

In 1980, America elected a President who supposedly wasn't confused about anything: Vietnam was a noble cause; Russia was an evil empire; the military-industrial complex was essentially underfunded. At the same time, there was also a deal shaping up about Vietnam. It went like this: Admit that Vietnam was a good war and we'll say that you veterans are OK; refuse to acknowledge the ambiguities of that war and we'll declare you number one; drop all confusion and we'll call you loyal and patriotic. It was a deal designed to appeal to men, especially those who had served in Vietnam.

To be male is, by definition, to search for solutions. From boyhood on, we are trained to do that. And life in the military is nothing but a steady parade of problems to be solved, along with textbook solutions to some of those problems.

As a male, I confess that I can handle ambiguity for only so long before I tire of it. But the problem with male impatience is that it arises not out of thought but out of fear. I hate to appear vacillating, weak, dumb. I want to look as though I know what I'm doing. Somewhere in that process, I drop my search for truth and begin protecting my image of myself.

That is precisely what we must *not* do as we search for the lessons of Vietnam. Of all the wars in our nation's history, that one was the most ironic, incomplete and ambiguous. It had moments of terrible beauty, thousands of incidents of incredible bravery, but it was also flawed from its inception, brutal in its execution and wasteful of lives, property and territory. As men, we must hold on to that ambiguity, we must live with it. It would be as stupid for us to jump on the bandwagon of those who would turn Vietnam into a virtuous action as it would be for us to accept the idea that all men who served there were baby killers.

Whenever I find myself searching for a simple-minded conclusion about 'Nam, I have only to think of the men I knew who served there, some of whom were on highly classified jobs. Their fates were ironic and unpredictable. How could they fit under one theoretical umbrella?

Mike and I served in the Marine Corps together, including some time overseas. He was killed in a chopper crash in Laos. You will not find his name on the Vietnam Veterans Memorial. Did you think that at least the memorial was unambiguous? It is not. Scores, possibly hundreds of men who were killed are not listed there: Air America pilots, Intelligence personnel, people on special duty attached to the military. Wars begin very quietly, you see, and they end quietly, too. Even the names of our dead are incomplete.

Ed was a head-hunter, a sniper who could put a .30-caliber bullet in the black from 1000 meters. He loved killing and enlisted for a second tour. Then a North Vietnamese sniper shot him in the back and severed his spinal cord. Paralyzed from the waist down, Ed now rails against the war, an assassin turned pacifist.

Jim stayed in the corps, a career man all the way. A company commander at Khé Sanh, he fought brilliantly, won the Silver Star, the Bronze Star and two Purple Hearts. He also had a casualty rate in his company of 200 percent. That is to say that he lost all of his men and then lost their replacements—all in a year's time.

David was a conscientious objector who joined International Voluntary Services, a precursor of the Peace Corps. He lived and died in the provinces and never touched a weapon. A total of ten I.V.S. people were killed in Indochina. Their names aren't on the memorial, either.

There is really no way I can encompass that war and its cost. I come to terms with it by admitting I'll never come to terms with it. And I tell myself that such confusion may be heavy luggage, but it's my job to carry it.

(1985)

The Healing Sky

I'd been on snowshoes for five days when I saw the deer. It was very alert and it seemed amused. I looked like one worn and tired humanoid, which is exactly what I was. I'd been running and hiding, slipping and sliding, for the better part of a week. There were people after me, too, and the object of the exercise was to see whether or not I could survive Marine Corps survival training in the High Sierras in January without being captured or frozen.

The valley looked like the moon. The deer bounced across my vision, disappeared, surfaced behind me a few minutes later, vanished again. I was fascinated with it. I was chewing pine needles and tree bark to give myself the illusion that I was eating. It helped.

My skills were limited in the mountains. I tried to break through the ice on a stream to find a fish, but all I found was more ice and a case of frostbite. I curled in my own handmade snow cave, nibbling the chocolate bars I had smuggled in my parka, conserving energy and staying out of sight, but the pain of the night's cold grasp and the dullness of the day's winter wind forced me to move on. Breaking trail in my snowshoes wore me out in a few hundred yards, yet I was supposed to traverse miles of snowscape to my pickup point.

I had no radio, no communications of any kind. I was too tired to

65

be scared, but I soon sensed that I was entering a dangerous phase, a moment when I might sink down in the snow and simply sleep until dead, imagining all the while that I was warm and safe.

The deer saved my life. By being there and by playing its continuous game with me, flirting and leading me on and prancing like a showgirl, it entertained me, motivated me, got me laughing, made me want to live. It even showed me the way out of the valley somewhere near Pickle Meadow, California.

On my last night out, I wrapped myself in my sleeping bag and listened to a rustling in the tree line and stared at the winter sky for hours. I felt small but strong, and I knew exactly where I fit in the universe. It was a fine feeling.

A few years later, this time on the desert near Twentynine Palms, California. I heard another rustling at night. I always slept well on the desert, not just because the work was hard but also because the sky was broad and comforting, wider than any sky I could imagine, wider even than the sky at sea.

The rustling interrupted my slumber, but I paid it no serious attention until dawn.

Dawn on the desert comes fast, and as black changed to gray, I opened my eyes idly. There, right in my face, was a rattlesnake curled like a whip.

I had the presence of mind not to blink. As I rolled, it struck the back of my sleeping bag. I jumped out of that bag and bashed the rattler with my entrenching tool.

At dusk, as I was getting ready to skin it, holding its jaws open to measure its fangs, the fangs sprang forward and it almost got me. I laughed, but I was frightened. I'd learned again that nature is unforgiving to the careless, a lesson you tend to forget in the city.

I was raised in a city, but I visited the country every summer. It was there that I learned about the sky. I felt a link with it, even as a child. I would often be dropped on the edge of several hundred acres of farmland with a lunch bucket, a Thermos and a hoe. For hours, alone, I would hoe cornstalks out of soybean fields. Sometimes, at night, I would sleep in the fields, counting the stars, watching them blink and occasionally fall. I loved the open spaces, and when I went back to Chicago, I felt as if I were putting blinders on. The sky narrowed, and with it my sense of freedom, of being tested, of being small but strong.

I have been fortunate to see any number of skies. The sky over the Bosporus is often as blue as the bluest vegetable dye in an antique Shirvan rug. The sky over the Pacific Ocean is like a veil made up of a thousand layers of silk. The sky over the Basque country of Spain is a patchwork of constellations, a reflection of the fields beneath it. It is possible that wherever we are, the sky interacts with the culture and the land, makes them what they are, informs them.

Once upon a time, when I thought I was being sent on a job that might kill me, it was the sky over a bay in Okinawa that convinced me that death was an illusion. That sky framed a scene that I had seen in tapestries and scrolls a thousand years old: small trees on the cliffs, bonsai shaped by the wind; fishing boats lanterned and in full sail; clouds like slow-moving butterflies; a fat and yellow moon that had seen centuries of men going off to war and seemed unaffected by it.

Nothing was new under that sky, I decided, and the odds were that nothing really died under it, either. Everything was recycled, one way or another. It was not that the sky was impersonal. It simply knew what I did not, and it was beyond fear or grief.

The struggle of our time is that we not lose our sense of identity. After all the manipulations to which we subject ourselves—after the $1,000,000-per-minute TV ads we must view and the political campaigns we must follow and the movies we simply must see and the gossip we feel a need to inhale—after all of this massive consumption and loss, there is something invigorating about finding the sky again, walking under it, studying it, learning from it.

I know this much: I learn more when the sky is open to me than when it's closed off from me. Cities don't do it. Open country does.

Once, a deer saved me, a rattler almost killed me, the moon comforted me, and I learned and relearned that I had limits and no limits. I had fears and courage, I was small and strong.

This summer, I hope to go to Kenya. The sky there, they say, is limitless.

(1985)

*The Road to Tenancingo*_____

The guerrillas had been active all night, bombing power stations around San Salvador and cutting off electricity to the city. The sound of demolitions and automatic-weapons fire kept me awake in my hotel room.

I was a member of a delegation of eleven Vietnam veterans brought together by Dr. Charles Clements, a Vietnam veteran himself. Author of a book called *Witness to War,* an account of his service as a physician behind the lines in El Salvador, Dr. Clements had asked us to accompany him on a ten-day tour of El Salvador, Nicaragua and Honduras in September 1985.

El Salvador was the first country we visited. Because we were veterans and politically undefined, we had access to many people— American-embassy personnel, Salvadoran military commanders, labor-union leaders, refugees, journalists, neutral observers. A trip into the hills to a town in disputed territory called Tenancingo would give us another piece of the mosaic.

I packed my knapsack with care: a laminated picture of my sons, a flask of water, some Halazone tablets, two bags of cashews, my camera and writing pad and pens, a Dire Straits tape, my Walkman, a metal mirror, a compass and a map. It would be my first time in a war zone without a weapon. I didn't mind. It made things simpler and more peaceful.

The road to Tenancingo branched off the main highway some 15 miles east of San Salvador at a town called Santa Cruz Michapa. The road became rough as it wound north into the hills. Just beyond Santa Cruz, we encountered a Salvadoran-army roadblock. The Salvadoran soldiers were young, angry, a little careless with their weapons. As they searched us, I knew the other veterans in the delegation were on automatic, just as I was. We were checking out gullies, looking for places to hide, watching out for one another, reading the silent signals of the soldiers, examining everything and saying nothing. When the soldiers allowed us to proceed, I think we all took the same deep breath. We had 12 miles to go.

We stopped the vans about 500 meters outside Tenancingo. Charlie Liteky read from a newspaper report by Peter Arnett that explained why a village that had held 2,000 people was now mostly deserted: "Tenancingo was the third Salvadoran town bombed...by the newly acquired A-37 aircraft provided the Salvadoran government by the United States....

"Tenancingo had the misfortune to be occupied by left-wing guerrillas who overpowered the local army garrison. The government response was to send in its new bombers as the first reaction....

"All the preparation I'd had in...other wars was no shield against the shock of coming upon Salvadorian victims sprawled in the streets where bombs had littered them....

"The children seemed to have been killed by the blasts alone. Four that I saw were frozen in the act of fleeing, arms and legs clutching at the air, mouths wide open in fear. Their mothers were mutilated by the bombs....We counted 17 dead in the streets...."

Liteky is a former Army chaplain who was awarded the Congressional Medal of Honor for heroism under fire in Vietnam. He read Arnett's dispatch in a slow, deliberate voice. Then we walked carefully into Tenancingo.

The church there stood on a deserted square. It was pockmarked by shrapnel and spattered with dog shit and graffiti. As if by signal, people began to filter into the square from all directions. A fully armed guerrilla arrived, followed by several men and boys, some with weapons. People materialized out of the tree line, out of the crumbling adobe houses: an old woman carrying wood, guerrillas with propaganda posters, older men with machetes, a young boy with a bandana across his face.

Our embassy had told us that the rural population was afraid of the guerrillas. If that is true, it is true somewhere besides Tenancingo. The *campesinos* we saw listened easily and respectfully to the guerrillas who spoke to them.

I listened for a time to a young man who called himself Esteban. Pale, thin, 22 years of age, wearing a large straw hat and a .38 pistol on his hip, articulate, humorous, Esteban talked earnestly to the crowd: "We are Salvadorans. We are not *Sandinistas* or Cubans or Soviets. We've always believed that the solution to our problems must be political." It was guerrilla rhetoric, just as predictable as embassy rhetoric. I listened, but I was bored. Rhetoric never changes.

Aaron Two Elks, Oglala Sioux and Vietnam veteran, asked us to sit in a circle and smoke a peace pipe. Aaron taught us how to do it, explained the significance of each gesture. During the ceremony, I could hear an observation aircraft, the kind I used to fly in, circling somewhere above us. I wondered what kind of radio traffic surrounded our visit and whether the soldiers at the roadblock would blow us away when we came back down the road, then pull back from their position and claim we'd been caught in guerrilla crossfire.

We left Tenancingo in midafternoon. I lay on the back seat of the van and listened to *Telegraph Road* and watched the sun through the trees. We had hoped to smoke a peace pipe with the soldiers at the roadblock, but they were too tense for that. They searched us thoroughly, talked among themselves, finally waved us through to the highway.

"Politically, we might be at a stalemate with the guerrillas," an American-embassy official said to me after a briefing, "but militarily we're way ahead."

I thought about that statement. It reminded me of many I'd heard before. If a political stalemate existed, wasn't it the only one that counted? If the battered population of Tenancingo supported the guerrillas, wasn't that significant? If a town some 15 air miles from the

heart of San Salvador was in disputed territory, wasn't there a lesson
in that? How many peace pipes would it take to lead to negotiations
and peace?

Maybe the ghosts of Tenancingo know the answers to those
questions. I'm not sure anybody else does.

(1986)

MEN AND WOMEN

The True Sister Profile _____

I was on Cable News Network's *Crossfire* some time ago, and I learned something interesting about myself and the world during that half hour.

Michael Kinsley and Pat Buchanan, the show's commentators, were trying to get things stirred up between me and their other guest, Gloria Allred, a feminist attorney from Los Angeles. As the show progressed, Gloria did a lot of the talking and seemed ready with an answer for everything. While I have no idea what she thinks personally of men, her public posture on the subject seems distinctly unappreciative. In the Public Gospel According to Gloria, men were at fault for most of the problems in the universe. We were selfish, we were uncaring, we had no issues of our own—and if we argued with Gloria's perception of us, we were crybabies and bad guys.

Suddenly, in the midst of the debate, it hit me: Ace, I said to myself, there are only two types of women in the world—sisters or shrews, menu A or menu B.

Allred was definitely a menu-B item, her brain trapped in some kind of feminist lockstep that showed no hint of kindness or compromise, no desire to understand men and their problems in this culture. We have seen a lot of that attitude in the past few decades, and most of us are quite tired of it.

I was also thinking about the many women I know who do not share Allred's seeming self-righteousness and self-absorption. They are not dyed-in-the-muff feminists, do not see men as oppressors and tyrants—they are women who like men and respect them and enjoy their company, and who acknowledge that much feminist rhetoric these days is sexist and excessive.

There in the CNN studio, while I stared at the television camera and listened to Allred's shrill voice through the earpiece, I remembered the many good sisters I have in my life, and I was especially grateful for them at that moment.

My luck with sisters has been outstanding, starting with—you guessed it—my very own sister.

Ducky Baber came into my life when I was three years old. I remember the day she came home from the hospital in her white bassinet. I was left alone in a room with her, and while psychologists will tell you that all siblings are jealous of new arrivals, I am evidence to the contrary. I remember looking at Ducky and feeling a great surge of love and protectiveness. To this day, Ducky and I have a wonderful relationship that is filled with laughter and affection.

Sisters? I have dozens of them across the country, from Laurie Ingraham in Milwaukee (a psychotherapist who often lectures, believe it or not, about women's prejudices toward men) to Barbara Dority in Seattle (who heads a group called The Northwest Feminist Anti-Censorship Task Force and is one of those rare feminists who support the publication of magazines such as *Playboy*). The list goes on, but you get the idea.

So, men, let me make a modest proposal: The time has come in this very strange and divisive age for us to reach out and support our sisters, to thank them for their support, to remember that they are out there.

How do we find and identify the sisters in our lives? What follows is a True Sister Profile. If a woman has the qualities listed here, it means she is probably a stand-up, back-to-back, no-bullshit sister. Which means she is invaluable.

A. *She has a sense of sexual humor.* No joke, guys, this is the acid test of sisterhood. One of the finest sisters in my life demands a minimum of one dirty joke a day from me. She loves to laugh about sex. She is no prude, and in that sense, I say with complete pride, that she is one of the boys—which is what all good sisters are from time to time.

B. *She likes men.* Unlike the shrew, most of whom basically dislike men and would have them banished (or at least under complete domination), the True Sister is a lecherous, loving, excitable, responsive wench who loves to do what I call comparative shopping. Her motto is "I get to look all I want." Her coat of arms pictures lace panties on a field of Chippendale. Her fantasies are as illicit as yours, and she finds herself continually amused at how much she loves life and sex. She was one of the first females to wear a SO MANY MEN, SO LITTLE TIME button. When the time comes, she wants the button buried with her.

C. *She listens to and respects men.* The True Sister, even in the midst of all her raunchiness, is looking for more than a pretty face and body. She is curious about men and male thought. She likes to converse with men, to hang out with them, to enjoy their company. She understands and accepts certain differences in expression between the sexes, and those differences interest her. The True Sister empathizes with men, can identify with them. In so doing, she breaks through certain sexual barriers.

D. *She distrusts feminist rhetoric.* The True Sister may be an old-fashioned feminist, a woman who works for equal rights. That's OK. Most men want equal rights for all citizens. But the True Sister is suspicious of most of today's feminist propagandists, especially the ones who bash men and blame them for all of the world's problems.

E. *She specifically supports fathers' rights in this culture.* This listing comes under the "last but not least" label. The True Sister understands that children need to be connected with their fathers as often as possible, whether or not there has been a divorce. She campaigns for things such as joint custody, and she has no respect for those mothers who alienate children from their fathers. The True Sister is true to the idea of the family (the father *always* included) in any of its possible forms.

The True Sister is more than a dream. She exists. Let's love her and thank her.

(1990)

New Rules for Her_____

American men did not organize or lobby or say very much as the Clarence Thomas-Anita Hill hearing roared like a forest fire through our culture this past fall. Indeed, American men didn't do much of anything except hunker down and hope that the flames of controversy would pass. For most men, it was a time for survival, not a time for debate.

Once again, the political momentum moved to the other side of the gender gap as various women's rights groups and women's rights lawyers and women's rights lobbyists and women's rights activists insisted that: (a) sexual harassment of women by men was rampant through America, (b) under the law, sexual harassment was to be defined solely on a reasonable woman's terms, and (c) under the law, a hostile environment in the workplace was whatever a reasonable woman said it was.

As men, we mostly sat there and took that abuse without objection. We knew that some men harass women in the workplace. But we also knew that to protest the direction against men that this issue was taking in our legal system might be fatal to our professional health. "If you question anything we claim about this subject," we could hear many of our female colleagues saying, "then you must be in favor of men harassing women. There cannot be two sides to this issue."

We hoped against hope that the Thomas and Hill grillings would not focus on us personally, that no one would ask us if we had used the term pubic hair in office conversation in the last decade, or had attended a pornographic movie while we were in college, or had rented an X-rated videotape at a local video store.

Such questions were potentially deadly, and they contained accusations that were impossible for us to disprove or defend against: In her terms, are you now or have you ever been a man who asked a female colleague out on a date once too often? In her terms, have you ever told an offensive joke at the office in mixed company? In her terms, have you ever made obscene gestures with your hands, or looked at her body in the wrong way, or placed pinups or cartoons that were offensive to her in a place where she might see them? In her terms, have you ever created a hostile environment—*however she defines it*—for her in your workplace?

"Damned if I know," most men said to themselves as the witch trials continued. "It is very hard for me to figure out what her terms are. I'm a guy. I can't think like a woman—especially a prudish and easily offended woman."

But most men did not say that publicly. We live in a time of sexual inquisition, and silence is deemed to be more prudent than confrontation. After all, if we argued or protested, the suspicion of sexual harassment might spread to us.

As men, our interests in this question of sexual harassment and how it is to be legally defined have mostly been ignored. We are in a new area of the law, one that has been shaped primarily by feminist influences. We are vulnerable in the extreme to false charges of sexual harassment, and we know it. As a matter of fact, we know that the term itself is bankrupt. "Sexual harassment"—what exactly does it mean?

Up until now, the focus of the discussion has been on male behavior. (That is one of the problems you will run into if you are accused of sexual harassment by one of your co-workers. Your behavior will be placed under a microscope, but hers may not.) So just for starters, let's turn the question around and ask ourselves this simple but serious question: "As men, what behavior do we now expect from our female associates in the workplace?"

Gentlemen, these are the five rules she is to follow. Read them to yourself, then read them to her. Because until men have equal protection under the law, it is your job to live defensively:

1. *Do not make sexual jokes with me, and do not laugh at any sexual jokes if I mistakenly make them with you.* We may have shared some good laughs together, but those days are over. I declare myself a corporate prude, and I ask you to do the same. Humor is tricky. It can turn on a dime and be easily misunderstood, and it courts a sexual harassment lawsuit by its very nature. So until the law is more clear, you cool it and I cool it.

2. *Do not tell me about your love life and I will not tell you about mine.* This, too, can be a fatal attraction in the workplace. Until things get sorted out, understand that sexual neutrality is my only protection as a male. Do not use me as a confidant for your marital or social problems. If you choose to report them in negative terms, discussions like that can lead to my dismissal or reprimand.

3. *Do not send me mixed messages.* Another way of saying this is "stop with the flirtation already." Nothing can confuse me more than a bright feminine smile and seductive feminine talk that is then followed by a personnel officer with sexual harassment investigation forms. That kind of communication can ruin my day.

4. *Be accountable for your own actions and responses.* Yes, Ms. America, I ask that you understand your own sexuality. If, in our working relationship, you are attracted to me, even temporarily, please admit that attraction to yourself and then act even more carefully around me. Nothing confuses me more than a woman who comes on to me like Madonna in heat and then suddenly gets insulted when I respond to that heat—especially when the EEOC is breathing down my neck. As it always is.

5. *If by any chance you and I form an intimate alliance outside the office, promise me that there it shall remain for all time.* This means that if said intimate relationship sours, there will be no professional retribution by you for that fact. You will not seek vengeance against me by setting me up for a sexual harassment lawsuit in the office.

There they are, men. Five rules for your female colleagues to live by. But if you're still confused, let me put it to you in our terms, man to man: From now on and until the law swings back to a more fair and neutral place for us, watch your ass and nobody else's.

(1992)

The Five-Sided Woman

OK, men, it's time to fess up and admit that we have been pulling a gigantic con on the universe. We pretend that we are mature and responsible individuals with reasonable expectations of our women, but we know that in reality, we are the neediest, greediest, lustiest, hungriest creatures on the planet. What is worse, most of us try to cover up our insatiable natures. We lie to the women we love about what we want from them, and we do it on a daily basis—because what we want from the women in our lives is *everything,* and we want it now!

"You don't want a wife, you want a mistress," women have said to me. I, of course, always lie and deny it.

"You don't want a mistress, you want a daughter," women have said to me. I, as usual, lie and deny it.

"You don't want a daughter, you want a mother," women have said to me. I lie and say I don't.

"You don't want a wife or a daughter or a mistress or a mother," women have said to me, "you want something so enveloping, so godlike and feminine and comforting that she could only be called a soul mate." That, too, I lie about and deny.

Well, I have to lie. You guys understand that. How could I ever

81

admit to the women who were pinning me to the wall that they had it right, that I want them to be all of the above—wife and mother and mistress and daughter and soul mate? That I want them to be masseuse and whore, virgin and nurturer, intellectual and primitive, confidante and adviser, audience and receptacle, lover and friend, child and spirit?

I mean, if I admit to all that, the women in my life will have proof that I am a neurotic, selfish, acquisitive, covetous, avaricious, desirous, grabby, grasping, lecherous, yearning, throbbing hunk of lust and greed who wants far more from any one human being than could reasonably be expected and who sets up failure in his relationships before he begins. That couldn't be me, could it?

It may be true that I am all of those things, but I lie to the women I know and tell them that I have very few needs and that I am a self-sufficient man. For some reason, they look suspicious when I say that, but what do *they* know?

"You don't want a wife, you want a mistress" is usually accompanied by another charge that we have all heard: "All you think about is sex." This charge is absolutely true, but it is disastrous to admit it. So I respond in a level, deceptive, neutered, logical, chilled-out voice, "That's not true. I want much more than sex. I want a long-term relationship with one woman I can call my wife, period." There is a problem after I say this. I want to laugh. At what? At my own hypocrisy. Did you know that yawning is a very good way to cover up laughter? So is stretching your arms and looking out the window as if there were a fire next door.

"You don't want a mistress, you want a daughter" is often accompanied by, "You can't handle a really mature and independent woman, can you? You have to run away to some obsequious floozy who will obey your every command." It is true that I can't handle the frequent fierceness of the independent woman, and it is true that I wish the world were filled with women who obeyed my every command, but I cannot admit all that, not even to myself, so I lie about it. "No," I say, this time in an angrier voice, which indicates that I'm being treated unjustly, "I love independent women who scold me a lot and kick sand in my face and find fault with everything I do. That's equality, and that's what I stand for." Usually, when I say this, the lie is so huge that I feel slightly nauseated. I get up and go to the window and stare at the horizon until I feel steadier.

"You don't want a daughter, you want a mother" is often followed by, "You're a groveling, slimy, dependent, perverted sex addict and hedonist who would like to live his life with a woman's nipple in his mouth twenty-four hours a day." No truer words have ever described me, as I well know, but if I give them that, I may as well give them the keys to the car and the deed to the condo, so I have a comeback that goes like this: "It's a cliché to suggest that every man wants his mommy back, so please try to say something original." Experience has taught me that as I say this, I will have an incredible urge to suck my thumb, so I advise you to sit on your hands before speaking. Against the hankering that you will inevitably have to pee in your pants and take a nap immediately thereafter, I have no proven defense. You might try opening the window and breathing fresh air. Or you might cuddle in her lap with your Teddy bear.

"You don't want a wife or a mother or a mistress or a daughter, you want an impossible creature with supernatural qualities called a soul mate" is always accompanied by, "Your demands and expectations about women are so unrealistic that I think you should be committed to an insane asylum or shot at dawn." Whatever you do, don't respond with a joke such as "Can I choose who I eat before they shoot me?" or "Do they make straitjackets for two?" This will only incite her to deeper and more accurate criticisms of your sensual nature, and unless you're into pain. . . . OK, I take it back; you're a man, so of course you're into pain, so kid her and be done with it.

What we want from women is no mystery. We want salvation and succor, pleasure and immortality, unconditional love and elegant eroticism. Simple needs for simple men, right? So what's the problem? We want five-sided women with all the qualities we cherish, and we want them to display the side we need at the time we need it. Isn't it amazing how difficult they can make it seem when we ask for that? You'd think they'd learn how to do what we wanted without so much fuss and bother. God, we're only asking them to be gods.

Pentawench, I call her, the five-sided woman of my dreams. She gyrates in the air like an angel in flames, and she glides across my psyche like a Madonna on skates. One day I know I'll find her—or die trying.

(1989)

Guerrilla Feminism_____

Most of the women in your life are still celebrating *Thelma & Louise*, a film released by MGM/Pathe last May. Directed by Ridley Scott, starring Geena Davis and Susan Sarandon, it made the cover of *Time* ("Why *Thelma & Louise* Strikes a Nerve") and the *New York Times* practically enshrined it ("*Thelma & Louise* is transcendent in every way").

Just a minute, now. Transcendent in every way? For whom, exactly? For most women, perhaps. But for most men, *Thelma & Louise* is a mixed bag of mixed signals. It mocks us and dismisses us, and it does so with subterfuge and shrewdness.

The fact that *Thelma & Louise* is a good movie makes its politics even more sly and seductive. The acting, directing and editing are excellent. But *Thelma & Louise* is also a film that trashes men. A strong element of antimale sexism runs through it, even though the folks connected with the film deny it.

"This is an adventure film," says Callie Khouri, the scriptwriter. "It's a film about women outlaws. People should just relax."

"It's outrageous for people to say, 'Poor men, they're being bashed in this movie! Ooh! Poor us!'" Davis says. "I think there's something

84

like seven or eight men in the movie, and in my opinion, they sort of cover a very broad spectrum. It's pretty darn fair."

"It could easily become a feminist lecture," Scott says. "The script is so beautifully disguised in its comedic aspects without smothering its message."

These kinds of disingenuous statements are examples of what I call guerrilla feminism. There's a lot of it in the world of this film—and in our lives today.

The story line of *Thelma & Louise* is relatively simple. Louise (Sarandon) is a wisecracking waitress who talks her good friend Thelma (Davis) into leaving her husband for a few days. Thelma and Louise drive off in a Thunderbird convertible, and a female buddy film is born.

As in all buddy films, something happens. Thelma and Louise stop at a bar for a few drinks. Thelma gets loaded. Liberated from her oafish husband (a man who never cooks a meal for himself—get it?), she ends up drunk as a skunk in a parking lot with a guy named Harlan (Timothy Carhart).

Now, you might ask what signals Thelma is sending Harlan with her behavior, since she has been dancing and drinking and flirting openly with him for some time, but let that pass (*Time* glosses over this question by writing, "They stop at a roadhouse for a drink. One of its resident lounge lizards mistakes Thelma's naïve flirtatiousness for a come-on.")

When Thelma resists Harlan's advances, he slaps her around. Even worse, he then tries to rape her. Louise happens upon the scene, pulls out a handgun, tells Harlan to stop what he is doing. Harlan stops but becomes verbally abusive in his own drunken fashion. Louise shoots him point-blank in the chest. Harlan dies. Pronto. Thelma and Louise take off from the scene of the crime and become fugitives from the law. On the run, the two women accelerate their liberation through increasingly bold escapades.

Thelma gets the hots for a young hitchhiker named J.D. (Brad Pitt), a cowpoke who sleeps with her, then steals her money and leaves her. She and Louise get the drop on a state trooper and lock him in the trunk of his car—but not before they steal his pistol and he weeps and moans and groans (you know how those male state troopers are under pressure). Thelma robs a convenience store successfully and, later, the two women destroy a fuel tanker driven by an obnoxious trucker.

At last, Thelma and Louis reach their finale. They are at the end of their road, trapped by insensitive lawmen and a police investigator named Hal (Harvey Keitel) who suddenly becomes meek and ineffective as the showdown develops (you know how those male police investigators are under pressure).

Thelma and Louise choose suicide instead of surrendering to the authorities. Sisters forever, hands raised and clasped in solidarity, they drive straight off a cliff. They fly courageously into the abyss of certain death and eternal companionship. Freeze-frame, fade-out, credits.

Thelma & Louise presents men as basically clumsy and cruel and powerless, but it also tells a good story with some good humor. In that sense, it often succeeds as a movie. Davis and Sarandon play tough, gritty, beautiful women. As a man watching them, I was attracted to them at first, and I did like them—until I realized that if I met them on the street, they would probably blow me away if I violated their standards of protocol and etiquette. And therein lies the meanest and deepest message of this slick cinematic exercise.

I remember a *Donahue* show of last May in which a woman who had been one of the many wives of an oft-married man was asked, "Why did you pull a thirty-eight on him?"

She did not hesitate. "Because he needed killing," she answered with a smile. The audience cheered.

The most primitive message behind *Thelma & Louise* is that a lot of men need killing these days. This is an acceptable, even amusing, proposition in our contemporary society. And I suggest that, as men, we had better be alert to it.

As men, we are accustomed to being considered expendable in both war and peace. But the standard feminist celebration of male expendability is relatively new to us, and very difficult to handle, especially when, like all good guerrillas, its perpetrators deny their motivations.

Thelma & Louise is appealing at times. It is also prejudiced and sexist at its core. It faithfully represents our era, a time when feminists can bask in the glory of their increasingly harsh sexism toward men—and even win Oscar nominations for it.

(1991)

Cherry-Blossom Boogie_____

It was unseasonably cool in Washington, D.C., even though the cherry blossoms were in full bloom and the tulips were as bright as paint.

As I always do when I visit Washington, I walked down to the Vietnam Veterans Memorial to say hello to some friends I miss very much. Then I circled back toward the base of the Washington Monument, hearing music and amplified voices in the distance.

Sunday, April 9, 1989, was the day of the now-famous abortion-rights march that drew an officially estimated 300,000 "pro-choice" activists to the nation's capital. My unofficial estimate is that the crowd was probably twice that size, and I would guess that three quarters of the marchers were women and children. Most of the women wore white and many of them sported yellow sashes and NOW buttons. Throughout the day, there was a wonderful rush of feminine energy in the crowd.

I enjoyed that energy, but I also felt slightly isolated from it. After all, this march was not mine. As a male, I had some unspoken questions about fathers' rights rattling around in my brain. Not only that but I also found the stated motive for the march to be off the

87

point and out of focus. This street demonstration would sway the Supreme Court's decision-making process? Doubtful, I thought.

Walking through the immense crowd that day, I had questions that I didn't ask aloud. The few times I did try to talk to women about the issues, I was met with reserve.

My major job in Washington was to cover a conference being held the next day called Women, Men and Media. It was cochaired by Betty Friedan and Nancy Woodhull, and it was sponsored by The Gannett Foundation and the University of Southern California School of Journalism. "Our goal? To examine how women are hired, promoted and portrayed by the media," Friedan and Woodhull wrote in an introductory letter.

Monday morning dawned warm and bright, and I walked into the National Press club wondering what was ahead of me. ASA BABER, *Playboy,* my name tag read. "Wear your name tag at all times," the woman at the reception desk said sternly. I nodded that I would do so, and as I put it on, she handed out other name tags without similar admonishment.

That woman at the desk was one of only three women to speak to me voluntarily that day. Confronted with my name and my presence, most of the women I saw avoided me. I was a white male writing for a magazine that bothered them and that most of them thought should be banned (as remarks later in the day proved). As such, I was sent to my own ghetto in the back of the room.

Friedan opened the conference by talking of the previous day's abortion-rights "march of millions." She also spoke of "the symbolic annihilation of women" in the media. She pointed out that while women make up 66 percent of journalism school graduates, they constitute less than 10 percent of top management.

The statistics quoted during the conference were (by now) familiar and unpleasant. They show that, on average, women still are not treated equally in the media business. According to the reports presented, women earn 64 cents for every male employee's dollar in media companies. Three percent of television presidents or vice-presidents are women (eight percent in radio). Ownership of media companies is primarily male, and fully qualified women are still running into a "glass ceiling," able to be promoted only so far and no further in their media companies.

No fair-minded man listening to these statistics can be proud of them, and I make no case that things should continue as they are.

But statistics tell only part of the story, and some funny things happened at the conference that proved to me, once again, that women are just as human as men—and just as prone to gloat and segregate, ignore and exclude, no matter how much they may proclaim today that theirs is a kinder, gentler psyche.

During the first panel discussion, a man named Joseph Ward, a student at Marymount University who described himself as a "young white male," stood up and asked Carole Simpson, a black senior correspondent at ABC-TV in Washington, how he would do in the present-day job market that seemed to him, in spite of the statistics, to be biased against him.

"I feel sorry for you right now," Simpson replied. "I think we're at a period of time where there is some compensatory time due.... Perhaps you are going to be at a disadvantage. That's new to you white males. And you'll see how it feels."

Joseph Ward sat down politely and the conference went on, but I thought a lot about the sexism that men like him will meet as this society struggles to make things equal. I thought of the blatant feminist sexism there in that room and in the culture, the ads on TV that mock men, the sitcoms that present them as nothing but jerks, the current feminist literature of sexual politics that gives men no shelf space. I wondered if Ward had registered for the draft, if he was ready for combat, if he was ready to see his rights to protect his children abolished by a divorce court.

Linda Ellerbee gave the luncheon speech. She was tough and funny and mostly fair-minded, and I would buy her a beer any day. "If you believe in equal rights, you are a feminist," she said. I knew that I fit clearly into her definition, but I also knew that it wasn't that simple anymore.

Somewhere in her talk, Ellerbee mentioned a female reporter who had threatened to kick a man's balls through his brains if he didn't get out of her way. The women in the audience roared their approval. I winced, and I imagine Joseph Ward did, too.

Late that night, I went back alone to the Vietnam Veterans Memorial and sat in the grass and talked to my brothers for a long time. They listened kindly and silently, and I felt at home.

(1989)

Catch-23

You remember Yossarian, the bomber pilot in *Catch-22*? Yossarian knew that he had to be crazy to fly bombers through heavy concentrations of flak and that such craziness could get him killed. So he went to the flight surgeon and asked to be grounded by reason of insanity. But the flight surgeon reminded him that there was a catch to his logic, Catch-22: By recognizing the madness of war, Yossarian proved he was sane, so he had to keep flying.

I think I'll write a novel called *Catch-23*. It will be about a vigorous male who feels as if he's always flying through flak. And he will experience today's classic double bind: He'll be accused of being sexist by feminists who are sexist, and he will be mocked for his maleness by people who are angered by his very nature. Like Yossarian, he'll look for relief from madness, and, like Yossarian, he will be hard pressed to find it.

Men have now had 25 years of sexists' calling us sexist. It is an amazing Catch-23. We've been living through a cultural revolution that has been largely unreported from the male side. We've been called evil and piggish and have been attacked at our core, and yet most of us have our own private check lists—unshared and unspoken—of sexist assaults against us. If we ever got together and compared notes, we might learn something.

Item: An English professor who admires my fiction suggests that I apply for a teaching position at his university. I do so. He calls me. "This is confidential," he says, "but the feminists on the faculty will not read your work, because it's in *Playboy*. They are boycotting it. You'll never get this job."

Item: A woman with whom I'm friends becomes angry when I won't close to an intimate distance. She is married, hiding our friendship from her husband, trying to make me a substitute for him. I won't cooperate. When she sees that my stubbornness is intractable, she writes me a series of letters. "You're not a player. You're just an observer, a voyeur," she writes. She labels me sexist, scarred, psychologically impotent. She claims virtue for herself. She knows how to love, she says, whereas I never will.

Item: Two women write an opinion piece in the *New York Times*. They rightly point out that no women were indicted in the Wall Street insider-trading scandals. They also correctly cite the sexism women experience in the field of mergers and acquisitions: Women are kept out of the locker rooms where much of the market gossip is traded. But then the writers go on to claim superiority for their own sex. Superiority, not equality. Women, they decide, simply are not as corrupt as men. "Perhaps absolute power corrupts absolutely—only if you're male," they write.

Item: I go to see *Outrageous Fortune*, a slick and sometimes funny movie, usually funny at the expense of men. I enjoy Bette Midler and Shelley Long, but I am troubled by Peter Coyote's role. He is every feminist's foil: a man who seems at first to be a nurturer but who turns out to be horrid. At the end of the movie, as Coyote misses a jump that Long makes and is falling to his death, she yells out to him, "Nine years of ballet, asshole!" I do not laugh, though most of the women I know think that is a hilarious moment. "I've never laughed so hard in my life," one of them says. Later, under the caption SHOCKINGLY REALISTIC, a gossip column reports with bemusement, "If you think it looks pretty realistic when Bette Midler socks Peter Coyote in *Outrageous Fortune*, it was. She connected so soundly that she actually broke his eye socket." I wonder to myself how it would be reported if Coyote broke Midler's eye socket. I suspect I would find a covey of feminists in high dudgeon.

I'm going to make a quantum jump now. I'm going to suggest that the Catch-23 process is more damaging than you may think. We've had a quarter century of male bashing, of feminists' claiming virtue for themselves while they call men sexists and ignore their own sexism. It's a form of induced schizophrenia, and it is a killing tactic.

The Centers for Disease Control recently issued a report on suicide among the nation's young people. By 1980, five young males committed suicide for every female. The suicide rate for young males increased 50 percent between 1970 and 1980 (compared with a 2 percent increase for females). "Further research is needed," the centers reported, "to explain the marked increase in suicide among young white males, to characterize their deaths more precisely and to develop and evaluate effective ways to prevent those deaths."

The reasons for suicide may always remain deep and mysterious, but surely the cultural dynamic of the past years has to be considered as one of the causes. The signals in this culture have been mostly antimale. Young men react to that, sometimes self-destructively.

As I watched *Outrageous Fortune,* I also watched a mother and her two young sons in front of me. The mother thought the movie was a laugh riot. The boys were confused. They initially liked Peter Coyote (he comes on as a grade school teacher, loving and likable at first, the perfect father). After he is exposed as a murderer and rogue, the boys didn't see one strong and decent male presence on the screen. I thought about the number of boys being raised with the idea that being male is a nasty condition, shameful and oppressing, limited and dull. Welcome to the world of Catch-23, I thought, a place where sexists trap you into believing that only you are sexist.

Yossarian survived his war, and it's up to us to survive ours. That's the male job: to survive at all costs, to keep on trucking, to never give up. One way we'll do a better job of surviving is by understanding the double bind we live under, by finding ways of getting out from under it and then by celebrating our outrageous fortune at being alive.

Yossarian did it. So can we.

(1987)

A New Breed of Woman

There is something dead at the center of most feminist rhetoric today. The ideas behind it are rattling like bones in a closet, and we sense that the keepers of this angry faith are mouthing clichés, not truths. Try this, for example:

"The other day a very wise friend of mine asked: 'Have you ever noticed that what passes as a terrific man would only be an adequate woman?' A Roman candle went off in my head; she was absolutely right. What I expect from my male friends is that they are polite and clean. What I expect from my female friends is unconditional love...." Anna Quindlen wrote this stuff in a *New York Times* column called "Life in the 30s." "I keep hearing that there's a new breed of men out there who don't talk about helping a woman as though they're doing you a favor.... But from what I've seen there aren't enough of these men to qualify as a breed, only as a subgroup."

Can you hear the wind? Are you huddled in your subgroup? Are you staying polite and clean as the coldness settles around you?

Take heart, men. A sexual springtime is coming. I've seen a glimpse of it. The good news is this: The Anna Quindlens of the world are going to be passed by, left to sit in their ice palaces. The sun is shining on a new generation of women, and they are far more ready to be our partners and friends and compatriots than the radical feminists who have blasted us for years. In its very shrewd and practical way, this new generation has come to bury Quindlen, not to praise her.

Yes, I'm talking about a new breed: the generation of women who are in their 20s and 30s. As I get to know them, I am truly impressed. They are bright and beautiful; but best of all, they are independent in thought and take nothing for granted, not even the insistent admonitions from some of their older sisters that the snows of disapproval must never melt.

The members of this new breed are postfeminist. Blind faith in any rhetoric is not their style. Tough, rational, scarred, uncertain of what's ahead, they are in the process of examining feminism and adopting only those elements that are useful to them. They are, as a generation, one hell of a lot fairer to men.

Take the Jogger, for example.

The Jogger is 25. She is redheaded, quick-witted, athletic. She has a stubborn chin, clear green eyes, a long neck, very long legs. I met her first through a series of letters she wrote to me about this "Men" column. We talked by phone, and when she came through Chicago on business recently, we did her version of lunch: a run in the sun instead of martinis in a restaurant. The Jogger has her M.B.A., is on the corporate fast track, makes twice as much money as I do and has the stride of a racehorse. The next time, I'll take my roller skates and clipboard; nonetheless, it was worth the strain and pain. I think the Jogger speaks for many women her age.

"I was born about the time feminism came on the scene, and I got very strong profeminist signals as a child. I remember in fifth grade, the teacher asked us to draw a picture of what we wanted to be when we grew up. Not one girl in my class drew a picture of a wife or a mother or a homemaker. We were all career-oriented.

"Nobody ever asked us what we wanted. We were simply told what we should be. It was assumed we wanted careers more than we wanted relationships, that we'd focus on business and let marriage and family happen later. The feminists thought they knew what was best for us. Sounds a little pompous, doesn't it?

"My generation is severely criticized by older feminists for not being feminist enough. I really resent that. I think they're missing the point. What are we supposed to do, mimic everything they did? We're in our 20s. We've watched our parents screw it up, and we don't want to repeat their mistakes.

"Sure, I run into sexism in business. I'd have to be blind not to see it. But I look at it as a problem to be solved. I don't get hysterical about it. When some male I'm working with tells me to go get the coffee, I see clearly that he's sexist. I get the damned coffee, go on to show him I'm very good at my real job, get him to trust and respect me, and then I talk to him about his attitude. It's very unemotional.

"I'm not interested in fighting the feminist wars. I'm much more interested in the question of choice—for men as well as women. Do we have the choice of doing what we're really inspired to do, male and female? If you want to stay home and raise a family, do you have the choice? If you want a career, is that option available?

"My generation doesn't see open choices ahead. We've led very insecure lives, and there doesn't seem to be much security in the years ahead. We live off plastic and see an economy deeply in debt and a Social Security system whose failure is going to hit us like a ton of bricks. We're being handed enormous obligations by the older generations. Why should we trust them when they tell us what to think? They're cutting off our choices."

We had a good run, the Jogger and I. She brought a new view to an old war. In her way, her vision is much tougher than Anna Quindlen's. Yes, in some ways, the Jogger seems too good to be true; but she exists, and as she looks down the road, what she sees is not pretty.

"My generation, male and female, is the new proletariat. We get our credit cards and business degrees and health-club memberships and mortgages and pretend we're in Fat City. But we're disposable. We're replaceable chips. This society will wear us down and use us up and then turn us in for newer models. We'll end up with no choices at all if we're not careful. Survival is going to depend on men and women working together. So we've got to stop fighting with each other."

I left the Jogger feeling that there was warmth after winter, spring after snow, and that the women of her generation were a special breed. I also felt winded and sore-legged, but that's what you get when you're in fast company.

I didn't mind. I had seen the sexual future, and it was sunny.

(1987)

Nuclear Feminism, Hormonal History

I was planning to drop a nuclear weapon on Chicago more than 27 years ago. I had all the maps, charts, weather reports and other classified data I could possibly need. Using special grids, I calculated that for a single one-megaton warhead exploding on the ground, there would be total destruction and burnout for some 2.6 miles in all directions. If, however, I ordered an air burst at 10,000 feet above the city, the area of burnout would extend to 60 square miles.

At precisely the moment that I stuck a pin into the map somewhere west of the Chicago Loop, my classroom exercise at the First Marine Division's A.B.C. (Atomic, Biological and Chemical Warfare) School at Camp Pendleton, California, was interrupted: I was told to report to the commanding officer's headquarters. There was an emergency telephone call for me.

I took the call and learned that my father had died a few minutes earlier from a heart attack. He had been seated at his desk at the Chicago Title and Trust Company in the Loop.

Publicly, I absorbed the news of my father's death like the young Marine I was supposed to be, but the strange conjunction of that morning's forces—death and nuclear weapons—has been vigorously linked in my mind ever since. (I wrote about this incident before in an article in the June 1981 issue of *Playboy.*)

Privately, I mourned the loss of my father deeply, and at times I still do. But, more important, what I learned in the Marines (and later) about our massive capabilities for nuclear, chemical and biological self-destruction changed my life, set my teeth on edge and led me to a career devoted to writing and speaking against nuclear war and its disastrous effects.

I wouldn't change a thing, but this antiwar stance of mine is not the shrewdest position to take in this culture. We live in a time of national uncertainty and anger, and as a people we seem prepared to go to war at a moment's rhetoric.

As a people, I said. *Male and female,* I add. Women are not immune to jingoism. I have found any number of female hawks, aggressive women who sound very hard-edged in their support of our militaristic policies. They have good role models to build on, from Jeane Kirkpatrick to Margaret Thatcher to Indira Gandhi, and they usually mock any male who strikes them as weak-kneed or lily-livered. Any male, veteran or not.

Questions of who wants war and who wants peace have always seemed to cut across sexual lines. Or so I thought until I read *Missile Envy,* by Dr. Helen Caldicott. It was there that I learned my male hormonal nature was at the root of war. It was there that I encountered the ultimate feminist argument: Men cause war.

"The hideous weapons of mass genocide may be symptoms of several male emotions, reflecting inadequate sexuality, a need continually to prove virility and a primitive fascination with killing," Dr. Caldicott writes. She proceeds to list familiar feminist clichés about the glorious nature of women and the dark nature of men. Some prime quotations:

> Men and women are psychologically and physiologically different.... A typical woman is very much in touch with her feelings.... Women are nurturers. Their bodies are built anatomically and physiologically to nurture life.... One of the reasons women are so allied to the life process is their hormonal constitution. After I went through pregnancy and the birthing process, I was emotionally and physically engrossed in my children.... To a certain extent, these feelings are induced by

the female hormones estrogen and progesterone.... Men, on the other hand, are men because of their hormonal output of androgen.... [Men are] typically more psychologically aggressive than women.... What is it about their most primitive feelings that makes these men enjoy killing? Women know almost from birth that they can experience the ultimate act of creativity, but boys and men lack this potential capacity.

When I hear words like those—and, like most men, I've had years of practice at it—I am amazed at the temerity and self-absorption of such thinking. How are we ever going to have any kind of peace if women are going to declare themselves so superior to men? How are those of us opposed to the arms race ever going to get together if we have to accept a hormonal theory of history?

As a male, how can I respond to such a limited view of my own nature? Does Caldicott really think she loves her children more than I love mine? Must I accept the idea that I love killing? Am I truly a victim of penis envy and missile envy? By my very nature, am I dumb and stupid and out of touch with my emotions? ("I am married to a very beautiful man," she writes. "But still he is a man.") If we gave every male in the world a hefty injection of estrogen, would we really solve the problems of war and peace? If it were that simple, I might even be for it. But it's not.

Take a look around. You'll find women who are walking away from nurturing roles as fast as they can. You'll find aggressive women, hawkish women, ruthless women, cruel women. You'll find women who are willing to turn children against their fathers—a kind of assassination if there ever was one—and women who are perpetually ready to go to war or, at least, to send men off to war, a role that has not been unknown to women over the past 1000 millennia.

We're fallible. All of us. We're conditioned in strange ways and we struggle with our tendencies toward aggression. We've got a lot of work to do if we're going to avoid nuking, gassing, germing ourselves to death. All of us. Male and female, conscious of our fragility and our equality, our weaknesses and strengths. But to charge that it is androgen that has caused our wars and estrogen that has promoted peace?

Helen, ye hardly know me.

(1987)

*The Dawn's Early Light*_____

When I was asked to be a guest on *The Oprah Winfrey Show*, I accepted the invitation with some hesitation. I respect Oprah Winfrey's intelligence, but my take on her show is that it's a bastion of female sexism. I've heard enough antimale rhetoric from her guests (and her audience) to last me several lifetimes.

When I got to the studio, I knew it might become a special hate fest, because my friend Nick Nickolas was also a guest on the show. Nobody angers feminists more than Nick Nickolas. Owner of Nick's Fishmarket and other eateries, Nick has the audacity to live the life of a *bon vivant*. He's a tough, energetic, humorous, hard-working man who often praises his Greek heritage and the strong sense of the conventional family it developed in him. He irritates feminists by consorting with beautiful women as often as he can and by flaunting old-fashioned dating etiquette. For example, he sometimes offers his dates the use of his credit card so they can buy themselves a new dress before they go out with him. You can imagine how disapproving Oprah and her friends are of that!

We walked onto the set, sat down and the taping began. I kept my mouth shut for the first half hour as I listened to the trashing of Nick Nickolas and wondered how our culture had grown so dark, so filled with feminist self-righteousness and anger. Men were slaveholders; men were Hitlers; Nick was a bad man because his dating behavior wasn't politically correct; he was a lecher because he bought gifts for his dates and (Oprah and company assumed) expected favors in return. It got even fiercer during the commercial breaks, when the off-camera conversation resounded with yelling and insults.

Eventually, I managed to cut through the clamor and say a few things. I pointed out that there was a tremendous prejudice alive in that television studio, a perverted belief that men represented only aggression and oppression, while women represented love and tenderness. I suggested that women were sending out very confusing messages these days, asking at one moment to be treated as equals, hiding at other moments behind traditional feminine poses. I asked how women could expect us to listen to them when they painted themselves as paragons of virtue and us as slaveholders and fascists. I asked them where the idea of personal freedom had gone, why they thought they had the right to judge Nick's personal behavior. "Give Nick his freedom," I remember saying.

It was a strange and strained time, and if that were the end of the story, I wouldn't tell it. After all, men have had 25 years of this judgmental shit from feminists. It's nothing new. But something happened after the lights were down and the audience was leaving that struck a spark in me and hinted at better things to come. It wasn't a huge moment, but it seemed significant. As I was turning to leave, one of the people on the panel, a staunch feminist, asked me a simple, profound question in a voice that was filled not with rage but with perplexity: "What are we supposed to do with our rage?" she asked.

"That's a good question. Did you ever wonder what we're supposed to do with ours?" I asked. She and I looked at each other for a minute. I would like to think that an understanding passed between us, that we both acknowledged that there is more than enough oppression and injustice and prejudice and abuse and manipulation to go around for both sexes. I hoped that we were silently admitting that neither men nor women get a free lunch in this turbulent culture, that life can be equally difficult for both sexes and that maybe, just maybe, we're starting to understand that fact.

If what I'm saying is true, then maybe, just maybe, there's a small streak of light on what has been a very dark cultural horizon, the light of personal tolerance and compassion that has been close to extinction for years.

That light glimmers for me fairly often these days. I find more women trying to communicate, to think independently of clichés, pat answers, party lines. Even those feminists who go on the attack seem to be more muted and thoughtful when they realize that men are not just going to roll over and accept the standard feminist versions of history and sexuality. Perhaps there's a mutual respect being born in the midst of the sexual wars. Maybe the light is shining out of a form of combat fatigue, an understanding that we can't go on beating one another up all the time without paying enormous, deadly costs.

Recently, I went out for what I thought was going to be a relaxed evening with friends. As had happened many times before, I got ambushed. One of the women in the group went on the attack: "How could you publish in *Playboy?* That magazine uses the camera as a penis. It violates women. It oppresses them. When you publish there, you support that." The harangue went on and on, angry and demanding and filled with accusations. I eventually got up and left. I've learned to do that after many years of such scenes.

But, again, something happened. The next day, the woman came by to see me. "I'm not even angry anymore," she said. "I'm just tired. Tired of the fighting and the anger itself." She handed me a pastel drawing she had just completed. It was a beautiful piece of work. "I want you to have it," she said.

Something's going on, some tentative gestures toward accommodation. Here at the magazine, one of my friends, a woman who has been a colleague for years, thought my performance on *The Oprah Winfrey Show* was "appalling." She didn't like what I had to say or how I said it or who I said it to, and she let me know it in no uncertain terms. But the point is that she said it to me at lunch, a lunch that was filled with a lot of laughs and affection, and when I came back at her with some statements in self-defense, she listened to me, as in *really* listened. There was mutual respect, mutual tolerance. A few years ago, it might not have happened like that.

There is light out there. It's not always easy to see, but if you look for it, you can find it. Most mornings, anyway.

(1988)

*How to Please a Man*_____

It had to happen, right? Eventually, there had to be some advice from a man to women about sex and life and love and ways to attract the opposite sex. Here on this page, a revolutionary concept is being born. The burden is heavy, but I accept the responsibility of explaining to women what men want. If any of you women out there have any questions about this, just call me. I'm a hell of a guy, and I think I can help you.

1. *Of course you can give flowers to a man.* Men are mellowing out, and you should not ponder this question. If you want to take him a small bouquet of forget-me-nots when you pick him up for your first date, that's fine, but be a little sensitive, will you? Tie a condom or a packet of cocaine to the stems and give him a big wink as you hand the flowers over. That way, he'll know you're sincere.

2. *Paying for dinner is fine.* This question is an old one now. Of course you can pay for his dinner if you want to, even if he's the one who asked you out. But is that all you play to pay for? If you really want to please him, do something like this: Pick up the check with a soft, feminine "It's mine," pause, take a sip of water as you hand your charge card to the waiter, gaze deeply into your date's eyes and say, "I've cornered the nearbys in soybeans and estimate I've just made

$140,000,000. Darling, half of that is yours." That is the kind of gesture he'll understand. But take heed: if he argues for a 70-30 cut his way and half your profits on the crush margin, tell him to get lost. That guy is a gold digger.

3. *Oral sex is permissible.* Some women may still be confused about it, but most men have their heads on straight about it. They absolutely do not mind receiving attention in this manner. It can even be argued that men are coming out of their shells, so to speak, and are willing to give instructions, directions, entreaties, orders and other ejaculations of that sort. Just ask him and he'll tell you how he wants it done, where he wants it done, how often. If he's shy, don't give up on him. Let's see, is there any other aspect of this subject we should be covering? Not that I can think of.

4. *If you play your cards right, some men will allow themselves to be picked up.* This is a tricky questions, because men in general can be so shy and unavailable when approached by women, but there are ways to break down male resistance. When you see a man you want to meet, think of a good opening line, one that is neither too leering nor too modest. "Aren't you that male stripper I saw on the Phil Donahue show?" is a very good opener and works 90 percent of the time. Two other possibilities: "With it strapped down to your knee like that, don't you limp when it gets hard?" and "What's life as a sex surrogate like, anyway?" Both of those intros are real icebreakers for most men, and you will have them at a disadvantage. They will *all* think you are being perfectly serious.

5. *The male is delicate, so handle him with care.* There are certain things that simply should not be said to a man. Common sense dictates most of those guidelines, but a refresher course probably won't hurt you women. A recent poll showed that the following statements cause hysteria in the men who hear them. I'm sorry to report that the context doesn't matter; these zingers hurt however and whenever they're said: (A) "Is it in?" (B) "There's my husband!" (C) I'm so glad you can't tell I'm a transsexual," (D) "Did you know your nose is your most prominent part?" (E) "You look just like the guy who gave me herpes," (F) "Smile! You're on *Candid Camera.*"

6. *If you want to score, don't mention death or taxes. Tax shelters are OK.* The average male is raised to believe that death is an inconvenient event that happens to those who weren't smart enough to get an M.B.A. Men cannot function unless they are fed with the

illusions that they are (A) indispensable, (B) highly successful and (C) immortal. Don't upset their fatuous applecarts. Play to their self-deceptions and you will get whatever you want. Don't say stupid things like "Gee, according to actuarial tables, I'll probably live 25 years longer than you will, sucker." That won't get you anywhere. The same goes for the subject of taxes. For reasons that can't be entirely explained, men feel threatened by a Government that can take about half the money they make. Picky, picky, I know, but that's men for you. Don't theorize with comments like "If Thomas Jefferson were alive today, do you think he'd approve of withholding?" That's just bringing up an unpleasant subject unnecessarily. However, there is no reason you can't discuss certain aspects of business and finance. If your uncle is chairman of the Fed, if you have secret information about the Russian wheat crop or, in particular, if you own an offshore bank that provides 10:1 write-offs that the IRS approved by mistake, let your fellow know about it, for goodness' sake. Why hide your light under a bushel?

7. *Men love flattery, even if they say they don't.* Inside every male, there's a little tyrant waiting to be worshiped. Men are so hungry for flattery that they'll believe anything you tell them. A woman friend of mine, when she can't think of anything else to do, compliments men on their breathing. "You really know how to breathe," she says to them. "I like the way your chest rises and falls, and I've never seen a man direct the air through his nose the way you do. I mean, wow, that is such a turn-on." She says it works, and I have to take her word for it. I'm a little hurt that she hasn't yet mentioned it to me, though. I think I breathe just about as well as any man I've ever seen, but you can't have everything. Damn it.

8. *The bottom line to the male psyche: Men want everything.* Oh, we do, we do. We all want beauty, fame, comfort, peace, excitement, wealth, love; and we want it while we're receiving hot-oil rubs from the persons of our choice. While you may laugh at our greedy natures, in our hearts we think we're being very sensible. And don't worry, the world shows us on a daily basis that we can't have it all, even when we go for it. OK, I admit it: We men are childlike fools. Just don't mention it, OK? You might interrupt our continuous secret dreaming, and you know how most men are when they're awakened by surprise. Unbearable.

(1984)

Happy As Pigs _____

The headline jumped out at me: "WOMEN REALLY TICKED OFF AT MEN, POLL SAYS." "Oh, no!" I cried. "Have I done something wrong *again?*" Suddenly, I felt very insecure. I hugged my Alan Alda doll even tighter.

I kept reading: "American women increasingly believe that most men are mean, manipulative, oversexed, self-centered and lazy.... And the women are getting annoyed." According to this report, The Roper Organization polled 3,000 women and found "growing numbers of women expressing sensitivity to sexism and unhappiness with men on many issues."

Forty-two percent of the women polled found men to be "basically selfish and self-centered." Some 54 percent of the women agreed that "most men look at a woman and immediately think how it would be to go to bed with her." According to 52 percent of the women, their mates do not help with the household chores.

What makes matters worse, according to the Roper poll (financed, incidentally, by Philip Morris U.S.A.), is that a similar poll was taken 20 years ago, and the latest results show greater female discontentment than before. In 1990, for example, 58 percent of women agreed that "most men think only their own opinions about the world are important"—up from 50 percent in 1970. And given the statement "Most men find it necessary for their egos to keep women down," 55 percent agreed today, up from 49 percent previously.

Ellen Merlo, a Philip Morris vice-president, was quoted as saying, "The frustration [of women toward their lifestyle] is expressed in hostility toward men. Women are looking to men for more support. And their attitude toward men has turned somewhat sour."

The Roper poll surprised me, of course. Sour women? Frustrated and angry women? Are they out there? I certainly have never met any women who fit that description. I assume from the steady smiles and constant generosity of the women I meet that most are very satisfied with the men in their lives. And I know—I absolutely know—that American men today are as happy as pigs in shit. For us, life is just a bowl of orgasmic oatmeal. We've never had it so good. And if you doubt me, I've got proof. It's called the Baber poll.

I recently polled 3,000 men. The results are astounding. Men, it turns out, have no criticisms of women, no sense of anger or frustration, no gripes. For us, women are ideal, loving, supportive and wondrous. They shine like beacons in an otherwise hopeless sea. And I can back this conclusion up with hard data:

• One hundred percent of the men polled by The Baber Organization agreed with the statement that "most women are basically kind, gentle and thoughtful." This was reflected in individual interviews, as well. "Women are great, just great," said Ronald Rexmard of Baggs, Wyoming. "They are a constant joy to me because they are never critical and they tickle me in funny places and make me giggle. I've never seen a harsh or overly aggressive woman, and I doubt that they exist. Women are, to a person, as gentle as baby doves in a grain field at daybreak in the springtime."

• One hundred and one percent of the men agreed that "women live up to every ideal I ever had for them, and they do it with subtle grace and exquisite charm." Maurice Shubertini of Dothan, Alabama, agrees. "I am awed by the way women comport themselves in these chaotic times," he said. "There is never a mean word, never a slip of the lip that causes me shame. As much as I hate to admit it, only men are selfish and cruel. It must be genetic. Men are doomed. But women? Women are perfect."

• One hundred and two percent of the men polled confessed that

they enjoy oppressing women economically. "Yes, yes, I admit it,"
sobbed Johnny Bluthcorn of Wainmanalo, Hawaii. "I do everything
I can to deny women their rightful place in the business community. After all, it used to be a man's world, and I want to go back to
that world as soon as possible. If a woman enters my workplace, I
try to get her fired, and I never recommend her for promotion. As
far as I can tell, all of my fellow males agree that a woman's place is
in the home, not the office—and that she'd better work at home for
free! We all know that men stand for slavery and oppression."

• Zero percent of the men polled found women to be "sexist and
unfair in their judgments of men." Arthur Windsock of Caribou,
Maine, put it this way: "The Roper poll simply verifies what we as
men have known all along. Women see us through very realistic
eyes. They don't expect too much from us, and when they are
disappointed in us, they don't overreact and stick pins in our doll.
Personally, I support the last quarter century of male-bashing. I
think we've deserved it. Of course, by the year 2000, I will
probably have had my sex-change operation, so it doesn't really
matter to me."

• One hundred and ten percent of the men *disagreed* that "women
look at a man and immediately think how it would be to go to bed
with him." Charlie Kravanaugh of Lake Mills, Wisconsin, said,
"That's what I like about women. They are very clear and clean in
their sexuality. Just take a look at the soap operas they watch, at the
movies they attend, at the videotapes they rent, at the books they
read, at the signals they give in social situations, and I think you'll
agree with me that women are basically in control of their sexuality,
honest and upright citizens of the republic who would *never* think
at first meeting what it would be like to go to bed with a man."

So there you have it. Which poll are you going to believe? Is it
Roper or Baber? Is it fiction or fact?
Write, don't call. And hurry.

(1990)

The Lysistrata Syndrome⸺⸺⸺⸺

Are you ready for 1986?

Let's talk about that for a minute. No, I don't want to hear your New Year's resolutions or your predictions for the economy. Come on, this is your old buddy Ace talking. Don't bullshit a bullshitter. I want to know what you *really* think about when you look ahead to the New Year.

You think about warmth and comfort and approval, right? You're wondering where those qualities will come from and in what abundance. Will 1986 be a good year? Who will be your partner in luck and love, and what will be the momentum of your sex life?

"My sex life?" you ask as if insulted. "My sex life is so fine it's divine, man. How can you even ask? Listen, I do OK, get it?"

Yeah, I get it.

You lie like a rug; that's what I get. You're like the rest of us. Your public image is that of a happy stud. But deep in your heart, there is a reservoir of confusion and uncertainty about your future. It's not something you can talk about, but it's there like a toothache in the middle of the night. You live through unpredictable seasons. When it is cold, it is very, very cold. You are wondering as the year turns how troubled it will be.

You're not alone, by the way. Take a look at your brothers-in-arms as they crack jokes and chug beer and pretend that all is well. The truth is that they're not really doing any better than you are. They get their water shut off, too. And, like you, they pretend that nothing severe is happening, their surfaces smooth, their emotions in turmoil.

No one wants to talk about it or name it, but there's an epidemic sweeping the Western world, an epidemic of rejection and dissatisfaction and discontent on the part of women against men. I call it the Lysistrata syndrome, and I say it's general all over America. Women are the purveyors of it; men have to deal with the residue of it. The Lysistrata syndrome: Women withhold, men suffer, and the temperature of the culture drops.

Two thousand, three hundred and ninety-seven years ago, a Greek named Aristophanes wrote a very funny play about sexual rejection. It is called *Lysistrata*. First produced in Athens at the beginning of 411 B.C., it tells the tale of a formidable woman named Lysistrata who decides to bring peace to the continually warring states of Athens and Sparta. "Ladies," Lysistrata says to the council of women she has gathered, "if we want to force our husbands to make peace, we must give up sex." The women argue for a time. An earthy creature named Calonice opposes the plan: "Give up sex? Never! Lysistrata, darling, there's just nothing like it. How would that help end the war?"

"How?" Lysistrata replies. "Well, just imagine: We're at home, beautifully made up, wearing our sheerest negligees and nothing underneath and with our triangles carefully plucked, and the men are all like ramrods and can't wait to leap into bed, and then we absolutely refuse—that'll make them make peace soon enough, you'll see."

The women lock themselves in the Acropolis (which is also the state treasury and contains all the gold), refuse to sleep with their men, beat the crap out of those few hardy fools who try to break into their sanctuary. As you'd guess, by the end of the play, the men, all hobbling about the stage with unquenched erections, frantically agree to stop the war. Peace comes, the women cooperate and life goes on.

Sound familiar? Think history repeats itself?

Don't get me wrong. I don't think the Lysistrata syndrome of today is based on anything as high-minded as a quest for world peace.

Women are rejecting men out of pique, distaste, irritation, competitiveness, revenge, confused identity, fatigue, anger—you name it, they're displaying it. Athens and Sparta are at war again, this time under our own roofs.

So if you swagger around and pretend that you're getting yours at all times, pardon me if I smile. I happen to know better.

It's time for us to do something about our predicament, however. The Lysistrata syndrome is a pain in the penis, and we men had better get ourselves together or each New Year will find us as rattled as this one. New strategies are required, new tactics must be employed.

If you are a victim of the Lysistrata syndrome, you have three basic choices:

1. *The matching-funds ploy.* This approach takes discipline. You feign as much disinterest as your mate. You mirror your Lysistrata. You yawn when sex is mentioned. You pretend to go to sleep as soon as you hit the mattress. You talk about continence as a reasonable way of life. When directly approached, you plead a headache or a difficult day at the office. Neutrality is a mask you hide behind. You may be surprised at how soon your Lysistrata becomes concerned and how soon your life warms up.

2. *The other-woman threat.* You've probably had some practice with this one. You splash perfume on your shirt, rub lipstick on your collar, take home matchbooks from the best singles bars. You write passionate letters to yourself, sign them with different women's names and leave them in your suit pockets, which also contain a package of condoms and crushed flowers. This tactic will get you either thrown out of the house or back in favor—50-50 odds.

3. *The other-man threat.* This is particularly effective. You put a SO MANY MEN, SO LITTLE TIME sticker on your car. You hum *It's Raining Men* while your significant other tries to discuss issues of the moment. You stop commenting on her female colleagues and mention her male friends instead: "That George is really a hunk, isn't he?" you ask with a vague smile. This strategy has its risks, you understand, but please don't write to me if it complicates your life. There won't be a thing I can do.

Happy New Year to you. And to all you Lysistratas, too. Peace.

(1986)

The Iron Fist in the Iron Glove_____

About four o'clock on the afternoon of Wednesday, October 30, 1985, Sylvia Seegrist parked her car at the Springfield Shopping Mall near Philadelphia, Pennsylvania. She got out of the car, wearing combat fatigues and sneakers and carrying a rifle. Without saying anything, she started shooting.

Seegrist opened fire at a woman standing at a banking machine, missed her, fired at two other people, moved inside the mall, killed a two-year-old boy who was walking with older relatives and worked her way through the crowded main walkway, aiming in one direction and then another. She fired more than 15 shots in less than five minutes, killing two more people and wounding six others.

A passerby, John W. Laufer III, finally moved behind her, grabbed her gun and held her until the police arrived. "It's, like, hurry up, man," Seegrist said in a clipped voice at her arraignment. "You should have killed me on the spot."

It turned out that Sylvia Seegrist had been having some major problems before she went on her shooting rampage. Prior to that event, she had tried to choke her mother, stabbed a mental-health worker, frightened neighbors with her aggressive behavior and carried a semiautomatic .22 rifle around for weeks before she used it.

Ruth Seegrist, Sylvia's mother and a columnist for the weekly *Springfield Press,* had written a column about the plight of parents who need protection from their own children. "What do you need? Blood on the floor?" Ruth Seegrist had asked as she sought help for her daughter.

The bet in this "Men" column is that there will be an increasing number of Seegrists. Violence, it is clear, finds those who will serve it, male or female. Women are not immune to its blandishments, no matter how we try to hide from that fact.

The violence of women is seldom discussed in this culture. It is a taboo subject. But in pretending it doesn't exist, we run risks, as some people at the Springfield mall would tell you. Although Seegrist was wearing the gloves of war, a woman climbing out of a car with a rifle in her hands is still less immediately threatening than a man in similar circumstances.

Some people will argue that Seegrist is a statistical aberration, but she is not. Talk to any cop who has to answer domestic-disturbance calls and you will learn that the police who break up family feuds *never* assume at the front door that the male will be the violent partner. They know better than most that women in those situations also have the potential for violence.

Sociological studies back up that fact: Women perpetrate spousal violence almost as frequently as men. This holds true across cultures and across economic lines.

Why are men so quiet about this? We're willing to examine our own acknowledged penchant for violence (as I've done frequently in this column), and we absorb feminist descriptions of our aggressive natures, but rarely do we look across the sexual boundary and see the violence on the other side. Or maybe that should be put another way: Rarely do we speak about it, even if we see it, even if we live with it.

"Yeah, my woman slapped me around last night. She was really pissed. I didn't know how to handle it or what to do."

Those are not lines you'll hear in any locker room. Men just don't talk about it. But taboos were made to be broken, and our self-censorship deprives us of needed discussion and feedback.

Once upon a time, I lived with a woman who physically abused me. It didn't start out that way. Like all romances, it began optimistically, but something soured, and her response to what she soon considered my unacceptable presence was to go on the attack. She raged, slapped, kicked, scratched, hit. Once, I woke up with a knife in the mattress beside me. Once, she cut every suit I owned into small pieces and then threatened to use the scissors on me when I discovered what she had done. Her violence escalated in proportion to my confusion, and I left the relationship—only to receive a call that very evening: Unless I returned to her immediately, she announced, she would kill me, then kill herself.

I chose to wait out that threat. It was the right thing to do. She stayed put, everybody lived, and we went on to separate, better lives.

The violence we survive is always educational, however, and that night marked the last time I ever romanticized women. As much as I hated losing my fantasies of shelter and refuge, I knew then that women were simply human beings, open to all the glory and cruelty that label implies. I saw the iron fist in the iron glove, and I knew that violence was androgynous, a hermaphrodite who could seduce any one of us if we let him/her.

The irony of my tolerating physical abuse from a person probably half as strong as I am was not lost on me. But what, as a male, do you do in such a situation? I asked myself that question many times. If you counter the aggression, you might really hurt somebody. If you talk about it, you'll be mocked by your peers and possibly disbelieved by professionals. If you're not careful, the rage you feel will eventually explode—or you'll crawl into your shell and question your own manhood. That narrow range of choices puts the male in a very tight bind.

Literally trained to kill, I had to resist the violence I felt when I was assaulted. I am glad that I did resist, but at the time, it was extremely expensive to my system and my sense of myself. I did not completely understand the forces at work on me, and I felt isolated, misunderstood, alone.

It is fair to say that the problem of domestic violence will never be solved until the issue is discussed in its entirety. Sooner or later, we're going to understand that today's simplistic perception—the idea that men are violent and women are not—is one that hides from the truth.

Sylvia Seegrist was neither the first nor the last woman to let vengeance be hers. Could we all admit that women, too, are open to violence? And then could we move on to tackle the overwhelming question of why we sometimes go that route—all of us, male and female?

(1986)

*Just Married*_____

Ah, yes, June. The bridal month. Hearts and flowers. White veils. Wedding music. Who could have known June would be the month The Greek panicked? He got married last June, and he's been on the phone to me ever since.

"Nothing's changed," he always says when I answer. The Greek does not bother with introductions.

"Greek, how are you doing?" I laugh.

"Terrible. Nothing's changed. Life after marriage is exactly the same as life before marriage. Maybe a little worse."

"Yeah," I say, "marriage doesn't change things a whole lot. People expect too much from it."

"I thought I'd have a mystical experience at the altar. Nothing happened."

"Nope," I say. "Usually doesn't."

"I asked my wife if anything happened for her. 'Why should it?' she said. 'I don't know,' I said. 'I thought maybe we'd see a light or a vision of the future or the dove of peace floating down on a cloud.'"

"Greek," I said. "you've got to stop waiting for a religious experience. Marriage isn't like that. It's a social contract between two people. Period."

"But nothing's changed," he laments. "I'm still in debt. My father hasn't sold the restaurant. He thinks I'll take it over when he dies. The investment club makes money some months, but we're under-performing the Dow. My job sucks. My marriage hasn't changed a thing."

The Greek is in his late 20s. He was in a short-story-writing class I taught. He's about six feet tall, maybe ten pounds overweight, much too conscious of his receding hairline. He is a very fine writer, a truly hot-shot writer who will one day publish a very funny novel about life as a contemporary Greek-American.

When he told me that he had finally decided to marry the woman he had been dating for years, I congratulated him. I'd read his fiction and assessed his maturity and assumed he understood that marriage was not nirvana. I assumed wrong. The Greek lives in a state of perpetual disorientation. He had counted on his marriage to save him, to clear up his life and end his trials.

"They don't need us, you know, Ace."

"Women?" I ask.

"Yep. They don't need us."

"I think that's a little extreme."

"My wife can repair our car. You know what she bought herself for Christmas? Tools. Tools and a machine to tune the engine with."

"Well, that's good, Greek. You're giving her space. Thirty years ago, she wouldn't have dared do that. Now she's got the freedom to express herself."

"Express herself? She's taking over. There's nothing left for me. I already gave her the checkbook. She's a lawyer. She does the taxes. She knows more about the law than I do. I get the feeling she carries blank divorce papers around with her. You know, one mistake by me and—wham—it's out of the briefcase and onto the kitchen table: 'Sign here.'"

"You're getting paranoid, man."

"Yeah? Well, think about it. They don't need us. What's my role now? She's making more money than I am. She travels more. She cooks better. My father likes her *souvlaki* more than he likes mine. I'm telling you, nothing's changed and its getting worse."

"Surely, you've got some territory of your own, haven't you?"

"Yes. Yes, I do."

"Well, now, see? It's not so bad."

"I have the *Wall Street Journal*."

"That's a start."

"I won't let her see it."

"Before you've read it, you mean?"

"No. I won't let her see it. Ever. I shred it after I read it."

"You shred the *Wall Street Journal?*"

"Yes. It's my territory, remember? She keeps asking me questions about the investment club I'm in. Me and four other guys. From before the marriage. From before we even started dating. I swear to God, if I let her read the *Wall Street Journal*, if I answer her questions about stocks and bonds and commodities, if I ever let her come to a club meeting, I'll be history. She'll take the club over. So I stonewall her. Mum's the word. 'What's a price-earnings ratio? How do you use a bar chart? What's a stock option?' My lips are sealed. I won't teach her a thing."

"That's a little extreme, isn't it?"

"I'm telling you, Ace, we're surrounded. Women can do it all. It's going to be a maleless society one day soon. We're useless appendages. When they fill up the sperm banks, watch out, man."

"You *are* paranoid."

"That doesn't mean I'm wrong!" he yells. The Greek is usually soft-spoken, but by this time he is yelling. "You know what men are becoming? Appendixes. Yeah, that's right: the penis as the appendix. A useless organ."

"Greek, you're going overboard."

"This whole culture is going overboard," he says. "Where my family came from, men had a significant role. When they came to America, my father was instrumental in their success. He worked like a dog in the restaurant business, he built up a clientele, he made the decisions. Sometimes, when he looks at me, acts like he's looking at a Martian. He just stares at me like I'm another form of life. We never talk about my marriage. But he can see that I'm a lost sheep. When I asked one of his buddies who's a private investigator to keep track of my wife, my father just shook his head and poured an *ouzo*."

"Detective work? You think your wife is cheating on you?"

"I know she is."

"Who's the guy?"

"Guy? Who cares about that? The other day, she went into Merrill Lynch and opened up her own trading account. Listen, with her luck, she'll have twice the equity in stocks that I have within the year. No way I could handle that."

"Hey, it's easy. Just buy low and sell high," I say.

"Thanks, Ace. Great advice. Have a nice month."

"Happy June," I say. "Happy anniversary."

The Greek hangs up on me. But that's OK. I expected it. He never could take a joke.

(1987)

The Female-Sensitivity Quiz_____

I hereby declare 1991 the year when we finally ask women if they are sensitive enough *for us!* Yes, men, it is now time to turn the question around. What follows is a sensitivity quiz for the woman in your life. See how she scores. If she chooses anything but the last option in any of these examples, she is an insensitive broad who owes you a lot of loving. And she had better start to repay you right now. Even as you read!

1. You and your wife are at parents' night at your child's grade school. You have had a long day at your office and are not as alert as you might be. But your child's home-room teacher is a vivacious blonde woman with Deborah Norville lips and incredible legs, and suddenly, you feel an amazing jolt of energy. "Boy," you say to yourself as you and your wife climb into your car after the meeting, "I wish I'd had a teacher like that when I was in school. I'd never have gone home." Your wife overhears you and she

    A. Hits you upside the head with her purse.

    B. Calls you an insensitive, sexist pig, gets out of the car and walks home.

    C. Rolls down the window and prays for the Spirit of the Arctic to attack your groin and testicles.

D. Says, "I'll get you her phone number tomorrow, honey, but in the meantime, how about a blow job?"

2. You have identified a perfect flag formation on the bar chart you are keeping of the Standard & Poor's 500. On several occasions, you have almost followed your convictions, but at the last moment, your courage has failed you. Now, convinced that the stock market is about to make a major move, you invest your savings in an S&P position that quickly deteriorates. The margin calls wipe out your savings. When you tell your woman, she

A. Hits you upside the head with her brass knuckles.

B. Answers all phone calls at home for the next year by saying, "Donald Trump's residence; profit is our only motive."

C. Has her attorney send you a bill for the money you lost, with the suggestion that the IRS may be interested in your entertainment deductions.

D. Smiles graciously, rips off your clothes, makes fierce love to you, then says, "Money doesn't matter, darling, and I couldn't care less that you gambled with our savings and lost, because you're hung like a horse and that's all that counts."

3. You and your woman are on a vacation cruise, traveling first class on an elegant luxury liner. The two of you are attending a formal dinner in honor of the ship's captain, but you are not at your best. It has been a long and boring journey, you are sunburned and overfed and irritable, you hate dressing up and, on this particular evening, you have consumed too many drinks. Suddenly, something inside you snaps. You drunkenly insult the woman sitting next to you by suggesting that she has great melons and you'd like to conduct a ripeness test. Then you tell the captain that he couldn't navigate his way out of a bathtub. Finally, you throw up in the punch bowl, call your steward a terrorist, then moon the entire dining room as security drags you away. Back in your stateroom, your woman

A. Hits you upside the head with a life preserver.

B. Informs you that she has been sleeping with both the captain *and* the steward, that they are great lovers and that your imbecilic behavior has hurt her reputation.

C. Agrees with the ship's physician that putting you into a straitjacket and preparing you for a continuous Librium I.V. *and* electroshock treatments is a fine solution.

D. Smiles graciously, says, "There, there, into every life a little rain must fall," and climbs into bed to hold you and rock you to sleep with your favorite lullaby.

4. You and your boss are on the golf course at his country club. This is a first. He is a respectable golfer and you are honored to be invited. Rumor has it at the office that if your boss golfs with you, he promotes you. But, as luck would have it, this is one of your awkward days. You slice every drive, you four-putt every green, you hold up play when you lose sight of your ball, you forget to laugh at his jokes and you forget to replace your divots. Worse, when he asks your advice about business, he seems distinctly unimpressed with your answers. Then, as the two of you are heading for the clubhouse, you take a turn too fast and the golf cart tips over. Your boss is thrown onto the gravel and breaks his hip. In your haste to make amends, you start to drag him toward the putting green. He screams in agony. You drop him, causing him even greater pain. You try to lift the golf cart back into an upright position, but it slips and falls and breaks your boss's arm. You finally decipher his screams: "You're fired!" Forlornly, you go home and tell your woman the bad news, and she

A. Hits you upside the head with her three wood.
B. Turns pale, screams, "Oh, no, I love him so and I must be with him in his moment of pain," and runs out the door.
C. Calls in the children and says, "See Daddy? Do you know what he is? He's a total failure. Remember, kids, you don't want to be like Daddy. You don't want to fail. Daddy's going to be a homeless person now. Wave goodbye to Daddy, kids."
D. Smiles brightly, fixes you a mint julep, wipes your brow with her panties and dives for your fly while she says, "Honey, it's tee time at the old rancho, so let's get out your driver and shoot us a round."

Remember—you have feelings and you're sensitive. But what about her?

(1991)

Are Women Fit for Combat? _____

This is one of those questions that we are going to have to answer, because the feminization of the American military is proceeding apace. The Service academies are sexually integrated, the Armed Forces now permit women to occupy most military billets and equal opportunity for women seems close to a reality in what used to be a masculine profession.

There still is, however, one sexually segregated area: Those jobs described as frontline infantry combat assignments go only to men. So the question occurs, Now that women are partners in everything else in the military, is it unfair to deny them this specific chance to serve their country?

Some quick responses to that question, and then a discussion: (1) Yes, theoretically, it is unfair to deny women any combat assignment; (2) it is also unfair to require only men to register for the draft; (3) the last time I checked, the concept of fairness was not really central to the way a military machine was most effectively organized; (4) the question Are women fit for combat? is only half the question and, for men, the lesser in importance. For us, the *real* question is, Are men ready to go into combat with women as their commanders, peers and subordinates? That's the biggie.

First, I think we all have to acknowledge that it is patently unfair to deny women any and all opportunities for advancement in the military that men receive. Especially in the Armed Forces, combat duty is the way to the top (or at least to the semitop; believe it or not, in addition to combat duty, to reach the top of the military profession, you'd better be a bureaucrat, politician and operator. Blood, guts and bluntness may get you to the level of a field-grade officer, but generals and admirals are made of shrewder stuff, and warriors who are good in the field but inept in the office are usually passed over for the highest promotions). So let's admit it: In terms of fairness, openness, democracy and equal opportunity, women deserve access to every military billet, bar none.

But as those of us who have been there and back will ask, Who said the military structure in this culture is fair, open and democratic? By definition, the system is unfair to men, because only men are universally required (under penalty of fine and imprisonment) to register with the Selective Service System at the age of 18 (and to serve if called). Inequity toward men abounds in the military maze, from the dictates of the draft laws to the dictatorship of the drill instructors to the randomness of death and injury in both peacetime and war. Fairness? Who ever mentioned fairness to me as I humped and grunted for three-plus years in the Marine Corps?

Are women fit for infantry combat duty? It depends on whom you ask. Brian Mitchell, a former Infantry officer in the Army (and a man who earned both the Ranger tab and senior-parachutist wings), thinks not. In his book *Weak Link,* Mitchell cites the Service's own studies that suggest women are less capable than men in their military careers. "They suffer higher rates of attrition and lower rates of retention. They miss more than twice as much duty time for medical reasons. They are four times more likely to complain of spurious physical ailments. When men and women are subjected to equally demanding physical regimens, the injury rates of women can be as high as 14 times that of men." Mitchell goes on to list psychological differences that he says make women less effective members of the military. "Military women are less aggressive, less daring, less likely to suppress minor personal hurts, less aware of world affairs, less interested in military history, less respectful of military tradition and less inclined to make the military a career." For him, women clearly are not fit for combat.

I think differently. I happen to know women—coolheaded, in great physical shape, aggressive, intelligent, capable—who I think would make excellent combatants in the field. I see no reason why they would not be outstanding members of their profession while under fire and in the trenches. Now, as women move into equal status throughout this culture, I firmly believe that there will be (and that there are today) qualified females who are fit for combat duty.

But the major question for men is, Are they ready to serve with women in frontline combat? Yes, it may be unfair to lock women out of certain jobs, but is it still necessary? Or, put another way, Will the presence of women in infantry combat units cause men to take unnecessary risks to protect them? Is the concept of chivalry and gallantry still very much alive in the male consciousness, and will men act differntly in battle if women are fighting alongside them? Will the presence of women, in other words, cost male lives? I believe the answer to that question is yes. And that presents one hell of a problem.

Of the history of women in the Israeli military, Mitchell writes, "In 1948, a handful of women did see combat with the *Hagana's* fighting arm, the *Palmach*, but their presence resulted in both sides suffering higher casualties. Israeli men risked their lives and missions to protect their women.... The women were withdrawn after three weeks.... Today, the Israelis use women far more conservatively than most NATO nations."

There it is. Much as I hate to admit it, as a man, I am psychologically conditioned to seeing men die in trench warfare. Genetically, subconsciously, most men can tolerate the losses of war if they have to. We do our jobs, we fight the good fight, and while somewhere deep in our hearts we mourn the deaths of our compatriots, we shut that mourning away until it is safe to display it. True, it haunts many of us for the rest of our lives. But the military job gets done. Add women to that dreadful mix of infantry combat mud, gore and gristle, and I fear that the male response to the female presence will be self-sacrificial. In saving women's lives at all costs, we will lose more of our own.

The lives of men are viewed cheaply enough in this culture. We should not debase that coinage even further. When men can easily accept women in the trenches as neutral and equally expendable peers, it will be time to allow them their full and equal rights in this bloody arena. But not until then.

(1990)

*Boss Ladies*_____

Last February, we passed a point that our fathers probably never dreamed of: The nation's 13,847,000 professional jobs split in favor of women—6,938,000 jobs for women, 6,909,000 for men. Women netted 29,000 more professional jobs, and there's little doubt that this is just the start of something big.

The U.S. Bureau of Labor Statistics called it a "historic milestone." Its figures were based on studies of 50 "knowledge-based occupations"—architects, engineers, scientists, physicians, dentists, pharmacists, lawyers, mathematicians, writers, artists, professional athletes, teachers, nurses, social workers, et al.

The gap between male and female pay is narrowing—men in professional jobs get a median salary of $581 a week, compared with $419 a week for women. The percentage of women in professions that were once bastions of male predominance is growing: Eighteen percent of lawyers are now women; so are 17 percent of physicians. And college enrollments clearly show that the explosion of women into the work force is going to continue to be a major story.

The feminist revolution, in other words, isn't about who opens the door at a restaurant or who gives flowers to whom. It's a revolution that promotes a basic restructuring of our culture and our lives, and it affects us in the profession and the wallet.

Given all of the above, there's another fact you have to face: The odds are that sooner or later, you'll be working *for* a woman. She'll be your boss and she'll write your salary reviews. Your job will be to follow her lead, take orders, assist her.

How do you think you'll do?

"I never thought I'd be working for a woman," Stan says. "And I'm not always sure I like it. My boss is a workaholic. It wouldn't surprise me to find a sign on her desk that says, THANK GOD IT'S MONDAY." Stan laughs. He is 38 years old, a wiry man in sports coat and slacks, an executive at a hospital-supply company. "She never stops. She's networking—believe me, I'm starting to hate that word—or going to grad school in the evenings or selling real estate out of her home. I put in ten-hour days, and on my last progress review, she said I was a little lackadaisical. Shit, I've never worked harder in my life!"

Rob shakes his head and smiles at Stan's frustration. I've asked them to talk about their female bosses, and they've agreed to—but only if I change their names. Rob is 27, a low-key man in a three-piece suit who works in a public-relations firm. "Every female executive I know works hard," Rob says. "Look, it's simple: They are first-generation bosses. They're on trial. They know they're setting a precedent. They're the first of their kind, and it's a lot of pressure."

"Wait a minute," Stan says. "My boss works hard for *herself.* She's never there when we need her to make a decision. We say we've seen her picture on a milk carton: She's missing. She pads her own nest with six businesses and then comes into the office and expects us to have everything done for her. I don't buy this idea of the hard-working, perfect female boss."

"OK, OK, Rob says, "I overstated the case. Big surprise. There are good and bad women bosses, just as there are good and bad male bosses. But one thing's for sure: Men are not adjusting well to this change. You can see it. We're improvising. All of us."

We talk for several hours about that. Stan calls the current crisis "working out the rules while working." His anger is based on how slippery and undefined the workplace is these days. "Male, female," he gestures. "I don't care how you cut it, there's always going to be sexual tension. Do you flirt with your boss or don't you? If you do, you're a pig. If you don't, you're gay."

"The sexual tension is there," Rob agrees. "I confess it: Sometimes I'm intentionally cute. I can't believe I'm admitting this. Hey, I can't believe I'm in a situation where I think I have to be cute."

"My boss thinks I'm just a little bit dumb," Stan says. "She gets patronizing; she winks at the other women sometimes when I'm arguing a point in a meeting; she's just waiting to be able to put the sexist label on my forehead. Because once that happens, you're dead, you know? That's the blackmail of the Eighties: If they color you sexist, they color you gone."

The discussion is intense, and it is clear that both men have thought a lot about their situation—yet both are floundering as they try to adapt to the new reality. At the end of the evening, we sum up a list of advice: Rob and Stan's Rules of Order. It comes from two men who have been there—and who hope to get back in one piece.

1. *Do not sleep with your boss.* In this case, the kiss of passion is truly the kiss of death. Don't date your boss. The potential for disaster is sky-high.

2. *If it's demanded, flirt.* Yes, this is a double signal. You can flirt but not touch, and some Boss Ladies want to be flirted with. "Professional distance, personal warmth" is the phrase Rob uses.

3. *Be professionally prepared.* Rob's first-generation analogy is not wrong. Most female bosses are under a microscope, and they need and expect professional support. They'll appreciate competence.

4. *Don't come on too strong in business discussions.* Today's Boss Lady is usually a tough and rational thinker who wants to hear facts and evidence, not *macho* posturing. The style of your presentation to her is as important as the substance.

5. *Courtesy counts.* You don't prove you're in favor of equal rights by slamming the door in her face or spitting past her ankles. Be polite. Or die.

6. *Strategize with your fellow men.* Few men are doing this now, but they will. To get a reading on how this Boss Lady treats everybody, what signals she sends, what behavior she rewards and punishes, you have to compare notes with your male colleagues.

7. *Just remember: Be careful out there.* With more competition and less forgiveness between the sexes, the soft focus of romance has been chiseled into the hard edge of the leveraged buy-out. Women are administrators and competitors, people of power and substance

who make decisions that directly affect our lives. Caution and consideration are the order of the day.

"We're all point men now," Stan says.

Yes, indeed.

(1986)

Snow White's Mirror

Chances are you know somebody who is slowly, secretly starving. Chances are it's a woman. You probably haven't perceived that she's starving—not unless she's in your immediate family and you're alert to the early warning signs of anorexia.

Eating disorders plague large numbers of women in this culture. Men are not immune from the predicament, but the number of anorexic or bulimic men is still relatively small. However, as men, we've got to learn how to recognize these serious, sometimes deadly diseases, how to live with them, how to participate in the healing of them. It's a difficult job, but it can involve the lives of the women we love, which makes it worth the struggle.

Women who suffer from eating disorders are haunted, driven people who live in a universe of obsession and fear. Think about it: Every morning, as you stumble out of bed and glance at your reflection in the mirror and make yourself as presentable as time will allow, there are thousands of terrified Snow Whites out there who have already been up for an hour or two, who have already done the first of their multiple daily workouts and who are staring in trepidation at their image in the mirror and asking overwhelming questions:

"Who's the fairest of them all? Have I lost weight? Will I be able to withstand the temptation of food today? Why isn't my body perfect? How can I deserve love if it's not perfect?"

No judge is as severe, no critic as unkind as these Snow Whites are to themselves. Indeed, many of them don't observe anything at all when they look in the mirror. Their anger and confusion are so great that they literally cannot see themselves. They are often without a self-image.

As a man, I cannot completely understand what that experience is like, but I know this much: It is truly scary shit, and it deserves my attention. I've spent a couple of years studying anorexia and other eating disorders, and what follows are some tips on how to live with the disease.

The Shock of Recognition. You first job is to recognize whether your woman has a problem. Anorexics live like spies. They try to hide their illness,, but there are telltale signs everywhere if you know what to look for: Is she hyperactive? Do her workouts increase in duration and intensity? Does she seem manic about exercise? Are there sudden changes in body weight? Does she toy with her food? Does she try to eat alone most of the time? Is she filled with self-criticisms about her body's shape and attractiveness? Are there exaggerated mood swings? Even though she seems attractive to you, does she complain about how heavy she is, how her clothes don't fit her anymore, how her body is simply too large? These are some of the clues. Rest assured that they will be subtle, inconsistent and hidden.

Food Is a Four-Letter Word. For the anorexic, food is an obsession that must be controlled but often isn't. The urge to go on an eating binge is ever-present. The stress of self-denial is painful. If the anorexic loses control and eats like a madwoman, some form of purging will inevitably follow (either intensive exercise or self-induced vomiting). Your job is to understand that the anorexic's obsession with food is as vigorous and all-consuming as any addiction. You can be talking about baseball, sex, business or the weather, and it may seem to you that she is listening, but it ain't necessarily so. Her mind is often on food, the great evil and the great temptation in her life.

Therapy Is the best Policy. The biggest favor you can do for the anorexic in your life is to gently steer her toward a professional therapist who specializes in eating disorders. There is no magic pill,

there are no voodoo rites, you do not have the words or the expertise
to deal with this complex condition by yourself. The roots of anorexia
lie deep in the mind and the history of its victims. Get help. I
promise you: If Lois Lane herself displayed signs of this affliction,
Superman would urge her to go into therapy.

Love and Sex Are Not Enough—But They Sure Can Help! It has
been my experience that women who are anorexic really don't
understand our male capacity for love and lust. The fact of the matter
is that men have no specific female body type, facial structure or
weight class to which we are exclusively attracted. Tall, short, plump,
thin, chiseled, soft, succulent, wiry, black, brown, red, white,
yellow—hey, we love 'em all! The frightened women who think they
have to be straight out of a fashion show for men to find them
attractive are simply wrong. They don't understand who we are. We
may have a predisposition for promiscuity, but we also have an infinite
capacity for appreciation, stimulation, enjoyment and love. We are
much more tolerant of female physical variety than we're given credit
for. Try us; you'll like us.

Cruelty, Thy Name Is Woman. I can't prove it, but I suspect that
anorexia is primarily fueled by (A) mother-daughter conflicts and (B)
women-to-woman cattiness, jealousy and cruelty. I know it is fashion-
able these days to blame men for all such ills, but I think that's off
target. Look at the messages women absorb through their own
magazines, soap operas, advertising, department stores. Listen to the
way they dissect one another's physical attributes with wicked humor
and near-fatal distraction. Watch them assess one another at health
clubs and spas, their eyes as shrewd and merciless as any killer's. I
don't know of a male who would choose to live at the center of such a
fire storm, and I don't know of one who could survive if he tried.
Until women learn to ease up on one another, anorexia will remain
with us.

If your spouse or significant other is a woman who is battling these
ghosts and goblins, there are some things you can do to support her.
But be prepared for a rocky road. She will not believe all of your
praise, she will not always trust the fidelity of your love, she will
occasionally challenge your psychological limits and spiritual endurance. That's OK. In a way, as one who loves her, that's what you're
there for.

Above all else, tell her as frequently as you can that she's the fairest of them all. Your Snow White will thank you. And she'll almost believe it. Some of the time.

(1988)

*Driving With Daisy*_____

This is a true story about gambling and cheating at cards. This is also a story about my grandmother Daisy. I guess you could say in addition that this is a story about female role models and what we can learn from them. As young boys, we watch the women in our lives very carefully. They teach us things.

Did I really have a grandmother named Daisy? I surely did. She was born Daisy Lycan and raised in Paris, Illinois, where she lived for more than 80 years. During my boyhood, I spent most of my summer vacations with her, a city boy visiting rural America and fascinated by it all.

Daisy had had almost no formal education. She talked like a character from *The Beverly Hillbillies*. Her grammar was often atrocious, and yet her use of language was exquisite, filled with country sayings and country laughter.

Daisy made a good marriage, or so it seemed at the time, hooking up with Fred Baber, my grandfather and the son of Asa J. Baber, my great-grandfather (and the president of the local bank). Daisy and Fred had one child, a son named Jim (the man who became my father). Fred, it turned out, liked liquor a lot and work not at all. He

132

died at a relatively young age, leaving Daisy a widow with some farm land and other holdings. She never remarried.

Daisy could swear like a trooper, drink like a trucker and gamble like a pro. She taught me about the potential richness and humor of earthy, bawdy women.

From my youngest years, Daisy and I had a secret life together. She nominated me early on as her partner in crime. For example, she and I bet on the horse races every day. I knew how to read a racing form by the time I was six years old. "Well, Ace, what do you think?" Daisy would ask me along about noontime as we studied the racing sheet in the apartment she kept in a downtown hotel.

"I think Portly Prince in the third at Aqueduct," I'd say. That was just before the bookie came up to collect her bets. Daisy would kid him and we would all laugh, and I would think that life was OK if at least some people had this much sass and wit.

Daisy sun-bathed in the nude on the hotel roof. This was not a fancy hotel, you understand. There was nothing on the roof except gravel. But we would sneak up there every afternoon during my summer visits, and Daisy would strip and bask in the Illinois heat. I am proud to say that my grandmother was attractive, even in her later years, and she taught me early that there is no reason to be ashamed of the human body.

After we had sun-bathed for a while, I would ask her to sing to me. She usually sang *Danny Boy* in a lilting and gentle voice that I can still hear today. When Daisy sang, she looked like a little girl.

When I was about eight years old, we began another of our traditions. We would drive over to Terre Haute, Indiana, every Saturday to see a movie and then go to The Apple Club. What The Apple Club had to offer was food—and poker and slot machines and a bar. What Daisy had to offer me was patience and generosity as she fed me nickels and steak and gambling advice.

I learned the basic rules of many a card game there by the Wabash, seated at Daisy's elbow. Sometimes, as we drove back toward Illinois on dirt roads in the moonlight, the Plymouth would skid slightly out of control on a curve. "Hold 'er, Newt, she's headed for the bushes!" Daisy would yell. We thought that was very funny.

Daisy showed me a lot of qualities that I admired. My own home in Chicago was impoverished and chaotic; hers was always clean and orderly. My mother was very possessive and sentimental; Daisy was as tough-minded as a commodities trader and just as fast with numbers. My neighborhood on Chicago's 47th Street was often violent and out of control, but life in a small town such as Paris had a certain peace and safety, a human scope and sensible limitation.

To top it all off, Daisy liked to drink and joke and laugh and swear and trade verbal punches with anybody who wanted to take her on. She was a live wire, a crafty fox of a lady who understood the give-and-take of life, a maverick who rarely went to church in a community that usually insisted on it.

She was also a hell of a card player. She had to be to survive the killer poker games that sprang up in Paris and often went on for days, like the one when I was about nine years old. Being a savvy little punk, I followed the games closely, even though the players paid no attention to me. What could a nine-year-old know about poker, anyway?

What I knew at one very strategic moment in one particular game was that Daisy was playing against a cheater, a man who slid an extra card out of his vest pocket and into his hand when I happened to be watching him. The pot was worth several hundred dollars.

Daisy had a full house. Humming *Danny Boy* to myself, I wandered behind the man and glanced at his hand. He had four of a kind. Still humming, I went back and sat by my grandmother. "He's got you beat," I hummed softly with a sweet smile. Daisy looked at me sharply. She was a very ethical gambler. We had never teamed up this way before. She did not like what I was doing. "He's pulling cards," I hummed.

Daisy got it. "Say there, mister, what in the goddamn hell are you doing with those extra cards?" she said sharply to the man as she slammed her cards down on the table.

The man did not argue. He turned pale and ran out the door.

Daisy won the pot. She gave me half.

The other thing she gave me was the understanding that there are special women in the world who can be as salty and funny and lively and wild as men.

Now, *that's* an education.

(1990)

*The Little Orphan Girl*_____

This is a column about my mother, and it is a tough one to write.

For most men, the mother–son relationship is complex, intense, loving and dangerous. It haunts us, thrills us and colors our lives forever. But it is also a relationship we bury deep in our hearts and rarely discuss.

I have never known a braver or more beautiful person than the late Dorothy Mercer Baber. My indebtedness to her is enormous. If it had not been for her, I would never have become a writer. If it had not been for her, I probably would not have survived childhood. And yet, at the same time, she almost ruined me with her possessiveness. She smothered me, pampered me, worshiped me and made me a substitute husband. It was, in every way except the completely physical, an incestuous relationship.

Oedipus could be my middle name. I basically married my mother and betrayed my father—and I know that I'm not the only male to have experienced that classical bind. There are a lot of us, and we have all been scarred by the trade-offs we made at an early age.

The Little Orphan Girl, as I often call her, was literally an orphan. Her mother died giving her birth, her father died shortly thereafter, and Dorothy Mercer was sent to live with her aunt and uncle in

Gibson City, Illinois. There, she was loved and protected by her aunt, but she was tyrannized by her uncle, a severe and violent man who would not allow her to speak at the dinner table or participate in the affairs of the household. It was truly an orphan's childhood, and from those early years rose her perpetual anxiety and sense of privation.

Dorothy Mercer grew into an attractive young woman with a stubborn demeanor and a great body. That last statement is not a joke. It is there for a purpose, which I'll get to soon.

My mother graduated from the University of Illinois in Champaign just as the Great Depression was looming. By that time, she was an established journalist who wrote for the campus newspaper and served as a stringer for several local news bureaus. If my mother were in journalism today, she would be an outstanding reporter for one simple reason: Her Scotch-Irish stubbornness would enable her to pursue a story anywhere it led, no matter the consequences. My mother had more courage than any other human being I've ever known, and I cannot imagine a threat or an assault that would stop her. Outspoken, blunt, undiplomatic, tenacious, beyond fear when challenged, she represented everything I would like to be as a writer.

Dorothy Mercer, like so many women of her generation, left her career in journalism as soon as she married my father. She devoted her life to her family. It had to have been an incomplete and frustrating choice for a woman of her talents. But she did it anyway, at great sacrifice.

Now we come to the dark side, the history I do not find easy to examine, my own early sexuality, my male understanding of what I call The Force and my infatuation with my mother, an infatuation that she returned and traded on.

Looking back on it, I understand that we were both orphans, in a way. My father, in his fierceness, was unavailable to us, so my mother and I took refuge in each other. It was a sanctuary that turned out to be both creative and destructive, an intimate harbor in a violent storm, a private nest we constructed together, mother and son. I can feel both shame and fascination as I write this.

The Little Orphan Girl did tend to flaunt her body around me. I suspect that few women understand how early in their childhood most boys feel attracted to their mothers. I watched like a spy as my mother dressed and undressed in front of me, bathed and played, teased and flirted. She had a gorgeous, youthful body and a sensuousness born out of isolation and inattention. And I have to face it: I had my own sexual precociousness. Perhaps it was genetic; I don't know. But I understood a lot about sexuality from my earliest years. I returned my mother's flirtations, and I was proud that I had somehow replaced my father in her affections. I felt like a little prince, and I didn't always mind.

But the price I was paying involved more than guilt. It involved the loss of male identity. First, I lost my father as a friend and role model. Second, my mother was overprotecting me, chaining me with a golden cord. Our long conversations, intimate discussions and intuitive understandings were of no help to me on the street or in the schoolyard, where my male peers demanded toughness and self-reliance. The more my mother clung to me, the less I was able to function in the real world.

I broke away, as most men do. That process had its own pain. I had to reject my mother, push her out of my life until I could discover my own sense of myself. I felt as if I had deserted her in doing this, but I had to confront an awesome choice: her or me. Either I faded into the soft folds of her all-encompassing love or I struck out on my own and led a cleaner, less devious life.

My mother wrote to me almost daily after I left home at the age of 14. I rarely read her letters carefully. I skimmed them for news, avoided the words of sadness and seduction, hated myself for my own brutality, tried to forgive myself at the same time. I knew I was trying to build my own life. I knew I could husband her no longer.

Later, we came to an uneasy truce, full of love, never mentioning the intensity we had shared. I tried to be a good son to her, within the limits I had set. And always, always, I loved her dearly.

When she died a few years ago in a hospital bed, I was brushing her hair. She took one last look at me. I comforted her as best I could, but I also steeled myself and refused to join her.

I am positive that she understood, The Little Orphan Girl. And I trust that she is now sailing near the sun, in league with my father, both of them waiting to welcome me to a healthier place when my time comes.

I'll be honored to be there with them.

(1989)

A Significant Shift_____

I went out on a limb in the September, 1991, "Men" column and defended the reputation of William Kennedy Smith. "As I see it," I wrote, "Smith is already as much a victim in this case as his accuser claims to be.... All it takes to lynch a man these days is the *accusation* of rape."

I wrote those words last June. Smith was being pilloried in the press and on TV, wild rumors abounded, nothing was said in his favor—and your favorite "Men" columnist sometimes wondered whether the words he had written might come back to haunt him.

Smith finally took the stand in his own defense and performed well. He gave a credible explanation of his actions and he effectively countered the more emotional testimony of his accuser. He handled the scorn of Moira Lasch—"So what are you, some kind of sex machine?"—without responding in kind. He thanked the jury for its sense of fairness ("My life was in their hands").

Harsh judgments against Smith in the court of public opinion have not completely disappeared, however. In some circles, he is still presumed guilty. For example, the verdict in Palm Beach did *not* clear Will Smith's name in the eyes of David Roth, Patricia Bowman's attorney.

Roth evidently believes in the presumption of Smith's guilt even after the acquittal of the charges against him. "A not-guilty verdict does not equate to innocence," Roth said in a statement that is stunning in its legal implications.

One wonders what Roth does equate to innocence in our system of justice. How could Roth claim that a unanimous verdict of six good citizens does not prove that Will Smith is *still* presumed innocent by all fair-minded people?

Roth is not alone.

"I'm privy to information that the jury did not have," said Amy Pagnozzi, a journalist, on ABC's *Nightline.* "As a woman, I feel he [Smith] was guilty."

Pagnozzi claimed that there were now *seven* women who had come forward to claim they had experienced attacks of a sexual nature against them by Smith, and that had the jury been allowed to consider those accusations, the verdict might have been different. (Pagnozzi did not mention that Patricia Bowman's sexual past was also declared out of bounds by Judge Mary Lupo; she also did not explain how an additional four women were now, at this late date, naming Smith.)

The second-guessing has begun, but something much more important and enlightening has occurred and I think it gives us a reason to celebrate.

There has been a significant shift in the public reactions of feminists to the Smith trial. And proof that something between the sexes might be changing.

Maybe, just maybe, we are about to enter an era of negotiation and compromise and rational discourse between men and women. Maybe the feminist movement is going to tone down its self-righteous rhetoric and reach across the gender gap in a gesture of reconciliation.

Listen to one of the toughest voices on the feminist front as she talked about the Smith trial: "The result was a just result," said attorney Gloria Allred on CNN's *Sonya Live.* "There was not sufficient evidence for a conviction to prove guilt beyond a reasonable doubt."

Gloria Allred? FYI, I debated Allred on CNN's *Crossfire* two years ago, and was stunned by her attitude. I had to listen to her quote about the Smith trial several times before I believed she had actually said anything that mild!

Susan Brownmiller, once a stern spokesperson for the feminist cause, author of *Against Our Will: Men, Women and Rape,* was equally rational and fair in her remarks about the Smith trial. It was, she said, not "an unfair verdict.... Given the testimony, I think there was reasonable doubt.... I was impressed with her testimony, but when I heard his, it was plausible. This was a case of bad exploitative sex, but that's different from rape."

Even Susan Estrich, who wrote *Real Rape* and whose pretrial comments about the case sometimes seemed harsh to me, gave Smith's testimony an approving nod: "He was a particularly credible witness," she said.

Is it possible that the feminist movement is growing up and maturing? Do we have a thaw in the gender wars? Are America's feminists ready to move from unsympathetic propaganda to peaceful coexistence?

Not once have I heard the usual rhetoric about patriarchy and male privilege. Not once have I encountered the customary guilt trips and mean-spirited accusations that accompanied feminist monologues as recently as the Clarence Thomas hearings. With the exception of a Catherine McKinnon op-ed piece in the *New York Times,* I have not heard women suggesting that all men are rapists and that Smith is just another male scumbag.

What has happened to the formerly strident spokeswomen of feminism? I believe that they have taken a look at the facts of the case and made a fair and impartial decision. They are not going to preach. "...Nowhere do I hear people saying that the trial was rigged," writes columnist Anna Quindlen. "They saw the prosecutor, heard the accusations, listened to Mr. Smith. Overwhelmingly, polls show, they would have made the same decision had they been on the jury."

We are not totally out of the woods yet, though. Gloria Allred still claims that "the burden should be on the man to find out if she's really consenting." And Sonya Friedman said on her own show, "I wonder how many other people felt Willie Smith walked away much too easily."

Nevertheless, things are getting better for us, gentlemen. The obvious prejudice and sexism of American feminism has not played well in this culture in recent years, and it looks like the movement might be cleaning up its act.

It's welcome. And it's time.

(1992)

Part Three

MEN, WOMEN, SEX AND CENSORSHIP

The Heat Is On⎯⎯⎯⎯⎯⎯⎯⎯⎯⎯⎯⎯

Strange days, indeed; most peculiar, Momma. The tension in this culture is high. There's something happening here, and what it is *is exactly clear:* There is an Unholy Alliance of extreme right-wingers and fundamentalists and feminists that is antimale, antisexual and anti-First Amendment. Three for three.

The heat is on. Censorship is the order of the day, repression the mode of operation. *Playboy* is being dropped from bookstores and newsstands, and the things men like to read, look at and think about are under fire.

The Unholy Alliance is trying to change or eliminate the habits and thinking of the American male. We men are, it seems, too rude, crude and unmannerly for the new world on the horizon; and unless we reconstruct ourselves along more tame and polite lines, the Unholy Alliance will consider us expendable.

Consider:

• I attend a writers' conference and am asked by two women to tape a reading of some of my "Men" columns and short stories. Their tape recorder is in their hotel room. As we ride the elevator, there are a few disparaging remarks about *Playboy.* It is clear that they do not

145

like the magazine and that they take me as a symbol of it. As we enter their room, one of the women turns to me and says, "Actually, we're here to shoot you."

She does not smile for a second. In the silence, I wonder if she could be serious. And I think that if it is a joke, it is also a luxury; if I said anything to her that was half as provocative, the *sexist* label would be stamped on my forehead. "I'm glad you didn't shoot me," I write to her later.

"You're welcome," she writes back. "Shooting you would have been so messy, anyway." Great repartee, right?

• Walking down Michigan Avenue in Chicago, I see a crowd of people picketing a large bookstore. They carry signs objecting to *Playboy,* among other publications. They want a boycott of the store until the magazine is dropped from the shelves. A group called Citizens for Media Responsibility Without Law (what does that mean? I wonder) is passing out a flier. Its members object to what they call this magazine's "Violent Objectification of Women" (what does that mean? I wonder again). They speak of the bookstore as a "Christian family-owned business" and say it "refuses to stop selling pornography." In blocking access to the bookstore, they say, "We perform these actions in the same spirit as the suffragettes... and Rosa Parks...." Such nobility while they go into stores and tear up magazines. Next thing we know, they'll be burning books and magazines and claiming that they're doing so in the spirit of Joan of Arc. Most peculiar logic, Momma.

• "*Playboy* will be gone in a short while (*hurrah*)," writes a so-called Christian in a letter addressed to Hugh Hefner and copied to me. "When you languish on your deathbed and cry out to know the state of your soul, it's a sure bet you won't ask to see a *Playboy!*" The language of the letter is apocalyptic, and it runs in the old, familiar pattern of fundamentalist preaching: "A society that allows free rein to man's baser passions will be torn apart by the lusts of its less-principled members. In short, *it's either vote for morality or be destroyed by your neighbor's lusts!*" I think about that and try to determine who among my neighbors I would first ask to destroy me with her lusts. There are several candidates. If you include the health club where I work out as part of my neighborhood, there are literally scores of possible destroyers. What a way to go!

Make no mistake about it: The Unholy Alliance is trying to make us ashamed of our maleness, our sexuality, our freedom, our love of humor and our love of play. To be a vigorous and happy male in this time and place is somehow dirty and wrong, the Unholy Alliance implies. Men are reading and enjoying improper words and images and thoughts. For that, we must be punished and censored. Our reading materials will be taken away from us and we will be closely monitored for signs of decay.

I wish I could report that men were responding to heat with intelligence and cool. Unfortunately, I think we are a little slow on the uptake. We don't have any role models to lean on—we're the first generation of males in thousands of years to be labeled unfit and improper in our thought and being simply because we are men—and we hesitate to take on the Unholy Alliance. After all, some of its members may live in our own homes.

Example: One of the bravest men I know, a Vietnam veteran and a very fine writer, comes to town and we have lunch. "I really like your 'Men' column, Ace," he says. He quotes details from several columns and talks about how my work has been of some help to him. He toys with his salad, momentarily embarrassed: "Uh, could you send me the magazine every month? In a plain brown envelope? My wife won't let me subscribe. She won't allow *Playboy* in the house." He does not look me directly in the eye as he asks this.

I think about how many times men have said this to me. Some make appointments with their barbers every month just so they can read my column. They can't have the magazine in their homes, either.

"I'll send you a copy of the column if you want," I tell my friend. He thanks me. He laughs at his own fear.

Here is a man whose bravery under fire in military combat is unquestionable, a man I would trust with my life. Yet under this other fire, he withers. I do not talk to him about it. I know he is uncomfortable. But I also know that until he stakes a claim to his own freedom of choice in what he reads, he will be an impoverished captive in a mean-spirited culture.

The heat is on. Believe it or not, that's good. The Unholy Alliance has come out of the closet and set itself up as prosecutor and judge and jury. And the bet in this corner is that men will not let aliens define them; instead, we will stake out our own territory, claim our own virtues and contributions and strengths.

The heat, in short, will help us thrive.

(1986)

The F.B.I. Is Watching!_____

They are out there, men. They have you under intense surveillance and your every move is being tracked. May as well face it, *amigo,* you are a deadass duck on the highway of life. The Feminine Bureau of Investigation is on your case, and you don't have a chance. This F.B.I. is the sharpest, brightest, most inquisitive and shrewdest intelligence agency ever devised.

I recently visited the international headquarters of the Feminine Bureau of Investigation in Washington, D.C. As you may remember, the F.B.I. is run by J. Evangeline Hooverette (Angie to all who know and love her). I am here to tell you that director Hooverette is a very tough cookie who does not suffer foolish men gladly.

"Asa Baber, also known as Needle Dick?" Angie said to me as I walked into her office. "Sit down and shut up, Butthead," she barked with a flinty smile. She was built like a fireplug. She had a strong handshake, too.

I sat down fast. "Needle Dick? How did you know that's what the women at the health club call me?" I asked anxiously.

"Oh, hell, Asa, this is the Feminine Bureau of Investigation. We've known all about you for years." She pulled out a very thick folder and

148

started reading from it. "'Asa Baber; Chicago, Illinois; 1990 update: "Thinks he's a stud but is only a pony." "Plays with himself all the time to see if that will make it grow." "Thinks he's a writer, but couldn't write a parking ticket if he had to."'" Angie looked up at me and laughed at the expression on my face. "Surprised? We've got wire taps and videotapes, transcripts and infrared photographs, credit checks and medical histories. We know more about you than *you* do. Had enough, Pudthumper?"

"Yes, yes!" I cried. "That's enough." I felt very shaken. I tried to collect my thoughts. "I'm not here to learn about my file," I said.

"Well, what are you here for, then, Baby Balls?" Angie asked.

"I'm here to learn how women got so smart and observant, why they are so far ahead of us guys," I said. "I want to know why they notice things about me that I would never notice about them, why they sense social situations more quickly than I do, why they think faster and talk better."

"You mean," Angie said, "why, if you wear socks with holes in them to the office—which, according to our files, you did two days in a row last month—all the women in the building know it within five seconds of your arrival? And why, if you even think about hitting on one of them, the word is out to all the others before you get back to your desk?"

"Yes," I said, "that's what I want to know. Women see more, they know more, they compare notes more often. It's very intimidating."

Angie leaned back in her chair with a smirk. "Well, in the first place, Crappy Columnist, we train our women well. Every woman in the world has been through our training program. Remember Eve? Of Adam and Eve? She started it. I'm just following up. It's genetic by now."

"You mean that throughout history, it's been like this?"

"Oh, yes," Angie said, nodding. "We're way ahead of you gentlemen in terms of intelligence gathering."

"Why?" I asked.

"Because you are always distracted when you're talking to women. You're thinking about sex all the time. You're usually mesmerized by women, aren't you? By the wink of an eye, the thrust of a breast, the shape of an ankle, the curl of a lip."

"I guess so," I said. "Aren't they interested in the same things about us?"

"Eventually, they may be," Angie said. "But first they are required to conduct a personal inventory. We teach them to do that before anything else."

"Personal inventory?" I asked.

Angie handed me a printed form. "Just follow me on this one, Liver Spot," she said as she read aloud: "*Personal Inventory Sheet, First Meeting, Form 101, Alpha Bravo:* height, weight, estimated age, color of eyes, color of hair, estimated value of clothing, estimated value of personal jewelry, estimated career potential, estimated cash on hand, number and type of credit cards———'"

"This is very cold," I interjected.

"No shit, Emetic Eyes." Angie shook her head and went back to reading: "'Type and expense of dental work, physical-energy level, vocabulary level, estimated penis size—not valid if pants are pleated———'"

"Wait a minute!" I yelled. "You mean to tell me that every woman fills out one of these forms on every man she talks to? You mean there are no casual moments, it's all business?"

"That's right, Panic Breath," Angie said.

"So while we're checking out the sex angle, they're making business decisions?"

"What else?" She handed me several other forms. "They fill these out and send them in. Here's a form about your domestic living quarters, here's one about your family and friends, here's your Colleague Evaluation Report, your credit-bureau record, etc. By the time she's done with you, the profile is complete. She sends it in, to us the information is added to your file and she gets a printout the next day."

"Guys don't have anything like that," I said.

"Guys never will," Angie said, smiling.

"Maybe if I warn them in my 'Men' column?" I asked.

"Be my guest," Angie said. "Men look at the pictures first, they look at the pictures last, they skim your shitty column sometimes. You're no threat to us."

I stood up and shook Angie's hand. "Thank you—I think," I said.

"Get some new socks, Jarhead," she said.

I could hear the director's laughter all the way down the hall. Outside, there was a beautiful woman in a trench coat in the parking lot. She had great legs and a warm smile and bright eyes. I was so intrigued with her that I almost backed my car into the fence. As I drove away, I saw the woman smile at me. Then she began making notes on a clipboard.

(1990)

Male Sexuality

Male Sexuality is up front, outstanding, penetrating, erecting, swollen—*there*. Sorry about that, but it's true. We spend much of our lives being haunted by our condition. But maybe it's time for us to stop blushing, banish the shyness and end the uneasy silence. The world depends just as much on our being *there* as it does on women's being receptive. If we refuse to admit our basic sexual nature, then we pervert any honest search for ourselves.

The image of the male in American culture has been thrown open to question by the winds of change. In some circles, men are seen as impotent wimps. To make matters more confusing, such weakness is praised at times. The more traditional male roles—guardian, protector, breadwinner, fighter—are considered too rigid and narrow, and so what some come up with is a muddled picture of the ideal male: John Wayne as Hamlet in drag, say.

But sexually speaking, such an image is wrong. For most of us, sex is joyful, direct and powerful. Our needs are frequent; our desire is strong. In this area, we are much more John Wayne than Hamlet. Not that we don't have moments of fatigue and lassitude. But those times are temporary. By and large, we function in sexual high gear for many decades of our lives.

Dr. Helen Caldicott, has been quoted as saying that "women are closer to the sources of life." She suggests that because women carry fetuses and give birth, they are somehow more intimately connected with the process of creation. She couldn't be more wrong. One of the glories of this life is that both men and women are in touch with the life force, in touch with it mentally and spiritually and sexually. It is now time for men to reclaim that equal status.

If there's one thing I know about my fellow men, it's that we possess sexual energy that is often excessive, definitely pleasurable, usually creative. Male sexuality is just beginning to be researched and understood, but what we are learning about the male animal supports the image of a vigorous human being frequently ready to re-create the race.

In her book *Night Thoughts: Reflections of a Sex Therapist*, Dr. Avodah K. Offit writes of some of the latest scientific studies into male sexuality. "We learn from these studies that male sexuality is characterized by a powerful and obvious excitement that may constantly afflict the healthy man with a desire to copulate," she says. In a study of men in their 50s, for example, it was found that "even under distracting laboratory conditions," those men spent at least 25 percent of their sleep in sexual arousal.

Another research team discussed by Dr. Offit "recorded male multiple orgasms prior to ejaculation. The graphs of heart rate, respiratory rate and anal contractions demonstrated conclusively that orgasm and ejaculation can occur independently in normal men. The men studied, ranging in age from 22 to 56, reported from three to ten pre-ejaculatory orgasms per session of lovemaking."

Offit, a woman after my own heart, understands the burden and the beauty of male sexuality: "Considering the factors that influence it, I am overwhelmed," she writes. "Very few experiences do not stimulate the libido of the apparently normal, healthy male. The feedback from all five senses, particularly vision and touch; the lure of beauty, adventure, sport, greed, dominance; the impulse to care for, protect, nourish; the desire to hurt or punish; indeed, every feeling and thought that a man may experience can lead to a heightening of the libido and a sexual response. Whether sexuality is the foundation of feelings or a relentless shadow that accompanies us, in men it affects everything."

Most men reading that will agree. We are live wires, stimulated by the energy of the world that flows in us, and sometimes, the craziest things strike up a response. "With so many stimuli, how do men retain their sanity?" Offit asks.

"It ain't easy," most of us answer.

Therein lies the male quandary: From a relatively early age, our sexuality has been *there*, plainly and obviously. Erections are hard to hide, and our struggles with that biological fact absorb a lot of our energies. We have to deal with excitement and guilt and the puzzles of love early on, long before we are really ready to do so. Our deepest instincts are primitive, aggressive, easily aroused, sexually ubiquitous. *Macho*, in other words.

And yet, because we are sociable, we try as best we can to keep ourselves in order, to lead lives of some dignity and structure, to push down the wilder elements of our sexuality. We search for controls and viable relief. That is one of the gifts we give the world, whether or not the world wants to recognize it. The fact is that our sexual energy is overwhelming ("Even rats whose penises have been anesthetized with tetracaine retain their libido and continue mounting behavior," Offit reports) and our struggles for self-control occupy the center of our lives. We start out most of our days with a self-amusing question: "Am I going to behave today?" we ask the mirror. The mirror splits its image; half of it says, "I certainly hope so," and the other half says, "Not if you get lucky." While most of us learn to laugh at that double bind and to be amused at our vacillations, no dilemma is peaceful.

If the current critics of male behavior protest that male sexuality is, by nature, too *macho*, then let them also criticize the tides and the seasons of the moon. The sexual make-up of the healthy male is a given: robust, playful, powerful, on the edge of wildness. And the fact that men go to great lengths to control their nature (in particular, in searching for a partner who will act as a governor and a sanctioned release) is one of those stories that don't get told much these days. But it is, nonetheless, a true story and heroic in its way. Society asks us to temper our instincts. And except for that small percentage of men who can't, don't or won't, we do—often at expense to ourselves.

"That's not small potatoes," John Wayne might say.

(1982)

The 1991 Low-Risk Dating Kit————

Ever ask yourself what's happening on the social scene that just might reach out and bite you on the ass?

Item: A man I know meets a woman at a bar, dances with her, necks with her on the dance floor in front of others. They join his friends outside and continue necking in the back seat of a car while they're driven to a party. There, the two disappear into a room and come out in about 30 minutes. All seems fine until a day later, when the woman goes to the police and accuses the man of rape. There is no physical evidence of rape, but the man is arrested, jailed, tried, sentenced and imprisoned. It is his word against hers. He loses.

Item: A man I know, a part-time lecturer at a city college, takes one of his former students out to lunch at her request. She is a bright but insecure woman who believes herself to be physically unattractive and says so. He says in response, and I quote, "You are a very attractive woman. If I were in your age group and single, I would probably ask you for a date." She goes back to the department chairman, reports that the man has sexually harassed her and insists that his contract not be renewed because he is a threat to women students. The chairman agrees and it is done. The man is dropped from the faculty, no questions asked.

155

Item: A sophomore at George Washington University is the sole source for a story in the school newspaper about two black men who supposedly raped one of her white friends. The assailants, as described by the student, had "particularly bad body odor" and allegedly told the victim after their attack, "You were pretty good for a white girl." The student, who a day later admits through her lawyer that she made up the report, says in her apology to the dean of students that she "had hoped the story, as reported, would highlight the problems of safety for women."

The bottom line? The war between the sexes has taken a uniquely virulent form in today's culture. False allegations of harassment and date rape are springing up like condoms in springtime.

Face the facts, men. You live in a high-risk social environment. If a woman brings false sexual charges against you, no matter how flimsy her evidence or belated her action, your protests of innocence may not be believed. This is The Time of the Werewolf Hunt. And the last time I checked, you look a lot more like a werewolf than she does.

Before you go out on a date, *before* you become trusting in a conversation with a female acquaintance, you'd better ask yourself some basic questions. What constitutes sexual harassment in her terms? Is it harassment for you to look at her with interest? To talk with her casually? To ask her for a date? To crack a sexual joke? To ask for a kiss or a hug at the end of the evening? Does she generally advertise that men are slime while women are victims? Better check her out. "Know before you go, bro'" should be your dating slogan. Write that down and paste it over your computer terminal. *Know before you go.*

For extra protection, I've devised a low-risk dating kit. You may want to take a look at it. Am I joking when I list these suggestions? Yes. And no.

• *Hire a private attorney.* Granted, his retainer is a few hundred dollars a day, and it is a little awkward having him around all the time, but remember: Dating is a high-risk proposition. Your attorney's job is to follow you 24 hours a day and advise you on your every move. (You should choose a male lawyer, of course, because if your lawyer is a female... well, you know, people might spread the story all over town.)

• *Have your prospective date sign a dating contract.* This is imperative. You and your attorney design the contract and print it.

With your attorney present, have her read the form, answer any questions she may have and then ask her to sign it. Among other things, she agrees on this form that she is responsible for her own behavior, that she is mature enough to handle a dating situation and that she has a genuine interest in dating you. No signature, no date.

• *Hire a television crew.* You need a cameraman to shoot a video record of your every move and probably an audio man to check sound levels. Better have a guy to carry the battery packs, too. And you need a special infrared TV camera for night work, along with a directional mike and extra videotape.

• *Arrange satellite surveillance.* The cost of this one? Could be in the millions, but think of what it saves in the long run. Insist on something like the KH-11 or one of its later versions. Used properly, this baby can spot a zit on your nose from many miles in space and it can follow you anywhere. You'll need a sophisticated team to program it and launch it, a satellite-dish operator and photo-analysis expert and some good code breakers to scramble your data so that *her* satellite transmission can't screw up *your* satellite transmission. (You bet, space captain, she may have her own satellite, too!)

• *Hire fingerprint and voiceprint analyzers, as well as polygraph experts, physical surveillance people and phone freaks who can tap into anything and everything.* Right, it's getting crowded with all these people following you around. Can't be helped, though. This is the Nineties. You might hire former FBI personnel for most of the surveillance jobs. And don't forget to take a lie-detector test after every date. Have her take one, too. Seal the test results in a bank vault. You may need them. Also, ask her to sign a release form after the date, testifying to the fact that in her opinion, you behaved yourself. Be sure to take your ink pad and towel along that first evening, too. Have to get her fingerprints, you understand. Nothing personal, just business. Because a guy can't be too careful these days, you know what I mean?

Yeah, I think you know what I mean.

(1991)

The Plot of the Vision Police_____

We may be heading back to a no-no culture, the Land of the Naughty-Naughty Boo-Boo, a place of censorship and deprivation where males will be told to deny their very natures—and where they will be punished by the Vision Police for simply being themselves.

Do you go to the University of Wisconsin? My older son tells me he can't buy *Playboy* at the student unions there. It's been banned. Do you live in Texas? A friend called to say that a district attorney in that state is planning to keep *Playboy* off the shelves. I received a news clip saying that the board of directors of a West Coast hospital has ordered that *Playboy* not be sold in its shop.

The Vision Police are everywhere, it seems.

It's really nothing new that this magazine is running into opposition. But when I hear that the guardians of public morality are on the warpath and are banishing *Playboy* from the marketplace, I feel a certain chill in the air.

That chill comes from the gulf that separates me from those who would tell me that it is evil and unnatural for me to enjoy reading *Playboy*, that there is something wrong in looking at pictures of beautiful women and that the text, cartoons, art and graphics of this magazine are dangerous to health and well-being.

Yes, I'm concerned about First Amendment rights. But for me, the

2

chill also roars in from another direction: The feminists and fundamentalists and right-wingers who would ban *Playboy* are essentially
trying to ban male genes.

We men are visual down to our genetic code. Telling us not to *look*
at something is like telling us not to breathe. For the healthy male,
looking is living.

It starts early, our way of viewing and being. We are taught by our
parents and peers and society that it is our job to watch out for
ourselves, and we take that warning literally. We use our eyes the
way our predecessors did, the men from whom we descend in our
extended family tree, the hunters who searched the countryside for
game, the sailors who scanned the horizon for storms.

We come from a tribe called Men. Our vision is an inherited
characteristic that leads into the center of our consciousness. We use
our eyes to stay out of trouble, assess our environment, survive,
protect, defend, enjoy. Life is a feast for male eyes, and there's no
reason we should apologize for that.

In this strange culture, at this strange time, there's a movement
afoot to reprogram the male. Through rhetoric, mockery, censorship
and rejection, certain segments of this society assume that they can
make men change, that our eyes can be blinded and our natures
neutered. But these people do not understand what makes us tick,
and in their own blindness—and possibly their own confused
sexuality—they attribute motives to us that we do not possess.

Take a look at this month's centerfold, for example... if you haven't
already.

Now, it will pain you to learn that the December Playmate is a
friend of mine. I get to see her on an almost daily basis, because we
work out at the same health club. She's attractive, funny, witty, in
shape, modest, realistic, a professional model with solid standards of
conduct.

I like looking at Miss December. I like her photos in the magazine
and I like seeing the real thing.

But listen: "What's wrong with *Playboy*?... Women and girls [*sic*]
are portrayed not as full human beings but as sexual 'objects'—as
breasts, vulva, buttocks. These 'objects' are presented as if men were
unconditionally entitled to them, as commodities that exist only to
satisfy men's sexual desires."

That's a quote from a leaflet published by Women Against

Pornography. According to them, the purpose of this magazine is "to promote the oppression, degradation and dehumanization of women." *Playboy* engages in "the graphic depiction of female sexual slaves" and, in so doing, it "contributes to the degradation of women's status in society."

The Vision Police do not understand us, but in their anger and conceit, they are always willing to speak for us.

When I look at Miss December, either on the page or in person, I do not assume for a moment that she is a commodity for my consumption or that I am unconditionally (or conditionally, for that matter) entitled to her in any fashion. I do not envision her as a sexual slave, and in appreciating her shape and form and spirit, I do not degrade her or humiliate her. I am, simply, a man who searches for beauty wherever he can find it. That does not make me a monster.

I learned early in my life that I loved looking at this beautiful, terrible, joyful, frightening world. And I also learned that outsiders can truly misjudge the motives of men. As a young punk from Chicago's South Side, I used to go to the Art Institute every chance I got. Without any training or education, I fell in love with the work of Van Gogh, Seurat, Monet, Manet, and I would sit for hours studying one or another painting, feeding my eyes as I needed to do. But because I was young and because I was from the wrong neighborhood and not well dressed, the institute guards would circle close to me, clicking their crowd counters and frowning at my leather jacket, boots, acne. "Let's go, kid," they would eventually say, "move it along," and they would usher me out, not always politely.

I knew that they had dark visions of my purpose. They thought that a delinquent child was only waiting for the proper moment to raise havoc and create destruction, slash a painting or cause a scene. Those Vision Police made the same mistake as the current ones: They forged their own fantasies into my head and then made judgments of me that they had no business making. I was—and am—finer and more focused then they knew.

Look, it's simple. Men love to look. You will never stop us—not even if you hang us for it.

And if it ever does come to that, do me one last favor, will you? Make the job of hangman (hangperson?) equal-opportunity employment. I wouldn't mind having someone nice to look at before she springs the trap.

(1985)

*Rise and Hate!*_____

It happens every weekday. How do I know? Because I watch it. Not every day; I don't have the stomach for that. But I see it as part of my job to tune in and chart the television industry's manipulation of the American woman as she watches Oprah, Phil and Geraldo and other talk show hosts.

I call it the several-hour hate. Yes, it's showtime, folks, every weekday on our nation's television screens. Women are encouraged to tune in and bitch and gripe and hate, to stick pins in our collective doll, to simplify and denigrate and curse us with an intensity that is hard to believe. For several hours every weekday, Oprah and Phil and Geraldo and others trot onto their respective stages and begin their ritual bashing of the American male. And their audiences, both in the studio and in the hinterlands, love it! They suck up every tale of womanly woe and male perfidy. They stir themselves into a feeding frenzy as they are presented with men who are evil and women who are victims, and it sells a lot of soap and gets very high ratings.

There is another side to this rise-and-hate syndrome, of course. Men who are considered OK occasionally do appear on the shows. Not all men presented are rapists and muggers and scoundrels—just most of them. Oprah, Phil and Geraldo sometimes offer their audiences politically correct males, men whom women are allowed to like. These include men who are TV stars, movie stars, feminist sympathizers, ballet dancers, etc. Cute and winsome men are adored, in other words, and *never* do the men presented give their hosts any shit. "It's just us girls together," these special men being interviewed seem to say, "and God forbid that we should speak out in defense of the average American male. He is definitely *dreck*, girls, and you have every right to hate him. By the way, please notice that I am a sweetheart and not at all like him."

All of this psychological exploitation is a result of today's cultural revolution. Many women, now the political majority in the population, truly love to hate the men who used to be the majority. Many women, now much more assured of their own spending power, are catered to by the sponsors who must hand them television programs they will watch. More than that, women form the major audience for daytime TV, so if Phil, Oprah and Geraldo did not exist, television would have to invent them. Oh wait a minute, that's right; television *did* invent them!

I'm trying to imagine the shows that Oprah, Phil and Geraldo have blocked out for the 1990 season. I submit that these will be the types of listings they will provide. Check them out—but be sure you leave home early every morning.

"Men Who Rape Their Children and Then Kill Them and Throw Them into the Sewers." This is a tossup between Oprah and Geraldo, but I think Geraldo will probably grab it first. On this show (or shows; this has the potential to be a monthlong series), men who have murdered their children are interviewed at length from their prison cells. They are asked to describe the murders in exquisite detail. There are many still photographs shown. The men are then asked if they are sorry for what they did. Those sickos who say they are not sorry and would happily do it again will be kept on camera and berated for a long time. "Is this what it means to be male today?" Geraldo will ask self-righteously. The audience will applaud him.

"Sexist Male Strippers Who Do Not Believe in God." This show just screams out Phil's name, doesn't it? He'll do it, for sure. First, we will see 25 minutes of male stripteasers in action. The audience will be shocked and outraged but very attentive. Phil will say "Oh, dear" a lot. Then, when he actually talks to these hunks, he will discover that they view women as sex objects. "How could you?" Phil will ask. Later, he will realize that several of them have no particular religious beliefs. "Is this what it is to be a man today?" Phil will ask in his motherly fashion. "First you titillate helpless females with your steroid-shaped bodies and baffling biceps, then you deny us all metaphysical faith?" The audience will be very pleased that Phil has stood up for purity and truth. As soon as the men have their clothes back on, they will be booed and hissed.

"Men Who Vomit on Airplanes and Then Hand the Bag to the Stewardess." This is a show just made for Oprah's incisive and unprejudiced interrogation. First, several men will be asked to stick their fingers down their throats and throw up on national television. The audience will be both amused and nauseated. "Look familiar, ladies?" Oprah will smile. "Look like the last time he came home drunk and disorderly after he said he had to stay late at work?" The men themselves will be fully confessional, in tears, ashamed that they have ever been airsick and expected help from a stewardess.

"I swear I'll never do it again," one of them will say.

The audience will scold him. "Don't put your puke in my palms," one of the women in the studio will yell. "You take that bag up front and give it to the pilot or the steward or some other man, understand?"

Oprah won't have to say a word. Her minions will do her work for her. Then she'll close with a haunting, perceptive question: "Is this what it is to be a man today?"

What it is to be a man today, of course, is to be an individual who avoids daytime TV. But maybe it's time for us to do our own gig, huh? How about it, men? Let's start our own talk shows and pick our own topics. What about "Women Who Kill Everybody They Know and Then Fly to France"? Or "Female Strippers Who Are Probably Lesbians and Don't Like Men Very Much Even Though Men Think They Do"?

Gosh, oh, gee, I think I've found a new career. See you at the hatefest, gentlemen. And don't forget to bring your sexist prejudices. They'll be reinforced. Promise.

(1990)

A Bookstore in East Berlin⸻

I spent the summer of 1956 in Europe. I was a college sophomore, it was my first time out of the U.S.A. and I had a ball. I rented a car and drove through France, Spain and Italy. Life seemed a continuous joy ride. But then things got serious.

Passing through Paris, I fell in with a crowd of East German refugees. They were charming and shrewd people, elegant in their habits and tastes. They also had plans for me. At their urging, I agreed to become an amateur spy and go deep inside East Germany to see what I could see.

Early one Sunday morning, I drove up to an East German border station. After some questioning, I was given a visa. "You will go to Berlin," the East German official said. "You may not go off the autobahn, you may not take pictures, you may not stop. If you do, you will be arrested."

As you can guess, I did exactly what I was told not to do, and I did it immediately. Once across the border, I left the autobahn and drove into the town of Eisenach. Thus began my odyssey through East Germany. There were maybe two dozen Russian divisions in the country at the time, there were any number of East German police and counterintelligence agents on patrol and there was me, a wiseass kid from Chicago's South Side, full of beans and bravado and ready to see firsthand what a Communist culture was all about.

The rubble of war lay everywhere in East Germany, and the streets and highways and farms were often deserted. There was poverty, inefficiency, corruption, brutality, languor. There was also rigid population control.

I learned this first as I exited Eisenach and tried to get back onto the autobahn. Getting out of town required passing by a guard tower built smack in the center of the cloverleaf, complete with young soldiers with machine guns. I saw the guard tower, knew I was illegal as hell and could not afford to stop and simply floored the accelerator and skidded by it. It was a foolish but effective tactic, and I used it a lot that summer. But those guard towers also taught me vividly that escape from East Germany was not an easy option for most in those days.

I got to West Berlin safely and decided to relax before I took a different route out of East Germany toward the West. I cruised the nightclubs on Kurfürstendamm, enjoyed the cafés and the zoo, felt the keen edge of the Berliners as they worked and played. I also visited East Berlin several times. This was before the Wall, and it was not hard to do.

The contrast between East and West Berlin was vivid. East Berlin was impoverished. There were statues of Stalin everywhere, there were miles of ruins from the Allied bombings and Russian shellings of World War Two and there was a general air of depression and fatigue. But it was in one of the state-controlled bookstores near East Berlin's Stalin Allee that I learned my biggest civics lesson.

The bookstore was huge, antiseptic and colorless. Most of the books were bound in identical bindings, and very few browsers were in evidence. The selection of titles was paltry. Marx was there, Trotsky was not. Dickens was there, the plays of Shakespeare made the shelves, but American authors were scarce. Those novels of Steinbeck and Faulkner that described American poverty were allowed; most other titles were not. Clearly, the East German state wanted to control the culture and not let in radical ideas from outside.

Even in those days, I yearned to be a writer. I realized that if I had been born and raised in a country like East Germany, my chances of publishing and of being read would have been slim. Original ideas, contrarian thoughts, unsanctioned suggestions would not see the light of day under that system. It was too dictatorial, too eager to promote only one point of view, too propagandistic. In that book-store, I was truly proud—and relieved—to be an American. I understood what the Cold War was all about, and I appreciated deeply the freedoms I had taken for granted.

The trip out of East Germany was interesting. There were times when the police would walk in the front door of a bar or a restaurant and I would run out the back. There was a moment in Magdeburg when I was almost shot as I photographed the steelworks. And there was a final argument at the border that almost got me thrown into prison as I tried to change my East marks back into West marks. I gave no end of shit to the Communist border guard who was armed and dangerous and very much flustered at my anger.

My anger was not really at him. It was at the East German state. The image of the bookstore would not leave me, and nothing pissed me off more than a society that censored and controlled thought.

I'm still angry about censorship today, but only marginally at my Government. Sure, Ed Meese and his cronies got *Playboy* taken off the shelves of many stores a few years ago, and sure, very few liberals protested that. But the Meese commission was a blunt instrument. Something much more insidious is going on.

Book publishing and television programming have become prime examples of contemporary thought control. They are sexist (antimale) in the extreme, and they guard their territory well. There is no equivalent literature or programming to match the feminist expres-sions of the past 25 years. This is not because men are not writing and thinking. It is because the agents and editors and power brokers who staff those industries are almost exclusively feminist, and they want no arguments, no male perspective, no contradictions. There is no shelf space for writing that questions the excesses of feminism. There are no TV programs of that nature, either. What we get in this culture is feminist propaganda, day in, day out.

"I wouldn't ever publish Asa Baber," a senior editor at a large publishing house said recently. It was the kind of remark I have heard often. "I consider him antifeminist," she said. "We publish some of the most famous feminists in America, so why would we publish him?"

Spoken like a true border guard, Madam Editor. You'd do well in Berlin. *East* Berlin of the 1950s, that is.

(1989)

Sexist Witch-Hunt_____

"So what should I do?" Jennifer asked. "I think I love them both. I'm orgasmic with each of them. They're wonderful lovers. I've never had it so good. I'm just afraid they'll drop me at the same time. What will that leave me with? My vibrator? Listen, I've got nothing against vibrators, but I hate loneliness."

We were eating in a Mexican restaurant, and Jennifer's voice bounced off the tiles. It was a fairly crowded room, but she didn't seem to care. She talked on, listing details—size, heft, endurance, technique; nothing was unmentionable—while I stirred the *guacamole* with my chips.

"George is into a lot of oral sex, OK? Hey, as long as it's fifty-fifty, I don't care. Ken has satyriasis. He can do it for hours. Literally hours. Am I happy? You bet. I don't want to give either one of them up."

"What happened to Andy?" I asked.

"Oh, he's still around, but he's boring. Missionary position all the way for old Andy. No imagination."

As Jennifer launched into a description of Andy's sexual defects, I sat there like a dunce and wondered why I was feeling so uncomplimented, so stressful, so *muscled*. There was something uneven about the situation, but I could not immediately define it. Jennifer, with her

168

red hair and keen eyes and tough voice, was on a roll, and it would not have surprised me had she stood on her chair and read a list of her fondest perversions to the crowd. Why did that threaten me?

"What's the matter, Ace?" she asked me. "Cat got your tongue?"

"That's it!" I yelled. "The cat's got my tongue!"

"What are you saying?"

"What were you talking about just now?" I asked her. "Your lovers, right?"

"Right."

"George and Ken and Andy and a supporting cast, right?"

"Yes."

"Don't you get it?" I said. "That was like male locker-room conversation—or what used to be male locker-room conversation."

"I talk like that because I enjoy it," Jennifer said. "I have nothing to hide. I'm not ashamed of my sexuality."

"I know you talk like that," I said, "but I don't talk like that anymore. And I don't know many guys who do. We just shut up. We don't talk about anything."

"What? You guys can't talk openly? What are you, prudes? What do guys talk about in the locker room? Football?"

"Yeah," I said. "You got it: football, business, weather; sometimes politics, but only if we really trust one another. Otherwise, the cat has our tongues."

Jennifer smirked. "You keep saying that, but it doesn't mean anything."

"Oh, yes, it does," I said. "Men aren't talking anymore—not to one another. Not to women, either, a lot of the time. Men are walking on eggshells. And I've just figured out why."

"From something I said?"

"No," I said, "from the things I haven't said. From the way I've shut up and let you ramble and had nothing to contribute. Guess what, Jennifer? The cat has my tongue. I am afraid to say anything. There you are, sexist to the gills, turning men into meat, laughing at their sexuality, taking over the role of the locker-room clown, and I say not a word."

"So you're chickenshit." Jennifer smiled without meaning it.

"Absolutely," I said. "I live in the middle of a revolution. I'm trying to stay alive. I remember how it was in the Fifties. People were terrified of being labeled Communist. In the Eighties, men are afraid of being labeled sexist. That's the death for men today. That truly cuts our water off."

"And well it should."

"We're scared into silence," I said. "Women can talk about anything, right? In your locker room at the club, I'll bet there are some pretty grubby conversations, right?"

"We get down to basics in there," she said, laughing. "As a matter of fact, when it comes to locker-room gossip, we could curdle your cream."

"I'm sure you could," I said. "But men are so afraid of being called sexist that we don't really talk like that anymore, not even with one another. It's like the McCarthy era. We're waiting for the House Unfeminist Activities Committee to subpoena us. 'Are you now or have you ever been a sexist?' they will ask. 'Have you ever known a sexist?' That's why it's so quiet in our locker room."

"You know what's more fun than dating?" Jennifer asked. "Talking about it later with my girlfriends."

"You talk about everything, don't you?" I asked. "His breath, his skin, the lines he used to get you in the sack, how fast he came—the whole schmear, right?"

"Right. Sometimes we all date the same guy and compare notes. It's such a scream!"

"It's a scream for you; it's a reign of terror for us," I said. "It's the time of the sexist witch-hunt."

"The sexist werewolf-hunt, you mean, don't you?"

"Absolutely," I said. "It's exclusively a hunt for sexism in males. You women can be sexist as hell and then chalk it off as merely amusing. But if men show even a trace of sexism, it's all over for us. We're charged, tried and convicted in about ten seconds."

"Couldn't happen to a nicer bunch of guys," Jennifer laughed.

"See, you get to swagger because I have to retreat," I said. "Any aggression on my part, any even trading, and you'll say I'm a sexist pig. And if I become known as a sexist pig, my life will get very lonely. That's the blackmail of the Eighties."

"And you're mad as hell and you're not going to take it anymore?" Jennifer asked with an arched eyebrow.

"No, I'll take it some more," I said. "I love women. I need them in my life. But I sure as hell feel as if I'm fighting with both hands tied behind my back."

"That's OK," she said. "You've got a cute butt. You look nice that way."

"I like your breasts, Jennifer," I said. "I never met a breast I didn't like."

"You're such a sexist pig," Jennifer said.

(1985)

The Dreamers Who Hate Our Dreams

You can't buy a copy of *Playboy* at a 7-Eleven store these days, but you can buy any number of romance novels. That says quite a bit about our culture. Among other things, it says that women's fantasies are acceptable and men's are not.

The next time you are charged with having an abominable imagination and a sexist attitude because of what you read, go buy a paperback romance by Barbara Cartland or Georgette Heyer or Nora Roberts or Anne Mather. You'll probably be bored as you read, but you'll learn something. *Both* sexes retreat into dreams and fantasies as a means of escaping life's trials, and women depersonalize men every bit as much as men depersonalize women.

There may be differences between the sexes, but not in the intensity of fantasizing. Here we are equal. Women make love and play around just as often as men in their fantasies, but since they do it under the cover of so-called respectability, they claim more virtue for themselves. They hunker down with a steady diet of romance novels, and then, after their excitement has peaked and they have had their fill of the tall, handsome hero of their dreams, they come out of hiding and scold us because of our reading and viewing habits. It's a wonderful con that could go on for decades if we didn't point out its hypocrisy.

The paperback-romance-novel industry is enormous. Harlequin Publishing puts out between 75 and 80 percent of the romance titles on the shelves. Last year, it sold 240,000,000 books and had total revenues of more than $230,000,000. Harlequin and its sister label Silhouette turnout 54 titles *per month*. Some 600 authors are under contract to the firm. Not small potatoes.

Just what is it that millions of women are reading? Take a typical plot, for example. Set it in Regency England. The heroine is always a virgin. She is sensitive, attractive but not gorgeous, and she is misunderstood by her family and friends. She is a woman of high energy and high intelligence, but these qualities are usually underestimated by the world around her. She is one hell of a lot smarter than the men she has to deal with.

Except for one. Ah, yes. Call him Cruel Eyes. He's the hero. He sneers a lot. He has had his share of women and has gambled and wenched his way through his careless, inconsiderate life. Jaded, wealthy, titled, a fighter and a lover, he's been in a duel or two and has killed because he had to. Cruel Eyes incurs our virgin's displeasure and wrath at first, because she can't stand the way he has used women to his advantage. Still, he does have a curious effect upon her sensibilities, often leaving her flustered—though, of course, she tries not to show it.

Cruel Eyes gains our virgin's love and respect in two ways: (1) He saves her in a crisis (he thwarts a kidnaping, saves her life, gives her his inheritance, becomes her guardian when her parents die at sea— little things like that); and (2) she teaches him to love her for her mind and her presence, and she sees that he accepts her limits on his sexuality. The beast is tamed, and our virgin has done it. Cruel Eyes cleans up his act under the tutelage of our good woman. He remains tall, handsome, gray-eyed, vigorous; but now he is hers, under her control, and the two of them head into the sunset to lead lives of sweet (feminine) fulfillment.

Two hundred and thirty million dollars' worth of romance novels sold by Harlequin in 1985? Ever get the feeling there's something going on and you don't know anything about it?

Fantasies, of course, can always be mocked when they are outlined in cold type and compressed without rhythm. What I am doing is not fair to the millions of female readers who climb into the shelter of their dreams. "ROMANCES MAY BE A NOVEL ESCAPE" reads one recent newspaper headline. The article goes on to say: "Housewives who read romance novels... may do so in part because the books are [an] effective way of screening themselves off from the rest of the family."

The point is not that I would disallow romance novels and feminine fantasies. Women have every right to dream as much as they wish to dream. If they like to imagine that some tall, powerful, good-looking male is about to throw a ladder up to their condo window and carry them off, so be it. I'm not tall or particularly good-looking, and I don't have a ladder of exceptional length (OK, you can laugh at that), so to some degree, their dreams don't do me any good. But what the hell, dreams should be free.

Maybe we should put that another way: If we're to stay healthy, dreams *must* be free. Once you start censoring fantasy, you've taken a giant step toward destruction.

Male fantasies are usually more directly sexual than female fantasies. But they are as necessary for wish fulfillment, escape and reverie as female fantasies are. We need our dreams as much as we need to breathe. It's time we gave each other space to do both.

Once upon a time, I was trained in the brutal art of interrogation. I learned how to get information from people when they didn't want to give it. There is a very simple way to do that. You don't have to beat people up or attach electrodes to their bodies or any of the other melodramatic crap you see in the movies. Nope, all you have to do to break a person is deprive him of his dreaming and his sleep. It is a frightening thing to see, over a relatively short time, a human being's energy and will power crumble because the dreams he so desperately needs are denied him.

We all need our fantasies. With no imaginary meadow to romp in, no seduction to enjoy, no triumph to celebrate, no secret lover to fondle or instruct, no breast to kiss or eyes to stare into, we are made to stay too much in this incomplete world. And without an escape hatch, we die.

Don't judge my fantasies or my harmless means to them, and I promise I won't judge yours.

That's called living. And letting live.

(1986)

*Romancing the Bone*_____

Rodney Dangerfield has a joke that goes something like this: The first time I had sex, I was terrified. It was late at night. It was dark. I was alone.

Oh, yeah, Rodney, I know what you mean. The same thing happened to me. And it seems to keep happening. As a matter of fact, I hope it never stops, because it isn't terrifying anymore.

Maybe one day, Roget's *Thesaurus* will have a list of the synonyms men have given masturbation: beating off, pounding the pud, milking the lizard, phoning the czar.... The list goes on, but you know what I'm talking about—one of life's major recreational activities, that's what I'm talking about.

Where would we be without the joy of solitary sex? Dead or in a straitjacket, I think. It's not easy being needy. When it comes to excessive energy, the healthy male is a nuclear-power plant, a Three Mile Island waiting to overload. We avoid meltdown by tapping the tank before it explodes.

Tapping the tank—another synonym.

When I was younger, I used to think that tapping the tank was a hobby that would fade in time, but that's not the case. "I can't believe it," a good friend of mine said. "The married men in this organization masturbate more than the single men!" He had just seen the results of the polygraph tests administered by his Government agency. "Do you believe that?" he asked.

"Why wouldn't I?" I said. "I'm married and I still do it. I haven't stopped; have you?"

"Are you kidding? I can't even give it up for Lent," he laughed.

That's right: Most of us won't give it up, not even for Lent. We flog that snake in all seasons. And we've been doing it for years.

You would think that all this romancing the bone would meet with society's approval. After all, we practiced pud thumpers hurt no one with our private workouts. We seek simple comfort, a release from tension, the tranquility of a remembered moment or a fantasized love. It's basic, it's creative, it's fun.

So why is it called self-abuse? And why is it an unmentionable topic in some company? And why is guilt about it still dropped around our horny hands?

Put it this way: You've heard of the separation of religion and the state, but have you heard of religion's separation of mind and body?

That's right, you eel stroker: Here in this supposedly liberated culture, we are, in our way, as hidebound and puritanical as ever. We are told from an early age that our bodies are evil things, mechanisms to be controlled and censored. Those of us who would obtain purity, we are taught, should copy those who have already obtained it. From church and synagogue and mosque, the message is remarkably similar: Religion remains unsexed, unable to deal with sexuality, primarily opposed to any open discussion about it and filled—in its silences as well as its words—with grim sexual lectures.

In some ways, it doesn't matter. There is a life force in us that transcends all the dire threats and warnings of those who would set our moral standards, and most of us doodle our noodles in happy abandon from the moment we first discover the warmth such doodling can bring.

Nonetheless, the attempts to connect masturbation with guilt are enormous in our younger years. It's too bad we don't have somebody who can demand equal time and say to us, "Hey, kid, it's OK. Go ahead and beat your meat. Everybody does it. Really."

I was lucky. I discovered the pleasure of my company at a very early age and I tickled myself whenever I could. Evidently, the smile on my face gave me away because shortly after my life's hobby began, an Episcopal priest chased me down the stairs of a church on Chicago's South Side.

"Ace! Ace!" The good father's voice echoed in the stair well. "I have to talk to you."

I didn't want to talk with him, and I kept running; but the bottom door was locked, and I was trapped. I was in my choirboy robes, and I looked like an angelic little shit. Looks, as they say, are deceiving.

"Ace," the priest said, "I want you to take this crucifix and hang it above your bed. I want you to pray every night. And I want you to learn not to abuse yourself. You're maturing very rapidly, and you must learn self-control. You know what I'm talking about, don't you?"

I was what? Nine? Ten? Somewhere in there. But even at that age, I was fascinated by the energy and strangeness of censorship: The priest's face was red, and he rubbed my shoulder while he talked, and there was a desperation in his warnings that I knew did not fit the so-called crime.

"Yes, I know, Father," I said, thinking that it would be better to admit it and get out of his clutches than to pretend total innocence. Boy, has he got problems, I thought.

I guess I still think that. I am not an irreligious man, but I have yet to find a religion that can acknowledge and incorporate all my energies into a way of living and being. Religious leaders and spokespeople seem desexed to me—soft and frightened and filled with forbidding messages about the life that flows through me. Those who tell me that the carnal part of me is unspiritual are people who have their own problems, and I certainly hope they can work them out. But I am here to tell the gurus of East and West that my sexual life has been, in general, a great joy to me, a proof that the universe has its friendly moments. The force that created sexuality was doing us a favor.

You know that Zen riddle "What is the sound of one hand clapping?" After a lifetime of jerking off, I think I know the answer to that one. The sound of one hand clapping is a happy, harmless sound, a celebration of life, a tranquilizing, reaffirming thing.

Like the old song says: They can't take that away from me.

(1986)

Intimate Ice

It's been a great evening. You've taken the woman of your choice out on the town. You've been a good companion, if you do say so, listening carefully to her, talking about yourself, joking and laughing, being a friend.

You've also been a considerate lover this evening. You take your time, luxuriating in the ballet you two are choreographing. And when it's over, you lie back, thinking that you've given everything you could possibly give. You've been tender, vulnerable, strong, passionate, mindful of her needs, imaginative, humorous, loving. In your mind, it's a ten out of ten, and you drift into a happy sleep.

For about two minutes.

"Are you asleep?" she asks incredulously.

"Huh? Me? No," you say, sitting up suddenly. You clear your throat.

"How can you sleep? I want to make plans. Let's talk," she says.

"Talk?" you ask.

"Yes, talk. About us."

"Us?" you ask. "We're fine, aren't we?"

"Oh, you know what I mean," she says.

178

"No, I don't," you say. You are truly baffled. "We had a great time, didn't we?"

"That was just sex."

"'Just sex'? Oh, excuse me. I thought we had an evening together."

"We did," she says, nodding. "But for you, the best time was the sex."

She may have you there, but you don't want to give it to her. Sex is one of life's high points for you, yet you're a little ashamed of that. Sex is a major release, a creative expression of warmth and beauty, a place of refuge. But when challenged about your love of it, you do tend to cover up.

"I want some communication," she says. "I want some intimacy. You don't know how to be intimate."

"I don't?" you ask, shaking your head.

"Sex isn't intimacy. Why do men think they've been intimate when they get laid?"

"Because it seems intimate to us," you say. "Doesn't it seem intimate to you?"

"Sure," she says casually, "but it's not *everything*. God, with men, it's *everything*. Men don't know how to love. They really don't."

You sit there in bed, puzzled and tired. You've heard it before and you know you'll hear it again: Men don't know how to be intimate; men don't know how to love. You feel like pulling the sheet over your head and hiding from the world. You've done your best, but it hasn't been good enough. That's the message you're getting.

Questions about men and intimacy fill the air these days. Take a look at a book called *The McGill Report on Male Intimacy.* It promotes the idea that women are creators of intimacy and men are ice cubes.

"Why aren't men more loving?" it asks. "Are men constitutionally incapable of intimacy, or do they consciously choose not to be close? . . . A woman's behavior is an open window to her feelings. . . . Love means many more things to women. Love has many more roots and covers a richer, fuller emotional range for women that it does for men."

Sooner or later, we're going to have to come up from under the bedclothes when such statements are made. As males, we've been too quick to feel guilty, too silent under attack.

Here are some of the things you can say in your own defense—

right in your own bed. But be careful: Feminists have had total control of this subject for 20 years. Who knows what they'll do if you suggest some of the following:

• *Intimacy is not the gift of either sex.* The sad fact is that most of us hide from one another most of the time. Intimacy involves risk, revelation, unpredictable rewards. Few of us know how to handle that.

• *The idea that "a woman's behavior is an open window to her feelings" flies in the face of most male experience of women.* Those supposedly open windows into the feminine heart are usually covered with drapes, curtains, fans, shades, gauze, screens, fog from fog machines and scrims of many colors. Most men do not see women as open souls, easily deciphered. Just the opposite, as a matter of fact.

• *Talk is cheap.* Some women operate on the theory that the person who does most of the talking is, by definition, being loving and intimate. Men know better. Men know that talk is often chatter, and aggressive chatter at that, on the attack and unrevealing. The silent partner can be the more loving partner.

• *For too long, women have defined warmth and love in their own terms—and then expected us to live by them.* Male trust, warmth, friendship, love may be expressed in different ways from what most women would wish. But communication between the sexes is a 50-50 proposition, and women should not assume that unless things are done their way, they remain undone.

• *Sex is central to our lives, and for us, anyway, it is intimate.* The current clichés about male sexuality are absurd. Making love is an intense and focused activity for men, never casual. We are vulnerable, open to mockery, needful, highly sensitized—and at the moment of orgasm, we know we're giving and dying, reacting and exposing, paralyzed and expendable. In that time, there is nothing we can do to defend ourselves, and we assume that we're giving a gift to be that helpless in that time. We don't see ourselves as plundering or exploiting or using. Sex and love are tightly interwoven for us. If they are totally compartmentalized for most women, who has the problem?

• *Intimate ice is the human condition.* We float somewhere between love and self-absorption, all of us, male and female. We play our cards close to our chests, then share, then become frightened and withdraw, then try to share again. It ain't easy. We can go from cryogenic to tropical in the wink of an eye, the blush of a smile, the curl of a lip.

But isn't it fun?

And aren't we supposed to be in this together?

(1985)

A Question of Focus_____

Psst! Hey, you. Yeah, you, the guy reading this column. You and I are engaged in a confidential transaction, did you know that? It's you and me and the printed page. There's no one else involved. Privacy? You have complete privacy here.

So let me ask you a question. I want you to give me an honest answer, no bullshit, no tap dance, no hiding and denying. The question is this: Are you a guy who fucks around?

Hey, stay cool. That question really makes you nervous, doesn't it? Relax. Nobody can hear us. It's just you and me, *amigo*. So let's try it again. Tell me, in all honesty, are you involved with more than one woman these days?

Come on, don't quibble with me. You ask, What *exactly* do I mean by "involved"? Well, it includes fucking, but it can also include sexual play. I am not talking harmless verbal flirtation or private personal fantasies here. I'm talking sex. Sexualized relationships. The question is simple: Are you wheeling and dealing with more than one woman?

How many women? Let's say a minimum of two women and a maximum of 2,000. Does your range of activity fall within those numbers?

OK, it's clear that you don't want to talk about this. I understand. Believe me, I understand. Time was when I was promiscuous as hell and didn't want to talk about it, either. Time was when my name was Asa "Hello, I Love You, Can We Fuck Now?" Baber.

You know what I mean? Most guys know what I mean. It's what all our sheep and chicken jokes are based on. Our sexuality is humongous, and it takes a lot of energy and wisdom to contain it.

Believe it or not, good brother, I think I have some limited wisdom about this question now. After many years of wrestling with it, I'd like to share something with you about promiscuity and the self-destruction it can bring.

It goes like this: Forget the scolds, forget the moralists who warn you of hell's fire and God's judgment if you stray. The fact of the matter is that fucking around is a self-destructive and self-limiting act. When you fuck around, you fuck yourself. It fragments your time and your psyche. When you fuck around, you send a signal to yourself that basically says, "Go ahead and mess up your life, sucker; start juggling two or three women at a time and split yourself into pieces; go ahead, numbnuts, and complicate your life."

Let's tell it like it is: At that moment of rationalization, *you* are the victim of your own sexual confusion. *You* are the person who will become more and more divided as the complications pile up, the little white lies accumulate, the juggling continues. When you start to wander, *you* voluntarily take an ax and split yourself into pieces. You lose your focus. *That is the central problem with promiscuity. It divides the self.*

Care to share a few laughs about the complexities of having an affair on the side? It gets confusing, doesn't it? You have to remember names, for example. In your sleep and in your orgasms, you have to remember to call the right woman by the right name. "I'm with Nancy today," you mutter to yourself. "Don't call her Sylvia. Or Jane. This is Nancy."

Better be alert on the street, too, dickmeister. Sure, you hope the women in your life never get together and compare notes—but what if they all ran into you on the same street corner at the same time? What if the god of synchronicity decided to call your name? Did you ever have a dream about that? All your women in touch with all your hypocrisy, and all of them standing at the same intersection as you arrive? You'd be mincemeat in five seconds, right?

Told one way, it's kind of funny. Looked at another way, it is very revealing. What does it reveal? That mincemeat is what you're looking to be, superstud. For some deep and dark and personal reason, you want to be divided at this point in your life. You *want* to be out of focus. Why? That is the essential question that only you can answer. Here are a few of the many possible reasons:

1. *You crave excitement.* What, a life with no diversions or complications? How deadly dull. You have fun living by your wits. You enjoy the chase and the seduction, the small lies and manipulations, the thrill of hiding affairs and holding secrets. It makes you feel alive. A little split, but alive.

2. *You need nurturing.* No question about it, given today's pressures and pace, many a couple can fall off the bed of nurturing. Some people never get back on. So the search for nurturing is out there. You may be after it. But since when did splitting the self comfort you?

3. *The unfocused perspective is all you know.* To be focused and centered is scary for some of us. We don't necessarily know how to do it. We've been divided for too long. We fear the responsibility we would have to assume for our own actions if we had no crises in our lives, no melodramas, no women crying or arguing or scolding, no domestic distractions. Imagine: You, without excuses for failure, without the diversions that keep you from looking at yourself—could you handle that?

4. *For you, commitment is a dirty word.* For some people, possibly for you, commitment is obscene, especially the commitment to the focused self. That is what you want to avoid. Or so you think.

But consider this, and consider it well: In the martial arts, in all the arts, in business and sports and parenting, the search of the wise man is *always* for focus, for clarity, precision, loyalty, unity.

The search of the wise man? Try it sometime. You may surprise yourself and the people around you. For a change, pull all of your selves back together. Enjoy the new cohesion. Don't wait. Do it now.

(1991)

Pumping Fur————————————————

Consider the succulent taste of a charcoal-broiled steak, the refreshing aroma of a brook trout grilled over a mesquite fire, the sensuousness of strawberries and whipped cream. There are incredible delicacies in life, aren't there? But could you list any greater delicacy than the exhilarating and provocative one that has no publicly acceptable name?

All bold men have tasted it; all wise men return to it as frequently as possible. I refer, of course, to the fine art of eating out. Purists call it cunnilingus. I call it pumping fur.

Have you ever noticed that there's a conspiracy of silence about this subject? Why do so few men admit to pumping fur while so many do it? In a society in which we publish restaurant reviews in every newspaper and magazine, why are we so unwilling to discuss *all* our eating habits?

Men, the time has come to pry open the lips of reticence and lick the problem in the bud. What follows are the questions most frequently raised about the fine art of eating out. The hope here is that by bringing this universal activity out of the closet, we'll be able

185

to trade information and offer advice that leads to better eating and better loving.

Are there conditioning exercises for pumping fur? I'd like to get in shape for it, but I don't know how.

This is an elemental question, of course. Cunnilingus is an athletic art. Think about it: With your mouth centered on the object of your affections, you try to become a human vibrator. "What am I, a hummingbird?" you sometimes ask yourself. Your neck aches; your knees hurt; your tongue tires. According to the National Sex Injuries Institute, 84.7 percent of all men who practice it are at one time or another injured while pumping fur. Clearly, this is no laughing matter.

I recommend a conditioning regimen that consists of (A) neck exercises (from a standing position, bend at the waist, raise your head and put your face against the wall, placing all your weight on your nose for as long as you can); (B) tongue twisters (say "Clit twit" rapidly 400 times); (C) tongue curls (use six-ounce weights tied to a tongue depressor); (D) chin bounces (do a headstand, then pivot on your chin); (E) knee scrapes (carpet your living-room floor with mattress ticking and walk around on your knees for a few hours each evening). Put it this way: While your friends train for triathlons and marathons, you're getting in shape for a fur pumpingthon. In your heart of hearts, which event truly deserves Olympic status?

I like pumping fur, but I'm never sure what rhythms I'm supposed to follow or how long I should do it.

There is a lot of confusion here. Different men have different answers, but on the basis of intensive interviews with 8,478 women, I suggest the headphones approach. Tape the following in their entirety and in this order: Ravel's *Bolero*, the Spike Jones version of *The Flight of the Bumble Bee*, Mozart's *Requiem* and Beethoven's *Ninth Symphony* (fourth movement only). The next time you are about to pump fur, put on your headphones, start the tape and go to work. The tape will give you some sense of the momentum, pace and duration practiced by the most successful fur pumpers. After a while, of course, you'll be able to take off the headphones and work from memory.

My lover claims that she doesn't like it when I pump fur. How can I persuade her to let me have the taste treat I'm yearning for?

You might throw some statistics at her. For example, did you know that the National Fur Pumping Institute has reported that men who pump fur for at least 20 minutes four times a week are far less likely than other men to have heart attacks or strokes? "It's fun; it's exciting; it's aerobic," you should tell her. "Don't you want me to live forever?"

I'm embarrassed to admit it, but I'm not sure I like pumping fur. Does that make me less of a man?

If you're looking for liberal sympathy here, forget it. Yes, if you don't like it, you are probably a latent transsexual who possesses Communist and atheistic tendencies. Any way you cut it, real men do pump fur. But before you despair too deeply, have I mentioned that fur pumping is an acquired taste? Remember your first beer? Oh, sure, you pretended to like it, and once you got a buzz on, you loved it. But remember those first few seconds, when it tickled your nose and tasted too salty and smelled unfamiliar? You get the analogy? All fur pumping takes is a little practice, *compadre*. Familiarity breeds contentment.

I can't stop pumping fur. It's all I ever want to do. Do I have a problem?

Any addiction is a problem, and there are a lot of women out there who will take advantage of your helplessness and use you ruthlessly if you don't go for help. Fur Pumpers Anonymous is an organization that will provide support and advice as you wrestle with your jones. Be honest; be blunt; admit that you're negotiating with your face too many hours a day, and healing will come in time.

I told my pastor recently about my love of pumping fur. He said it was a tasteless and subversive act and he was ashamed of me. Help!

It's anything but tasteless, right? And if it's subversive, does that mean nobody in the FBI does it? Ask your pastor why he goes to the dentist every week for a haircut. He'll shut up.

Sometimes when I'm pumping fur, my wife calls me by other men's names. So far, she's called me Arthur, Barry, Jonathan, Tom, Jeff, Gary, John, Peter, Walter, Steve, Jim, Reg and David, but my name is Mortimer. What should I do?

First, pay no attention to the fact that she's naming most of the editors on our *Playboy* masthead. I'm sure that's just a coincidence. Second, change your name. Third, if she ever calls you Asa, remember that it's a Biblical name, as common as clay in soap operas and the book of *Kings*. And finally, please fix the headboard of your bed so it doesn't squeak so much, and don't forget to feed the cats before you go to work.

All right, men, let's get pumping!

(1986)

*The L Word*_____

OK, men, before you do anything else, please take the following test. It's simple and quick, and I promise you'll learn something about yourself.

    1. I rarely get an erection.   T F

    2. If I ever do get an erection, I usually don't notice it.   T F

    3. If I do notice it, I don't do anything about it and it goes away soon.   T F

    4. If it doesn't go away, I simply shrug and whistle a happy tune.   T F

    5. Sensuality repels me.   T F

    6. My interest in women is spiritual, not physical.   T F

    7. If a beautiful woman asked me to make love to her, I'd call the police.   T F

    8. If the police were busy and she were pushy, I'd run away. T F

    9. If she ran after me, I'd scream for my mommy and hide. T F

    10. Every day, in every way, I'm growing less and less lecherous.   T F

Let's call this the Universal Male Lechery Test. Were you honest in your answers? How many "false" responses did you give? Ten for ten? I'd bet you came close to that number. I know you did.

Now let's try an experiment. Please take the Lechery Test again. Only this time, answer it as if you were going to hand it in to a committee composed of (A) your spouse or significant other; (B) the governing board of the National Organization for Women; (C) a group of religious leaders from your community.

Finished? How many of you scored a large number of "false" responses this time? May I see a show of hands? Why don't I see any hands? Well, then, let me ask it this way: How many of you reversed yourselves and scored mostly "true" responses? I can't believe it. Most of you changed your answers? You were afraid of going public with your lechery?

Don't worry, *amigos*. It's happened to all of us. We're afraid of the L word. Call us lechers and we shrivel up and die a little. We feel defenseless against that charge, so when it's leveled against us, we lie and duck and cheat. "Who, me? Lecherous? Not on your life."

That describes the past quarter century of male life in this culture. It's a hell of a way to live, isn't it? Why are we so fearful of the L word? Why have we chosen to deny our basic makeup?

There are two reasons: (A) the powerful nature of our sexuality, powerful from our childhood years; (B) the feminist and fundamentalist attack upon that nature.

Let's face it, we're a horny bunch of guys. A wonderful, vigorous, amazing sexual force comes into our lives at an early age. We can't hide from our own hard-ons—not that we'd want to—but we're also confused by them. The signals we get from many directions are antisexual. The New Puritans imply that our aggressive sexuality makes us rapists and pillagers by definition. That's a heavy charge, and it hurts us. So here's this new gift, this warm glory, this beautiful force, yet the message we get from the culture cuts against it, diminishes it, suggests it's evil.

The male experience of early sexuality is inherently a happy one, however. We love the new toy we've found. We play with it and pamper it. We like our bodies. Very few shameful signals come from within us. We stare across the schoolyard at recess and ask ourselves how girls can be so naïve, so protected, so unsexed. We tell one another jokes while they skip rope. We yearn for them while they giggle and dream. Our horniness is obvious; our needs are great. We lust and fantasize and masturbate—yet through all this early development, we hear a subterranean symphony of shaming that continues through our lives. We are, we're told, monstrous and unsociable in our sexuality.

Consider the fuss made during Jimmy Carter's Presidential campaign—over his remark that he had lust in his heart. Or consider the recent persecution and assassination of Gary Hart. "GARY HART, BEDEVILED BY DEMONS," one headline read. Lives there a man with soul so dead who couldn't list and identify those demons? Do we not shiver just a little when we hear the knives being sharpened for Hart as the L word is branded on his forehead?

Try this: "Under the sway of his sensual passion, and when conquest and possession were the issue, he could be very intense, according to confidants of several of his partners. But once the passion was consumed, the fantasy fulfilled, and the specter of the start of a relationship reared its head, Hart would shrink back and—clang!—that inner steel door between his two selves would slam shut." That's Gail Sheehy writing an analysis of Hart in *Vanity Fair*. I have to wonder as I read that paragraph if it doesn't describe a major dynamic in the male psyche—a dynamic that is natural and self-protective, not demonic and dark.

One day soon, gentlemen, we'd better stand up and cheer for our nature. We'd better take the Universal Male Lechery Test and mark it honestly and hand it in to that committee with pride. "This is how we are," we'll say. "Now deal with us instead of trying to condemn us. And clean up your own house before you come over and criticize ours."

Oh, yes, that reminds me: After Gary Hart's appearance on *Nightline* this past September, a friend of mine called me from Washington, D.C. "That guy gives me the creeps," she said. "He makes me gag. I wouldn't trust him for a minute. And boy, oh, boy, do I feel sorry for his wife. Why does she take that shit? If I were her, I'd throw him out of the house."

I listened, but I didn't say much. How could I? I was too busy laughing. Only three months earlier, my friend had been on the phone to me describing her latest affair, one that her husband didn't know about.

You don't suppose we should construct a Universal Female Lechery Test, do you? You don't suppose women go clang! too? They don't have problems with intimacy or sexuality, do they? None of the women candidates who've run for various political offices have ever slept around, have they?

Hey, I'm just a dumb, lecherous guy, and I'm only asking.

(1988)

Feminist U————————————————

Read the catalog of any self-respecting university these days and you'll find a women's-studies program in full flower—lots of courses, lots of teachers, heavy enrollments. Clearly, the college students of today can find out all they ever wanted to know about the history of women and feminism, and they can do so for credit. That is all well and good, but read the same catalogs in search of equivalent programs in men's studies and you will be sharply disappointed. Men's studies simply do not exist in any meaningful fashion in the academic environment of this country.

A good friend of mine attends Dartmouth. She sent me the college catalog and the brochure that advertises a vigorous women-studies program. Two women cochair the program and women make up about 80 percent of its faculty. As a student at Dartmouth, here are just some of the courses you can take: Women in Africa; Women in China; Women in Russia; Women in Myth; Women in Classical Literature; Women in Modern Europe 1750–1950; Women, Economic Development and Social Change; Women and the Tragic in French Literature; Telling Their Own Lives: Women and Autobiography; The Aesthetics of Female Writing; The History and Theory of Feminism; Women and Culture; Women in the Past: A

Historical and Literary Perspective; The Second X: The Biological Woman; Women and Change in the Third World; The Educated Woman; Childhood and Revolt; Sex, Sin and Grace: Can There Be a Feminist Theology?; Mistress, Muse or Maiden?

There are also special seminars for advanced credit in women's studies, and there have been several conferences with titles such as The First Decade: Feminist Studies at Dartmouth and The Gender Gap in the 1984 Elections. A student can obtain a special certificate in women's studies. Again, there is no men's-studies program on campus. None.

"I went to the the admissions office and asked for the brochure on women's studies," my friend reported. "The woman behind the desk was glad to give it to me. 'Is there a program in men's studies?' I asked her. 'Excuse me?' she asked. She looked very irritated. 'Is there an equivalent men's-studies program?' I asked again. 'No! Never!' she said. 'Not in my time here!' Then she backed off a little. 'Although I suppose if some liberals start asking for it, we may have to do something.' She really didn't like my question. I'm sure it was the first time it had ever been asked."

Why this monopoly of feminist thought on today's college campuses? What's happening here? It's obvious—and generally unmentioned in college classrooms or in national debate. Sexism takes many forms, and today's academic feminism is one of the most virulent. Equal and independent men's-studies programs are *verboten*. They have not been considered much and they still are not allowed. The feminist arguments against them are prejudiced and cavalier, but who's surprised? Feminism is living today on its excesses: Men, you will hear, have controlled all of academia since time began, and now it's women's turn; men are the oppressors who wrote all the books and interpreted all the history and there is no reason to give them even more power and priority; men, the poor fools, are not as worthy of study as women are.

Whatever the excuses and arguments for this academic blindness, they are basically arguments against a body of thought and study, obstacles to a complete education. Sooner or later, they will have to fall, but I'm sorry to report that it looks as though it will be later, not sooner. Monopolies do not crumble overnight, and some college men are having more than enough trouble simply surviving the women's-studies courses they sometimes take.

"CHALLENGE IN WOMEN'S COURSE ROILS UNIVERSITY OF WASH-INGTON CAMPUS" read a headline in the *New York Times* last April. It profiled the problems of 22-year-old Pete Schaub, a senior at the University of Washington in Seattle who had enrolled in an introductory class in women's studies. Schaub was asked by his instructors to withdraw from the course after he repeatedly challenged the feminist assumptions he heard in class. He was eventually reinstated but with an interesting limitation that should make any educational institution blush—he was told by associate dean James Nason not to attend the class after readmittance. "Mr. Nason said he thought it would be best for the class," the article reports.

"'From the first day on, they started in about how all men are wife beaters and child molesters and how the traditional American family, with a mom and a dad, doesn't work,' Mr. Schaub, a business major, said. 'You read the course description and they say the class is supposed to foster "vigorous, open inquiry" into all issues regarding women, but then they classified everything I had to say as racist or sexist. Where's the freedom of inquiry?'"

The answer to Schaub's question is that by definition, there is no freedom of inquiry concerning men's issues today in our colleges and universities. This nation's curriculum in gender studies is skewed in favor of women's issues alone—and as long as it has that bias, it will continue to remain captive.

Once, I was a tenured professor at a major state university, I had a lifetime job if I wanted it. I resigned that position for a number of reasons, and one had to do with my disaffection for university life. It seemed constrictive, without much risk, even dull. I loved teaching in the classroom, and I was good at it, but I found the university bureaucracy impenetrable and the opportunities for establishing new courses and new ways of looking at things extremely limited.

I'm saying this because I know how difficult it is going to be to establish valid, independent, exciting men's-studies programs at the university level. Feminists *are* the establishment for gender issues on many campuses, and their arguments against men's studies are well practiced and refined. But nothing is more needed right now than that addition to the college catalogs. We could then study one another equally—learn, debate, surprise ourselves, thrive.

It's worth a try.

(1988)

The Class of 1992 _____

Welcome to college, gentlemen. I assume you have the only three skills necessary to profit from the education you are about to receive: (1) You know how to tap a beer keg; (2) you know where to buy condoms; and (3) you know how to sleep in class with your eyes open and a smile on your face.

Anything else? Well, it helps to know where the bookstore and the library are. You may have to take your parents by them on Parents Day. And don't forget the golden rule of every college student: Ask for money from home *before* your first semester's grades are posted.

OK, it's been a long summer, you miss your high school friends, you wonder how you ended up at a university that seems to be little more than a huge commercial enterprise and you're lusting after several women on campus who have little interest in you. Welcome to the world of the college freshman. You are not alone. Soon you'll have a new crew of friends, people who will be your compatriots for life. Be patient. It will happen.

While you're sitting around, sipping your suds and reading this edition of *Playboy*, check out last month's "Men" column. It's called "Feminist U" and it applies directly to you and your new world. In it, I talked about the proliferation of women's-studies programs on the

196

college campuses of America, a phenomenon of the past two decades of feminist activism.

As an example, I listed some of the women's-studies courses a student could take at Dartmouth (Women in China, Women in Africa, Women in Myth, etc). I suggested that no equivalent series of courses for men could be found in the Dartmouth catalog—and I noted that this was the standard situation on our college campuses at the present time. Men's-studies programs equal in rank, stature and budget to current women's-studies programs are nonexistent today.

"Why this monopoly of feminist thought on today's college campuses?" I asked. "It's obvious—and generally unmentioned in classrooms or in national debate. Sexism takes many forms, and today's academic feminism is one of the most virulent."

What does this have to do with you? Everything. You're being denied an education about yourself. Worse, you're living in a culture that assumes you have no problems worth examining. So your assignment, gentlemen (and fair-minded ladies) of the class of 1992, is to improve the impoverished condition of your university's course offerings. You have four years to work on it, but I hope you get started now. Men's studies is a worthy idea.

To help you along, here are some suggestions for some courses that might constitute the beginnings of a viable men's-studies program. Use what you can, forget the rest, add your own. Just give the idea some thought, then translate that thought into action. If you do, I promise you this much: You'll have an interesting four years. No topic provokes more heated discussion, none is more sensitive at this time than the question of male and female roles in our society. If you argue that the men deserve an independent program of their own, you'll catch some flak. But if by 1992 you've helped balance the curriculum of your school, you will graduate with the sense that you've done more than just drink beer and go through the motions of getting an education. Try it. You'll like it.

Proposed men's-studies courses:

The Biological Male: A study of male physiology, the athletic male, male health problems, the nature of aging, questions of male longevity and ways to increase it.

Fathers, Mothers, Siblings: The male's relationship with his family, burdens and opportunities, patterns of love and resentment, creativity and destruction.

Male Sexuality: The psychological and physiological elements of sexuality, differences between male and female sexuality, an examination of homosexuality and homophobia.

Men and the Law: Questions of divorce, child custody, property settlements, cohabitation agreements, the military draft, men in prison, the death penalty, abortion, date rape, sexual harassment.

Role Models: Biographies of representative men, with a focus on role modeling as a major learning experience; each student in this course writes an autobiography.

Contemporary Feminism: The feminist movement from a male perspective: its history, its value and usefulness, its excesses and how to deal with them.

Hero/Antihero: How men are portrayed in literature, drama and film and the expectations produced by those portrayals.

TV, Advertising and the American Male: The cultural suppositions behind the images we are fed, the devices used to manipulate us, the differing images of the male.

Fathering: A "how-to" course, including a historical and sociological perspective, from prenatal care to relationships with adult sons and daughters.

Pornography/Erotica: A study of differences in male and female perceptions of sexual excitement, also focusing on issues concerning pornography and the First Amendment.

The Myths Men Make: Issues of self-perception and identity, how men motivate themselves, what they notice, hear, see, remember (and what they don't), ways of self-improvement.

History of the Common Man: Not the usual study of the campaigns of Napoleon or the decisions of American Presidents but a history of the unnoticed man.

Men and War: The history of the male in any society is often the history of men in combat; a study of war and its impact on all men.

Gender Studies: This is the biggie, the seminar that should cap both the men's and the women's-studies programs; in it, you draw from all you've learned about yourself and the opposite sex, and you practice problem solving on a group basis.

That's a start. It gives you some ideas to take to the dean. I wish you luck. Now tap that keg, smile that smile and may the sleep you get in class be peaceful.

(1988)

A Cultural Lynching⎯⎯⎯⎯⎯⎯⎯⎯⎯⎯

This column is dedicated to William Kennedy Smith, whatever happens to his indictment for rape in Palm Beach, Florida. It is early June, and the safe thing would be for me to wait until all the facts are in before I write about Senator Ted Kennedy's nephew. But I believe we should talk about his predicament right now.

As I see it, Smith is already as much a victim in this case as his accuser claims to be. What has happened so far to Smith is nothing short of a cultural lynching. In the media, in the gossip of the day, in the public statements of people who claim to be experts, Smith has been named, accused, pictured (and what a photograph at first!), analyzed, charged, convicted, jailed—and hanged by a lynch mob from the highest tree.

Smith's guilt has been assumed in most of the talk so far. Rarely has he been referred to as an *alleged* rapist; he is simply *the* rapist. And now there is something worse: NBC's *Hard Copy* has done a show that, while consistently referring to the *alleged* rape, gave me the impression that Connecticut police are interested in evidence gathered at the Palm Beach scene in regard to the sex murder of a 15-year-old girl in 1975. That strange and insidious half hour of air time has silenced all but the hardiest of his defenders.

The treatment that Smith has received by the public should be chilling to us all. What has happened to him from the beginning of the investigation has very ominous implications for every man in America. Whatever the technical charge, I see this as an instance of possible date rape, and it therefore touches us all. Think about it for a minute: *It could happen to you.*

Remember this, good reader, and conduct yourself accordingly: All it takes to lynch a man these days is the *accusation* of rape. At that moment, the male so accused is considered guilty in the court of public opinion. At that moment, before any indictment, before any fair or reasonable investigation or trial, a man's reputation is shattered and his future is at risk.

Once accused, the male in America becomes fair game for all those people who think deeply about the rights of women but who couldn't care less about the rights of men. (Indeed, in many circles, a mention of "the rights of men" invokes a cynical chuckle.)

What is even more threatening to men today is this: Project a trend line of popular attitudes about date rape into the twenty-first century, and it appears that every American male who wants to have a social life will live with the possibility of sexual blackmail.

Here is the scenario: Whimsically, angrily, justifiably or not, any anonymous woman can destroy a man's good standing in his community by pointing her finger and naming him as a date rapist. In Smith's case, his accuser remained anonymous to the American public for two weeks and no purpose would be served by naming her here before the trial. When she was finally named, long after Smith's face and name had been smeared across the newspapers and TV screens and magazines of this country, there were great debates about her rights to privacy. There were few, if any, about Smith's rights to privacy. Indeed, the cultural assumption is that a man accused of date rape has no rights of privacy.

The trend in this complicated arena of sexual politics is definitely against us, gentlemen. A lynch mob could be just outside your door. In William Kennedy Smith's case, a lynch mob has already placed the rope around his neck.

Let's face the facts: As men, we are a political and demographic minority—and not a very popular or respected one in certain sections of our culture. The image of the male as inherently evil has been pounded into the American psyche for decades. Hannibal Lecter lives. So we had better take note of this cultural dynamic and do something about it. A few suggestions:

1. The stigma attached to a male who is accused of date rape is just as severe as the stigma attached to the accuser who has charged the man with sexual assault—if not more so. It is extremely harmful to be called an oppressor and an attacker and a rapist. Could we have recognition of that fact in the media?

2. Neither the name of the accuser nor the name of the accused should be published when the accusation is made. If an indictment is handed down, then both names can be made public.

3. The charge of date rape is, by definition, more complex than that of brutal rape by an unknown assailant. Until an investigation has been made, and until both the accused and the accuser have had a chance to face each other in court, date rape should be the phrase used in describing the accusations.

4. More than ever before, men need to educate themselves about the law and its applications to their issues. More than ever before, the only thing that stands between men and a lynch mob in this tricky area of date rape is the law itself. We cannot count on the media and the public to treat us fairly if we are accused of date rape.

5. As risky as it may seem to you, and as unpopular as it may make you in certain circles, it is your job to argue the case for men's rights in the date-rape debate. Don't sit silently by when people suggest that only the accuser feels traumatized, only the accuser has rights. Once again, someday *it could happen to you!*

6. Finally, we live in an environment of antimale sexism and prejudice. You'd do well to remember that image of us and be careful out there.

William Kennedy Smith, if the courts of law find you guilty of rape, then you deserve appropriate legal punishment. Rape is a terrible crime. But let it also be stated on the record that you were lynched early, and lynched well, before you had a chance to defend yourself.

(1991)

*Johnny Wadd Lives!*_____

The king is dead, long live the king. John C. Holmes, a.k.a. Johnny Wadd, died March 12, 1988. A lot of men took note of his obituary. It is rumored that he died of AIDS brought on by a bad drug habit and the sharing of I.V. needles. "His death was not the result of the excesses of sex but of the excesses of drugs," said Bill Margold, a former porn actor and longtime associate of Holmes's. "The result of a whole series of abuses to his body in one way or another."

No doubt, the man abused his body, but in some wonderful way, Holmes was a universal male role model. He is a man we're going to miss, the guy who lived out our fantasies on camera, the man who brought a smile to our faces and helped us pretend we were superlovers all, gigantic and invincible. The king may be physically dead, but for most of us, he lives on in our imaginations as a symbol of enjoyment and virility. The puritans in this culture will scold us for that, but it's true: Johnny Wadd is a vital part of male history and psychology, and to us, he's as famous as any movie star.

Holmes starred in thousands of heterosexual sex films, most of them "loops," ten-minute specials made for exhibition in movie machines in adult bookstores. He claimed that he had had 14,000 women as sexual partners. By rough calculation, that means he made love to an average of 460 women per year, assuming he started his magnificent career at the age of 13.

I don't know how to tell you this, Ms. America, but in our heart of hearts, most men chuckle at such a thought. In fact, if God Himself came down and spoke to most 13-year-old males and said, "Son, I have good news and bad news: The good news is that you will be allowed to have sex with several hundred attractive women per year; the bad news is that you'll die at the age of 43. Care to go for it?" I am here to tell you that most of those 13-year-olds would be stuck for an answer. They would debate that one, I guarantee it. That may irritate you, Ms. America, but it's an accurate description of who we are as men—horny little fuckers from an early age.

Holmes was a scrawny white guy with an enormous schlong that was reported to be 14 inches long. In the simple, primitive male consciousness, a bodacious tool is an object of respect and glory. We do salute it, yes, indeed, and in that salute, there's a tinge of wishful thinking. I know I always wished I could borrow Holmes's dick for a weekend—not for myself, of course, because I'm hung like a horse and have no sexual insecurities at all—but I have a couple of buddies who are uncertain of their sexual appeal and could use some help.

The typical Johnny Wadd film was a compendium of male fantasies. The early loops had no sound track and involved straightforward fucking without many preliminaries. They were amazing, really amazing. Johnny didn't have to talk a good game or pay penance for years or go out for dinner and dancing or buy jewels and precious gems before he could get it on. There were no tests or trials, no criticisms or rejections. It was sex sans bullshit, a condition to which, in fantasy, many men could relate. An attractive woman would greet Johnny in an apartment, at a swimming pool, on the beach, wherever, and within seconds, he would be under tender assault, his fly unzipped, Mr. Happy springing to attention under the caresses and oral ministrations of his partner for the moment. The lovemaking would be rigorous, uncomplicated, joyful, and the positions chosen were often surprising and educational. Usually, the loop ended with a blow job, a copious come shot, a sedated Johnny Wadd, a worshipful, supposedly satisfied woman smiling at him through his sperm. Typical male fantasies, as I said, and for those women reading this who are saying, "Yukky, gross, yukky," I have no apologies. That is the way we are, and no amount of disapproval is going to change us. We are the simpletons of sex, and proud of it.

Seka, Aunt Peg and a host of other women appeared with Johnny and seemed to enjoy his presence, but insiders say he was basically a loner off the set. "He was virtually friendless by his own decision," Margold said. That loneliness was undoubtedly exaggerated by a fierce marijuana-and-cocaine habit that led him into debt and violence. He was linked to an infamous murder case, spent time in jail after refusing to testify, found his own career starting to deteriorate, ran into severe health problems and died a difficult death. Not exactly an advertisement for a life of sex and sensation, I know, but that's not the point. Here we are celebrating his memory, his decency on camera, the humor and gentleness he frequently displayed while making love.

"I would love to be able to sit back and drive a truck and be a nine-to-five guy like everybody else and forget everything that's ever happened," he told his ex-wife.

Well, maybe. But I've driven a truck for a living and hauled freight and furniture through Iowa and Illinois and put in some long hours on the loading dock, and I'm not convinced that Holmes would have truly enjoyed that life. He found his line of work and performed well in it.

There is a potential porn star in every man, and most of us are envious, in some secret way, of the little dude with the big enchilada who got to play for pay. I guess I've always been confused by concepts of pornography in film and TV. I've never understood why lovemaking is banned and killing is exalted. I've never comprehended why murder—from *Murder, She Wrote* to *The Godfather*—is considered an innocuous subject, while sexuality in its most unrestrained forms is kept under wraps. For me, Johnny Wadd was a far more honorable actor than all those hunks who play detective and mobster and commando and sheriff and kill people with icy abandon.

Here's to you, Johnny Wadd. You taught me some things about sex, you made it look pleasant, you seemed to care for your partners and you seemed to be able to laugh at yourself and not take anything too seriously. Thanks for the memories.

(1988)

Ripped-Off Mozart

They're taking away our role models. In movies, books and television shows, men are being trivialized, and the message is this: You guys are mostly dumb, frivolous, awkward and mouselike—and if you don't agree with that, you're sexist.

You've seen *Amadeus*, right? That's the film about the gifted but infantile composer who giggled like an idiot and then died of indigestion. Great vision of Mozart? The way you always thought of him? Peter Shaffer called his screenplay for *Amadeus* "a fantasia based on fact. It is *not* a screen biography of Mozart and was never intended to be."

That disclaimer doesn't do it. Most people viewing *Amadeus* think they're seeing the real Mozart, and as they leave the theater, they have to be wondering how such an imbecile could produce such a good sound track.

The Mozart I know about was a man of infinite variety and great strength. He was a playful man, no question about that. He was also vigorous and direct, and his music was a concrete and vivid reflection of his energy, talent and perception.

Take one day from Mozart's life. He wrote to his wife about his schedule: He rose at five A.M., and took a long walk, treated himself

205

to some cutlets (*"che gusto!"*), played two rounds of billiards, sent for black coffee, smoked "a splendid pipe of tobacco," quickly orchestrated the third movement of the *Clarinet Concerto*, dined on "a delicious slice of sturgeon" and other delicacies, and then, since he had "a rather voracious appetite," sent his valet back for seconds.

This is the same Mozart who was bled of two to three quarts of blood during the last 12 days of his life, yet had the strength to stand up and rehearse his *Requiem* ten hours before he died.

Not a giggling, bawling jerk, in other words, but a man who led a varied and difficult life and who met his many challenges bravely.

Why didn't we see that Mozart?

The fast answer to that is simple: He wouldn't sell. The handle, the gimmick, the trick these days is to make a mockery of any male whose life goes beyond the narrow range of wussie and wimp. *Amadeus* is the perfect vehicle for the Eighties—the greatest composer of all time wasn't a man, he was a mouse. It's the message this culture seems to want to hear.

Meanwhile, of course, Diane Keaton and Sally Field and Sissy Spacek have been busy playing cinematic superwomen, none of whom giggles inanely or loses self-control at a moment's notice. Women, we're being told, have their shit together. Men never have. Not even the best and most creative of them.

Men are disappearing nowhere more obviously than in contemporary fiction. Find a novel that is not a spy or detective story and you're likely to find a feminist tract. Women form the bulk of today's literary consumers, we're told. Why shouldn't they? The standard novel of the Seventies and Eighties describes a brave but lonely woman who discovers that there's life after men. Or should that read "after mice"?

Example: "He was still handsome . . . but the beauty had something desiccated about it, like a dried flower. . . . He was a slim, proud-looking man, more delicately built than his sister. He should have been the girl and she the boy."

That is a description of Julian DeVane, the most prominent male in Gail Godwin's latest novel, *The Finishing School*. Julian, poor mouse, will go on to kill himself at the end of the book, but who's surprised? It's obvious he won't be able to hack it. Here's how he plays the piano: "His eyes were almost closed, and he touched the keys with a slight restraint; he looked as though he had sent himself into some other realm and had to be careful not be swallowed up by it. . . . Several times Julian hummed aloud, or emitted abrupt, guttural sounds as he played."

Well, at least he doesn't giggle.

When the next editor you meet laments the fact that men are not buying novels the way they used to, you might ask why they should. So they can watch themselves being annihilated? Or you might ask that editor what it's like to be male and walk into a bookstore these days. Usually you're greeted with shelves of feminist fiction, and then you turn around to face the special section on women's issues. It's a double whammy, and it proves that publishing's matriarchy is alive and well. Men sense that and stay away.

What's going on? It has to do with money, among other things. The feminist audience is the largest, the most easily identifiable, the one most clearly on the ascendancy. Women now constitute a significant portion of the work force, and their search for role models has been given top billing. Turn on your TV and you'll see what I mean.

P. J. Bednarski, former television critic for the *Chicago Sun-Times*, wrote recently about male roles in the TV wasteland: "Something has happened to the TV Guy. Some things have been surgically removed from men: brains and spines and morals and scruples.... Men are the old Women on TV. Ornamental. Subservient. Dullwitted. And most often, very good-looking." Bednarski goes on to cite examples of dumb guys we're all supposed to laugh at: Ted Danson and the late Nicholas Colasanto in *Cheers*, Tom Poston in *Newhart*, Thom Bray in *Riptide*, Pierce Brosnan in *Remington Steele*, John Ritter in *Three's a Crowd*, John Forsythe in *Dynasty*, Tony Danza in *Who's the Boss*— the list goes on.

The trivialization of the male today is conscious manipulation of our national psyche to create and then please a market. The money people doing this have no real understanding of who men are. Nor do they seem to care.

It's time for some new bumper stickers. How about MOZART WAS A MENSCH, NOT A MOUSE? Or FREE TED DANSON? Or TAKE BACK THE CULTURE?

Honk if you agree.

(1985)

Naked at Gender Gap_____

The headline caught my eye: "STUDY: BOYS' FANTASIES MORE OUT-LANDISH THAN GIRLS'." Oh, no, I said to myself. If the world figures out that we men are in reverie much of the time, that fantasy is as central to our lives as breathing, what secrets will we have left?

Fortunately, that article had its limits. It described a study that had been conducted by Malcolm Watson of Brandeis University. Under the auspices of the National Institute of Mental Health, he had examined the fantasies of 45 youngsters at a day-care center. What he found will not surprise any of the men I know. But I think I can speak for all of them when I say that I'm glad that Watson confined his research to boys and did not go on to discover that men are no different.

"Little boys pass as much as a quarter of their playtime fantasizing spaceship rides, ray-gun duels and other outlandish adventures," the article said, "while girls are far less likely to act out unrealistic escapades."

Big news. Who's surprised? I'm not, and neither is my spaceship. I take a ride every day. I used to go behind the moon and over to Mars, but recently I've been trying to get out to the edges of the universe, because that's the territory that truly fascinates me. Usually I have a partner on my space explorations. Usually its Debra Winger. Sometimes it's Goldie Hawn. OK, once in a while it's Seka, but I certainly wouldn't admit that publicly. Our trips are very nice, though fraught with danger. Often I have to climb into my space suit and repair the magvite magtrometer on the external computer gyroscope. This is dangerous and difficult work, but boy oh boy, do I get rewarded when I'm safely back in the ship. Those women are glad to see me. All three of them. They ask what they can do for me and I show them.

Watson found that "bizarre, often combative, daydreams filled with magic and the supernatural are the almost exclusive domain of little boys.... Sometimes preschool boys pretend they are spies and superheroes.... Woven through these illusions are conflicts between good guys and bad guys."

Did you hear that? "Illusions." Who the hell does Malcolm Watson think he is? Illusions? Listen, just yesterday, I was in Berlin, OK? It was 1939. I was a newspaper reporter. Look, if you're going to mock me, just stop reading this right now, all right? Because this really happened. I was in Berlin and Goebbels was pissed off at me because of my dispatches to the *Chicago Daily News*. A beautiful blonde who looked a lot like Goldie Hawn had given me information that there were concentration camps outside Munich, and I had sneaked through the forest and photographed the barracks and the crematoriums and then had gone back to my hotel to write about them. That series had won the Pulitzer Prize, and Hitler was furious. After Goebbels chewed me out, Hitler wanted his turn. As I marched into his office, I pulled out my Xenon Laser Relativity Gun. The great thing about this gun is that you never kill anybody with it—you just send him into a deep freeze in outer space for 6,000 years. "Adolf," I said with my Humphrey Bogart smile, "there are good guys and bad guys, and guess which you are?" I disappeared him—*zap!*—like that. I stopped World War Two. Let me tell you, that blonde back in Munich was grateful.

"Girls the same age also spend lots of time pretending, but their fantasies are almost always realistic domestic dramas.... In fact, the girls studied never drifted into the unrealistic never-never land that so fascinated little boys."

There he goes again. "Never-never land." Why is it that researchers are so condescending? What do they know, anyway? Take my trip to the French Riviera a few minutes ago. I suppose that's a never-never land? I broke the bank at Monte Carlo. Seriously, I did. I started with only 50 cents and through grit, pluck and luck, I worked my way toward a small fortune. There was this big Sicilian guy at the roulette table, and I challenged him to a series of bets—pick a number, pick a color, pick any combination. Debra Winger was so nervous, she could hardly watch. Man, I was hot. We played for 16 straight hours and I won, lost, won again, lost again; and then, at dawn, with the sky the color of smoked glass, I broke the bank on one last brilliant bet. Whew, that was a close one, I suddenly realized. Debra Winger scolded me, but I could tell that she was actually very proud of my coolness under pressure. She gave me a massage and then tucked me into my bunk on our yacht.

The most dangerous part of Watson's study—the part that could show that not one of us emperors ever wears clothes—reads as follows: "Watson found the high fantasy among boys four or five years old but not toddlers who were two years or younger. 'This shows that it *increases with age...*' Watson said" (italics mine).

It is to be hoped that Watson will not continue along these lines of inquiry. This is very troublesome territory. If he proves what we men already know, and if our tendency toward fantasy is successfully exposed, we will never hear the end of it. Daydreams and night dreams are where we frequently live, but we cover our tracks by appearing busy, industrious, organized, mature. We know we're not any of those things, but we hope nobody else knows.

The answer, of course, lies with me in my secret life. I will take care of the likes of Malcolm Watson. I will deny everything. Watson and I will be debating on national TV. The whole country will be watching, and I will lie like a rug for my fellow men, claiming that real men don't fantasize, that our minds are always on our jobs. I will be triumphant and resplendent, and the issue will be put to rest.

Of course, I will also be a little sweaty, because I will have just come in from my rock concert, where my fans loved my music so much that they wouldn't let me go. Nevertheless, I will win the TV debate with Watson, and people will be impressed. George Will will shake my hand. "I always thought you were a Communist," he will say with a warm smile, "but you certainly protected the reputations of us men this evening." My arm will be hurting a little because nobody can come back with only one day's rest and pitch a perfect final world-series game for the Cubs and not feel some pain. But I will grin and bear it. And when the shouting's over and I'm walking back to my limousine, Debra Winger will hug me, Goldie Hawn will giggle, Seka will pout and I will smile.

Not just at them, either, but at my trusty spaceship, too.

(1985)

No More Reprints, Ladies _____

Three women, all good friends of mine, all people I truly respect—and each one of them suddenly announced to me *on the same day* that *Playboy* magazine is not something she can easily buy, read or share with her friends.

It is a coincidental series of confessions that leaves me just a little fatigued. I am used to hearing that *Playboy* is offensive to some people; but to these women who are also my friends? What is happening here?

To make things worse, these women are talking about the April issue of the magazine, which happens to contain both a "Men" column ("The 1991 Low-Risk Dating Kit") and an article by me titled *Call of the Wild*, which I hope people will read and take seriously.

My three friends know that *Call of the Wild* is in the April issue. They claim they want to read it, but they say that they are having problems getting to it. They do not like dealing with the nature of *Playboy* itself. To them, for various reasons, it is offensive.

For Jill, the problem is in the pictorial *Give Us a Break!* This magazine called *Playboy* went to Daytona Beach, South Padre Island and Palm Springs and took some pictures of college kids on vacation. Not to make the pictorial sound artificially innocent, there are candid

212

pictures of wet-T-shirt contests and topless coeds and beautiful, naked women—you know, all those things that most of us guys hold near and dear to our horny little hearts. But Jill is offended by the photo spread, and she says so in a phone call to me.

"I open the magazine, and what do I see? There is a girl with a sign on her that says, I SUCK DICK. I'm telling you, it made me sick. I had to close the magazine and put it away. I couldn't read your article, Ace."

Now, when people I know and trust are offended by *Playboy*, I am a little surprised. It has been published for almost 40 years, and the legal record is clear: *Playboy* has never once been judged—in any jurisdiction, at any time—to be obscene or in violation of any Federal, state or local law. As Burton Joseph, special counsel to the magazine, wrote not long ago, "First Amendment jurisprudence, the integrity of the magazine and the good judgment of judges and juries have always vindicated *Playboy*."

So I have this problem. I want Jill to read my article, but I also know that by her standards of taste and decorum, she cannot bring herself to open the magazine again.

"Look, I've already got some reprints of the article," I say in my dumb and helpful way. "Text only, no pictures, just black print on a white page, OK? You want me to send a reprint of *Call of the Wild* to you?"

"That would be nice," she says. She is pleased.

"OK," I say. "Consider it done."

After talking with Jill, I look at *Give Us a Break!* I cannot remember seeing a woman with the I SUCK DICK sign. Finally, I spot her. It takes an observant eye to do so. She is taking part in a body-painting contest. She has painted those supposedly offensive words on her tan belly. She looks cute and feisty and fun-loving. She is certainly not offensive to me. What's the problem?

My day is not over. After talking with Jill, I have lunch with Dana. She has been able to read my article, but she has another difficulty. She wants to show the article to the man in her life. "He should read it. He'll get a lot out of it. But I can't show him the magazine, Ace. It's too threatening to me. I'm not one of those young cuties anymore. The pictures threaten me."

"How could they? You are one of the most beautiful women I know, Dana."

"But I don't measure up to the women in that magazine," she says. "And I don't want Joe to start looking at younger women that way."

I don't say, "Dana, he's a man, so he's looking at everything all the time, anyway." I don't say, "Dana, you girls look at men a lot, too. You're just more hidden about it." And I don't say, "Dana, we're talking about pictures, not reality, and guys understand the difference." Nope. I say what I am supposed to say. "OK, I'll send you a reprint."

"That would be nice," Dana says. She is pleased.

The third time's a charm. Lorie hits me with her objections to the April issue in a phone call later that same day. "It's your 'Men' column, Ace. I hate it. You're talking about date rape and you're making a joke out of it. I won't read any magazine that makes a joke out of rape."

"I'm writing about how risky it is for men to date today, how vulnerable they are to phony charges of abuse," I say. "I try to show to what ridiculous lengths men would have to go if we were to be completely protected from false allegations of rape and harassment. You know: hire a lawyer, have a dating contract, set up surveillance, have your date sign release forms. I'm telling the male side of the date-rape story."

"I don't care. Your column is very offensive," Lorie says. "Send me a reprint if you want——"

And here, I crack. Here, I stop being the nice guy and I stand up for myself. "No way," I say. "No more reprints."

"Well," Lorie huffs, "you certainly can't expect me to read your article in that context of boobs and butts."

"I don't expect anything from anybody," I say, "but I'm not ashamed of where I publish or what I publish. Read me in the magazine or don't read me at all."

Later, there is a column by Anna Quindlen in the *New York Times* that basically trashes the April issue of *Playboy*. Several of my women friends send me copies of the Quindlen column, just to make sure I read it, I guess.

Funny, though. Quindlen never mentions my article in her critique. And, no, I won't send her a reprint.

(1991)

Part Four———————————————————

MEN, WOMEN AND FAMILY

The Decade of the Dad_____

The Nineties are upon us. Whatever else happens in the years ahead, this will be the decade in which fathers claim and take their rights. We will organize, lobby, endorse and demand. We will be a force.

In our culture, the father has *always* been seen as a dispensable item. Portrayed as either a tyrant or a wimp, prejudiced against in divorce and child-custody actions, viewed in the media as an unnecessary appendage, considered unqualified to be included in the enormous question of abortion, available to be sent to war but rarely honored and accepted in times of peace, the father in America has been toyed with and excluded, forgotten and banished, mocked and misinterpreted.

We hereby announce an official end to all discrimination against fathers. We simply refuse to take that crap any longer. The Nineties are hereby designated as The Decade of the Dad. As fathers, we know that we are vital to the healthy growth of our children and our society, and we will be trivialized and deported no longer.

The Decade of the Dad Club has certain rules and procedures. To join, you must be a father who loves his children. Contrary to popular perception, that includes almost all fathers. We really are a loving bunch. Our motto: *"Semper fidelis."* Our pledge: Come hell or high water, we will always be faithful to our children. Our mascot: the bulldog. Our symbol: the profile of a father and child, hand in hand. Our colors: blue (for our loyalty), red (for our love and energy) and gold (for the light we bring to our children).

Listed below is what I call The Father's Bill of Rights. I do not say it is complete, but it is a start. Read it, amend it, add to it or subtract from it. But whatever you do, my fellow fathers, bulldogs and friends, help us stake our claim as honorable men who deserve constant access to our kids. This is *our* decade. Let us grab it before it slips by.

THE FATHER'S BILL OF RIGHTS

Our children are our children; they are not objects for barter, ransom or withholding. By definition, this means that joint custody will be the law of the land. It means that there is no legal presumption that mother love is superior to father love. And it means that for the first time in our history, fathers will be as likely to receive child custody as mothers in divorce actions. Fathers stand for equal-opportunity parenting, nothing less. Let the courts now truly enforce that idea.

Our children are our children from conception onward. This throws a wrench into the abortion debate that has been the exclusive property of the feminists and the fundamentalists in this country, but that is as it should be. Until now, a father's rights in this thorny area have been ignored. The controversy has focused on the divine right of motherhood (and the subsequent disenfranchisement of fatherhood). "It's my body," many women say, as if the issue were thereby closed and the male who is the father had no function or rights after impregnation. It is one of the most pompous positions women take in the current sexual debate. "But there's another body inside your body," fathers want to reply, "and I have a right to at least be consulted about the fate of that body. It is mine as much as yours, and I decline to be so easily dispensed with."

We have the right to generous time with our children, and the business community had better adjust to that fact. The common corporate assumption? That a man with children should not plan to see them if he wishes to be paid and promoted. But that is a tyrannical and shortsighted view that is helping ruin the American family. Businesses should give fathers in the workplace more free time (including paternity leave, without prejudice toward those who take it) to spend with their kids. Why? Because every successful parent knows the secret of that parenting: Being there is all that is needed. Give them tough love, give them gentle love, be a saint, be an asshole, offend them, delight them; it doesn't really matter. For your children's sake, *be there* on a consistent basis. That is what they yearn for, that is what they deserve, and in this Decade of the Dad, you have the right to insist on unfettered time to do that.

If we do lose custody of our children, we still have a right to unimpeded visitation with them. The greatest story never told in this culture involves the cruelty and manipulation that some mothers engage in after divorce, behavior that is almost never treated with appropriate legal admonishment. If a father withholds child support, his wages may be garnished and he may go to jail. But if a mother plays games with visitation? Rarely will anything concrete be done about it. In the Nineties, we are going to get equal treatment under the law.

We are people who believe that the role of the father in the child's life is vital, and we are going to band together, organize and do the work necessary to guarantee our rights. If you had done nothing but listen to TV morning talk shows over the past 25 years, you would have assumed that (A) fathers were expendable and (B) women could do it all anyway. But we know that neither of those points is true. We know that the fast lane to trouble is often taken by the fatherless child, that children without fathers tend to do poorly in school and carry deep psychological scars into their later years, and we are going to do something about that. For starters, we are going to support and participate in fathers'-rights, divorce-reform and joint-custody organizations. We are going to make the effort to find out which groups are doing this kind of work in our area (most divorce lawyers can tell you, especially if they are sympathetic to the male in divorce proceedings) and we are going to join up. We will attend meetings and conferences, send money, write letters, get out the vote, help monitor courtrooms and legislatures and just generally do the dirty work that democracy expects of its concerned citizens. It is going to be a great decade.

Welcome to the club.

(1990)

Fathers and Sons_____

My father looked like Humphrey Bogart. He had about him, as did Bogart, a muted air of anger, a temper close to the surface, a thin line of steel behind the eyes that glinted when he was crossed. He was a rebellious man who sat on his wildness for the sake of his family, an alcoholic who never took a drink after I was born, a Willy Loman in a three-piece suit.

My father and I did a few things together, but we were never that comfortable with each other. That fact hurt both of us. The distance between us brought mutual pain, and it was not easy for me when my father died before that gap could be closed. Like many men—perhaps like most men—I wish I had known my father better.

History is filled with such stories: Oedipus and Hamlet, those Freudian archetypes, haunt us men more than we usually admit. We don't go around talking about it much, but the son who kills his father and the son who searches for his father's killer are often the same person, a schizoid alien balled tightly inside the male heart.

Present or absent, our fathers are a major force in shaping us, yet there are few moments when we discuss that with anyone else. It is a silent struggle. Still, we watch our fathers the way we watch mirrors, and we assume that we will be like them, come what may. I doubt that any relationship is ever more important to us.

In his autobiography, *Please Don't Shoot My Dog,* Jackie Cooper (a child movie star in the Thirties) writes of a trip he took across the country as a young man, driving his Jaguar XK120 from California to New York. Late one night, as he boomed along at 100 mph, the canvas top of the Jaguar shredded in the wind. Cooper slowed down, only to find himself caught in a severe thunderstorm. There he was, on a highway somewhere in the state of Kansas, just before dawn, getting drenched. It looked as if he had a long and uncomfortable ride ahead of him, but as fate ("or perhaps something a little stronger") would have it, there was a sign in the distance: CONVERTIBLE TOPS REPAIRED. Cooper stopped at the garage, knocked on the door and spoke to the proprietor, who very kindly said he could make a new top in a couple of hours.

The man set to work, but it was clear that he recognized Cooper. When the man asked him, Cooper smiled and said yes, he was who the man who thought he was. Cooper waited for the next request (an autograph? A picture for his kid?), but the man did not ask for those things. Instead, he pointed to a dimly lit window over the garage. "See that window there?" the man asked. "That other fellow I live with is your father."

It was a stunning moment—one that most men could relate to. Cooper writes of it: "A hundred thoughts flashed through my mind in the next few seconds as I stood there and stared at that window. Who was my father? Was it John Cooper? Was John Cooper still living? Why had he left me? Where had he been all those years I needed him? Why had he deserted my mother? And other mysteries, private mysteries I had spent a childhood wondering about."

You'll have to read the book to find out whether or not Cooper chose to see his father. But there's probably not a man alive who can't see the drama in that story. Those of us who have lost our fathers must wonder what we would do in a similar situation. If it were me, I'd bounce right up there and break the door down and give my old man a hug. We never did hug much.

The "private mysteries" that Cooper mentions are not that mysterious to us, though men are isolated creatures, unable to articulate our deeper feelings, often making the mistake of assuming that we are alone. If we ever do start talking with one another, we'll find out that we're not alone. We all yearn for the approval of our fathers. Few of us grow up with any firm sense that we have it. It may not be an exclusively male quest, this search for our father's love, but it is universally male.

I can't prove it, but I think men are going through a revolution regarding fatherhood, a revolution largely unpublicized and rarely mentioned. I think those of us with children take fathering very seriously, enjoy it, commit ourselves to it as best we can. That is not to say we always do it well, but the importance of trying to be a good father is high on our list of necessities, often higher than career or, indeed, marriage.

Men and women are exchanging roles in an ironic fashion: While women go public and establish careers, men are going private, turning toward themselves and their families, refusing promotions that require frequent moves, spending less time with peers and more time with their children, requesting child custody in divorce. Men, in short, are warming up.

On a recent *Newsweek* "Sports" page, George Gervin, star of the N.B.A.'s San Antonio Spurs, is quoted as saying, "My family is my whole life. I want to establish strong communication with my children, to give them a lot of good memories of growing up with a father who loved them and cared about them." To some folks, that may read as either self-congratulation or slick PR, but I believe Gervin. More important, I do not see him as singular or unique. He's in the mainstream of fathers now. As the outside world grows colder for men, and as we are challenged in every arena, fathering assumes more importance than ever before.

The questions arise, of course: How will my kids view me? How did I father differently from my own father? Without much to go on, have I learned to provide and nurture and define? Have I been strict when I should have been flexible?

But the major question is this: If my kids and I had been separated for years, and if they were driving across the country without knowing where I lived or what I was doing, and if fate or something stronger led them to stop by my window, would they come in to see me? Would they feel free to do that and would they think I deserved their company?

A lot of men think about things like that these days.

(1982)

The Vineyards of Vengeance⎯⎯⎯⎯⎯

This column is dedicated to every divorced father who has lost custody of his children after he sued for it. You will see that it speaks to a very dark fantasy that many of us have shared.

When a father loses custody of his children in divorce court, he feels as if they have been kidnaped. No matter how soft-spoken the judge or how slick the lawyers, it is a traumatic moment. Strangers come into the father's life and take his children away. Worse, these same strangers award custody of his children to his ex-wife—a woman he probably does not trust anymore. To the caring father, that is a violent action.

Every father knows that the numbers are stacked against him when he enters the divorce/child-custody process. Fewer than 3 percent of all children in the United States live with their fathers only (while 21.4 percent live with their mothers only and 3 percent live with neither parent). On the face of it, these numbers prove that the disenfranchised father is a common character on the American scene.

The day inevitably comes when the divorced father has to say goodbye to his kids. That is a day of maximum pain. As I turned Jim and Brendan over to my ex-wife's custody, I felt angry and gypped (to put it mildly), and I was desperately worried about their future. How

223

well would my boys fare without me? What would they think of my absence? I knew that I was qualified in every way to have at least joint custody of my children; I knew that I deserved equal treatment under the law but had not gotten it; I knew that I was a good father who spent a lot of time with his kids and loved them totally. But there they were, leaving my life for all but a few days a year (*if* visitation were honorably enforced), and it hurt like hell.

I gave my boys one last hug, and as I walked away from them, I felt as though I had just lost every claim to masculinity I ever had. I couldn't protect my kids? I didn't even have a right to live with them? Then, by definition, I was not a man. The phrase battered father occurred to me, and it fit. I was in the middle of a certain kind of violence, and I had just lost the biggest fight of my life. I was ashamed of my fears and ashamed of my loss.

As the years went by, things got worse. Internally, I was struggling with a darkness that almost overwhelmed me. It was as if I had watched a kidnaper haul my two boys into a car at gunpoint and speed away with them—and I had stood there and allowed it to happen. Born and trained for action, filled with the need to protect my sons, I had peaceably surrendered them to the system that had screwed me.

There were times when my self-image was so distorted that I was close to self-destruction. I raged inwardly at the injustice of the situation, but I still tried to be a good father from an awful distance. I paid more than my share of child support, wrote to my children and called them often, visited with them whenever I could, endured various disruptions of communications from the other side, and the pain of the loss stayed in my psyche like a chunk of hot shrapnel.

Somewhere in the lower depths of that terrible time, I had a thought. "They were kidnapped from me," I said to myself, "so I'll just kidnap them back." That idea took hold of me and became my favorite fantasy. Having been dealt with unfairly by the courts, having had my rights as a father dismissed in a cavalier fashion, having my children raised in ways that I could not tolerate, I saw no way out of my pain other than revenge.

The fantasy grew: I would show up in their town, tell them to hop into the car, and away we would go, The Three Musketeers united again and forever, wrestling and singing, laughing and joking. "Why not do it?" I kept asking myself. No one could execute a kidnaping faster or more efficiently than I could; no one could disappear more professionally if need be. After all, I reasoned, the three of us deserved to be together after so many years of cruel and unnatural separation. In one dramatic moment, I could redress my grievances, prove to my sons that I cared, show my ex-wife that I could not be muscled and ensure the safety of my boys. Such a deal!

Indeed, that is a common fantasy for many divorced fathers, it turns out. After talks with hundreds of men about this experience, I know that many of us go through the same cycle of fantasized vengeance. There are some of you out there who, as you read this, are saying, "All right, Ace, I'm going to go get my kids right now!"

I understand your eagerness. *But don't do it.* That eagerness is misplaced and that fantasy could be destructive to your children. Don't act on it. That's the message for today, as tough as it is for me to write it and you to absorb it. Don't bring even more violence and dislocation into your children's lives. Take the pain and deal with it on your own. That is your job as a man. Stay in touch with your kids, shield them from your sadness and be a great father to them every time you get the chance.

You and I have consumed the same bitter grapes, but we should remember Jeremiah's lamentation. "The fathers have eaten a sour grape, and the children's teeth are set on edge," he wrote. Think about it. How can we help our children avoid the bitterness we have been forced to consume?

It is our job as men to eat our share of the sour grapes of divorce and *not* pass them on to our children. Once the court has made its decision, it is our job to take a dive, to get fucked, to lose. Maybe one day we can get justice in the legal system. Maybe one day fathers will not be dismissible evidence. We should fight for that. But our children should not be fodder in that fight.

My sons eventually came back to live with me, and the courts had nothing to do with it. It was a natural progression. The grapes I ate were poisonous and sour, but I lived. And every grape I ate was one grape they didn't have to deal with.

You there, you good man with an intense love for your children, don't turn kidnapper. If you remain constant with your kids, they will figure it out. Listen to Jeremiah instead of that voice inside you, and you and your children will thrive! Sooner or later, you'll be united again.

(1990)

*This Day's for You, Dad*_____

Father's Day is on June 16 this year. Are you ready for it, Dad? This Father's Day will probably be a very amusing day in your life.

Take the gifts. Please.

How about that clock-radio made in Sri Lanka that will work for only a week? How about that pink-and-green bow tie, the same tie you got last year (and the year before that)? What about the pet turtle that was probably alive when it was packaged in plastic wrap and electrician's tape the night before, or the tissue box with red ribbon tied around it that is filled with free religious handouts? Let's face it: Father's Day is a funny day, and the gifts prove it.

Then there's the food. Take the food. Please.

How about that chicken that your kids just cooked on the grill? Notice how it's strangely purple inside, with tiny white worms still wriggling around in it? How about that spinach salad with silver crayon bits mixed in the salad dressing, along with small pieces of mystery meat that smell like anchovies but might be rat fat? And that Father's Day cake, isn't that neat for your teeth? The consistency of chocolate cement, right? Chocolate cement topped with sour whipped cream and rancid maraschino cherries. And how about those exploding Father's Day candles that almost put your eyes out?

Laughter? Oh, yeah. Take the Father's Day cards. Please.

They are either sappy ("To the greatest dad in all the universe from his totally adoring and appreciative kiddie-widdie-poos, with thanks for the incredible guidance and for being there for us every minute of every day") or New Age mystifying ("For Dad: I held a butterfly/by the wings at sunset/and as it struggled against the cosmos/and tore itself apart/like a helicopter/I looked at the clouds in their brief glory/and thought of you"). And, yes, the cards are sometimes brief and blunt ("Hey, Dad, fuck you!").

The bottom line? Father's Day is made for laughs, and that is as it should be.

But let's tell the Father's Day story in its entirety, gentlemen. There is another side to it, not quite so lighthearted. And it goes like this: For those of us who are fathers, Father's Day is also a day of self-examination and self-doubt, a time of secret introspection and private regrets. As fathers, we are men who have learned the hard way that fathering is a superhuman task. We know that fathering is not always a lark, and most of all, we know that sometimes we really fuck it up.

The truth is that for us, Father's Day has its share of difficult memories. Certainly, we remember our own fathers and our complex relationships with them. That's part of it, and that is tough enough. But, more important, we remember our kids and the mistakes we have made with them—the unjustified moments of anger, the impatience that rose out of fatigue, the times of insensitivity and awkwardness and absence that we would take back if we could.

I can talk myself into a funk in about five seconds if I chart the blunders I've made as a dad. And I would sign a pact with the Devil if I could be allowed to go back and do it all over again with the knowledge that I now have. In my instant replay as a father, I would never lose my temper, I would always be there for my kids and my home would be a nurturing and supportive place, a safe haven in an insane universe for two of the most treasured people in my life.

When I say this, I know that I am not alone, that I am speaking for most of the fathers in the world. We may look unaware and stupid at times, but we know what's going on. We know where we have failed.

Understand that this subject is something that we rarely discuss among ourselves. The perils of fathering? The secret sadness of Father's Day? We'd rather talk about commodity options or new cars or the odds on the Chicago Cubs' reaching the play-offs.

But I want to help us all through the darker side of Father's Day. And I want us to learn to deal with the subject in a more straightforward fashion, without the denial and guilt and remorse that can drive a wedge deeper between us and our kids.

You know, for all our faults and fuck-ups, for all our occasional absence and distance, our love for our children is immense. It is in many ways the deepest love we will ever experience. And, yes, that includes many of those fathers who have disappeared, dropped out, given up, those fathers who find themselves alone on Father's Day, who get no cards, open no gifts, have no meals cooked for them. They, too, are usually very loving.

So here you are, Dad. Some statements to carry with you on June 16.

• As a father, you have helped someone gain the gift of life, and you should be proud of that.

• No matter what the law or the culture says, you are vitally important to your child's sense of self. All kids need a father. Desperately.

• In many ways, children are better than adults. They are certainly more forgiving, no matter what their public pose. Extend a peaceful hand to a child, and that child will take it eventually.

• You are the adult in the situation, so if this Father's Day finds you isolated from your children, *it is your job to make the first move.* It is your job to see that contact between you and your kids is reestablished.

• Choose a new and more creative mind-set for yourself: Look at the past with clarity, at the future with hope, and screw the regrets.

• Do not give in to self-pity or self-censorship. Your kids need you. Whatever has happened in the past can be overcome if your love is evident to them. So show it, *amigo.*

Happy Father's Day, Dad. Now, tie that tie, eat that chicken and smile!

(1991)

Divorce: A Judge Talks_____

I wrote an article several years ago about the hazards of being male in divorce court *(Who Gets Screwed in a Divorce? I Do!*, *Playboy*, December 1978).

"If you are an American male, and if you get married," I began, "the chances are approximately one out of two that you will eventually get divorced." I went on to outline the typical male's experience in divorce at that time: If he sued for custody of his children, 96 percent of the time he would lose; he could count on paying his ex-wife's court costs and at least some of her attorney's fees; he'd probably lose his home, as well as his kids, and if debts had to be settled, he'd get the larger share of them; both alimony and child support could cut into his earnings to the point where financial reversals were inevitable.

Life after divorce wasn't exactly a ball for men, either, I reported. Rarely would anything happen to a woman who refused to grant her ex-husband visitation rights with their children, but should he withhold alimony or child-support payments in retaliation, the chances were high that he would be prosecuted and possibly sent to jail.

Those tough facts established, I went on to describe the ways men could learn to cope with divorce: how to choose a lawyer, the value of men's-rights groups, what various experts recommended for male survival, a manual of dos and don'ts for men (don't move out of your home unless ordered to by the court; do close joint checking accounts and cancel credit cards, etc.).

One of my best sources at the time was Judge Charles J. Fleck, Jr. A man who heard hundreds of divorce cases a year, Judge Fleck gave me a great quote: "I guess I'd have to admit, when it comes right down to it, that the male may be equal under the dry rubric of the law, but he probably isn't always equal in the way the divorce law is administered. Men who complain about unfair treatment frequently have legitimate complaints."

Soon after Fleck made that statement, he was appointed presiding judge for the Domestic Relations Division of the Cook County Court system. He was 38 years old then and had a reputation as a fair and imaginative magistrate.

I had lunch with him recently to ask him if that quotation still held. Charley Fleck is an attorney in private practice in Chicago now, having left the bench to make a living.

He doesn't look like a former judge. He's thin, youthful, quick in thought—the kind of guy you'd expect to see in front of the bench arguing, perhaps, but not sitting behind it. Somehow, the image doesn't fit, particularly in Chicago. He's 45, has a two-year-old daughter and a good marriage. "My family life is the most important thing to me now," he says. And as for the fate of men in divorce court?

"No matter what the law says, change comes very slowly," Fleck says. "To my mind, the courts follow society, they don't lead it. Judges don't necessarily know they have social prejudices, but they do, and there is still a strong tendency by the courts to protect women in divorce actions. They assume the male is the stronger of the two sexes and that he will survive.

"I guess I'd say that the courts may not protect women to the extent that they used to, maybe. But the tendency is still there.

"One of the reasons change comes so slowly is that unless a judge is a strong and courageous individual, it's simply easier to follow the crowd. Judges are human beings, they're often afraid of criticism by lawyers or by the bar and, like all of us, they can be afraid of offending the norm.

"The prejudice and discrimination against men are subtle and hard to prove; but they're there.

"One thing that is changing is that younger women today who are secure in their abilities in a corporate society won't ask for maintenance. They consider it an insult to do so."

I asked Fleck what advice he could offer the 30-year-old male who's considering marriage.

"I'd say this: You can't guarantee a good marriage, but there are some things you can do to protect yourself. One, make sure you're comfortable with your prospective wife's personality. Comfortable with every bit of it. Two, write up a prenuptial agreement. Make a complete disclosure of what you own and how you'll split it if the marriage falls apart. I'd even advise you to videotape the procedure or have a court reporter there at the signing. When I was on the bench, the argument was always made that the partners didn't know what they were signing. Get the evidence that they do. And don't fudge when you list your assets, or the agreement can be thrown out later."

What about men's rights in general?

"Men aren't organized and don't have the voice that women do. Women have been active for the past 15 years, but there's no male equivalent in power and stature to NOW. The men trying to draw attention to these problems are voices in the wilderness. Men should organize, if that's possible.

"In child-custody cases, which were always the toughest cases for me, you see how slowly men's rights have moved. Women are getting it both ways today. They have new rights and opportunities in society, but they're not sharing those responsibly in divorce court. There's an invidious discrimination against men, a subtle presumption that the woman will get the children.

"But the best thing we could do would be to change the system. Put funds into establishing mediation as the way divorces are settled. License mediators, use experienced personnel to talk with both parties—and, face it, both husband and wife are often out of control in a divorce—take the time to really understand the issues and the people. Arbitration, mediation, that's the way to go. That would be a more just system. And men really need that."

(1985)

You Can Call Me Mom_____

Hell, yes, I'm tough. I'm surprised you even have to ask. Have you been reading this column or not? I've been telling you for almost four years how tough I am.

I was a Marine. I killed a rattlesnake. I fought in a boxing tournament. I'm so macho my dog calls me Butch. How could you doubt that I'm tough?

Is it the apron? Don't tell me it's the apron. This is a perfectly respectable apron. I don't like the frills on it, but I have to wear an apron when I'm baking bread and making soup.

Soup? I make a great lentil soup. I empty a package of lentils into three quarts of boiling water and cook them for about half an hour. Then I throw in leeks and carrots and onions and parsley and garlic and lemon rinds and celery, lots of celery.

Bread? Cornbread, mostly—high in nutrition, easy to make, no mess afterward. I don't like to do too many dishes.

Yes, I do the dishes. You see these hands? Do you know what they did before they got tiny and red and wrinkled? Once upon a time, these hands threw hand grenades and pulled lanyards on howitzers and ripcords on parachutes. These hands became proficient in karate.

Listen, you take these hands out of dishwater for a couple of days and they look like a real man's hands.

I do windows, sure. In fact, there's not a job around the house that I don't do. I clean the cat's litterbox and do the laundry and fix a lot of meals and shop for groceries and spend time with my kids. I'm a regular Mr. Mom, and there are a lot of us out there.

That's a big secret, by the way. Most women won't agree with it, either. "A lot of Mr. Moms?" they will ask. "Just find one for me, would you? My husband won't wash his own socks, let alone the baby's diapers."

I used to buy that, but I don't anymore. I think men are making big contributions at home. And it is definitely a story you don't hear much about. Men are becoming Mr. Moms out of necessity. Between working wives and working husbands, survival depends on everyone's pitching in and doing as much as possible to keep the house going.

Maybe we should have a term for all the change we're going through. Let's call it cultural spin. Culture is, after all, a concrete thing in our lives, the culmination of all outside forces that try to shape, use, modify, exploit, entertain us. Our culture is spinning like a top, and most of us are learning ways to stay on board.

When it comes to cultural spin, men have truly been spun. In the past 20 years, almost nothing has remained constant, and nowhere is that more true than in the question of sex roles at home.

Just who is supposed to do the dishes, anyway? Who's in charge of the cleaning, the cooking, the child raising? The answers are being worked out in new forms of negotiation and compromise, but this much is certain: The home in which the husband is pampered and coddled and uninvolved with his family is a thing of the past. We're a nation of workaholics now. All of us, men and women. Maybe one day we'll understand why this has happened, but few of us will argue with the fact that it has happened and that the adjustments we're being asked to make are tremendous.

Becoming a Mr. Mom is not easy. There are few role models for the job, and we work by improvisation, learning as we go. We suck in our guts, tuck our egos into our pockets and fulfill domestic functions that our fathers would never have dreamed of fulfilling.

For those of you who are just becoming Mr. Moms, here are some household hints from a man who has been an outstanding mother in his time. Remember as you read that you are not alone, and the sooner we men admit that we're all Mr. Moms these days, the better off we'll be.

1. Even though you're fatigued, harassed and at your wit's end after a day of baby-sitting and bottle washing, do *not* use the cat's litterbox as a sandbox for your children. For one thing, they will simply splash around and spread litter all over the floor, which you will then have to sweep up.

2. Fathers undergoing the painful transition into Mr. Momism should learn playground etiquette before they take their children out to play. There are several rules: (A) Fathers should always stand by the swings and should not speak to mothers unless spoken to; (B) if your child gets into a fight by the teeter-totter and bashes some kid on the nose, do not gloat openly; say, "No, no, Daddy says no" and spank the child lightly, but don't forget to give him a sip of your beer when you get home; (C) there is a code you must learn if you are to succeed as a Mr. Mom on the playground: If an attractive mother sidles over to you and says, "I really admire men who involve themselves in child raising," what she is really saying is "This playground routine bores the crap out of me, so what'll it be, my place or yours?" Your response depends on what you want, but if you ask her, "What time does the ice-cream truck come by?" the hour she mentions will be the time her husband gets home.

3. If you find yourself lapsing into baby talk at cocktail parties ("Doesums wantums 'nother drinkums, baby poo?") or retreating to the host's bedroom to watch *Sesame Street* reruns, there's a chance you've overdosed on Mr. Momism. Don't worry. It happens to everybody sooner or later. I knew I was in trouble when I began writing the alphabet in red crayon on the kitchen walls while singing songs from *The Sound of Music*. It's just a phase. What you need at that point is my Mr. Mom Survival Kit. It includes things that will remind you that you're a full-blooded male, such as a Rambo rubber duck, a GO AHEAD, MAKE MY DAY apron made out of black parachute silk, four Heavyhands baby bottles that allow you to flex while feeding, a

year's supply of camouflage diapers, the Green Beret guerrilla-warfare coloring book and a plastic Uzi submachine gun that looks like the real thing but shoots oatmeal.
Hell, yes, you're tough.

(1985)

*Custody Is a State of Mind*_____

You're in your 30s, a professional man with an accelerating career. You're married. You have a couple of young children and a life that appears to be successful. You own your own home—well, the bank owns it, but your name is on the door—and the patterns of your family life are meaningful to you. On weekends, you barbecue in the backyard, talk with your neighbors, watch baseball on TV, take the kids to the park, trim the hedge and cut the lawn. Home is often where your heart is.

That is especially true when you think about your children. You love them without reservation. You know that love had never been defined in your life until your kids came along. They upped life's ante.

But deep in your heart, you know there is a fault line down the center of your being. You dress well, you behave maturely at work, you put on a good pose, but you know you're flawed. Your restlessness goads you. "Is this all there is to life?" you ask yourself. "Am I stuck in this rut forever?" You feel guilty that you can ask such a question. "Be happy, you dumb bastard," you scold yourself, "or you'll ruin more lives than your own."

You hate to admit it, but you and your wife have grown bored with each other. The fault line trembles, the earthquake occurs. Maybe you crack first, maybe she does, but whatever it is—infidelity, emotional cruelty, financial madness—the marriage falls apart like a doll left out in the rain. You are thrown onto a roller coaster of emotions, and as the depositions and court calls and lawyers' fees sweep over you, there are moments you'd rather be dead than put your children through the pain of divorce. I can't live with my wife and I can't live without my kids, you think. The double bind tears at you.

One of your biggest decisions will be whether or not to conduct an all-out custody fight. This much you should know: If your children are young and if your wife wants them, the odds are heavily in her favor that she will get them. How heavily? We're talking something like 95 times out of 100. The courts are reluctant to take young children away from their mothers. It's called the tender-years doctrine. Most divorced fathers have heard of it.

Like a wounded bear, you sit in court and watch the judge award custody of the children to your ex-wife. You get visitation rights: a weekend or two a month, a few weeks in the summer, special holidays sometimes. "Visitation rights?" you ask yourself. "These are my kids, too. How can I be told I'm just a visitor?" But a visitor is what you are under the law, and a *paying* visitor at that. Child support has been demanded of you, possibly alimony, certainly a change in financial status.

Most men who've been through it will tell you that nothing hurts like the loss of child custody. The state steps in and takes your children away from you. It is, somehow, a very totalitarian moment.

What follows is some advice about how to handle that situation. Believe it or not, there's life after custody loss. With planning and effort, you can stay in touch with your children. Custody, you will learn, is much more a state of mind than a condition of the law. Your kids intuitively know that. They are waiting to see whether or not you know it, too.

Five rules for the divorced father.

1. *Always pay child support.* It is not easy to send money to an ex-wife who just got the gold mine when you got the shaft. But both legally and psychologically, it is self-defeating to skip out on your child-support payments. Skipping out deprives your children of

certain necessities. It tarnishes your case in future custody action. Worst of all, it hurts you in your own eyes.

2. *Fulfill visitation rights.* If your ex-wife is vengeful, this will be a difficult chore. She will do her best to make visitation appear to be a toy that can be played with. Dates will be changed, appointments broken, last-minute crises invented. Put up with as much as you can and, if necessary, go back to court to settle her hash and reclaim your rights. But don't give up and don't avoid seeing your children. Even with the most cooperative ex-wife in the world, visitation will still be a chore. Your children will be adjusting to their new lives, and it's probable that they'll test your patience. What they are really testing is whether or not you still love them. You prove that by being with them whenever you can. It's as simple as that.

3. *Don't talk about the divorce.* During visitation, as you and your children try to get to know one another again, it will be tempting to focus on the divorce as the favorite topic of conversation. Don't do it—not even when the kids ask about it. The question "Why did you and Mommy get divorced?" is answered by "There were a lot of reasons, but they don't affect you and me. I never divorced you guys and I never will." That's what your children really want to know. If your ex-wife has filled them with her side of the story, your children will sometimes sound like Munchkins for the Prosecution, but it's your job *not* to go into a detailed defense.

4. *Don't overindulge your children.* This means that when your three-year-old points at a red Mercedes and says, "Daddy, me want!" you don't buy it. Not even if the kid cries. Not even if his mother bought a blue one as she cleaned out your joint checking account. Kids have a wonderful and greedy sense of the world, and they will prod you for all they can get. But secretly, they want you to have limits. Because that's how they learn limits.

5. *Like it or not, you're a role model, so be a good one.* Imitation is more than flattery—it's the essence of learning. Your actions and lifestyle and values will be observed and absorbed by your children, so it's your job to set the example. Kick yourself in the butt and clean up your life and stand tall for your kids as a man who has lived through divorce and come out in good shape. Who knows? Your kids may even come back to live with you one day. Mine did. I never gave up custody in my head. And my reward for that was total.

(1985)

*Dealing With Lady Macbeth*_____

The memory lingers on, years after the fact: I am driving in a modest neighborhood in Manoa Valley on the island of Oahu. There is a rainbow in the distance, as there often is in Hawaii. It is a Friday afternoon, and I am supposed to pick up my two sons, Jim and Brendan, ages eight and five, for my legal and assigned weekend's visitation with them.

I can see Brendan playing with a group of children at the end of the street. Suddenly, he breaks away from them and races toward my car. He looks frightened. He is calling my name over and over again. To this day, I can see him in detail, brave and fearful, loving and lonely. I stop the car, jump out and hug him, feel him shaking in my arms. "Where's Jim?" I ask him.

"He's with Mommy. They went away in the car this morning. Jim's not coming. Mommy said you might hurt him."

Brendan hugs me very tightly, and I simply hold him for a while without talking and wait out the lie. "Do you know I'm not going to hurt you?" I finally ask. He nods his head yes. "Do you know I would never hurt you or Jim?" He nods yes again, but he is not sure of anything at this moment.

We get into the car and go to the beach. We make sand castles, and then we wade in the warm Pacific surf. Brendan stands on my shoulders, uses me as a diving board for hours. I love it, but I miss Jim, and the pain that I feel for Brendan and for Jim—for the three of us, really—is enormous. Why can't the three of us be allowed uncontested time together? Why is visitation so often up for grabs? Why is the spirit of Lady Macbeth so alive at visitation time?

Many noncustodial fathers ask such questions. The fact is that visitation is often canceled or delayed by mothers who want revenge against their ex-husbands, mothers who are willing to use their children as pawns in a ruthless war. This is the story that is rarely told when we hear the usual reports of absentee fathers and lonely children. Sure, some fathers are irresponsible. But irresponsibility cuts both ways.

In spite of what you read and hear, most fathers do not vanish from their children's lives simply because they are selfish or unloving or cavalier. Noncustodial fathers—second-class citizens, by definition— are often driven away from their children by the heartless tactics of their ex-wives. This is a truth that should be more highly publicized as we seek ways to bring fathers back into the family dynamic.

The statistics concerning fatherless children are not encouraging: More than 21 percent of all American children live in families headed by women only. That is almost twice the percentage who did so in 1970. A study of more than 1,000 children from disrupted families (published by the University of Pennsylvania and covering representative samples nationwide from 1976 to 1987) found the following: (1) More than half the children whose fathers did not live with them had never been in their father's homes; (2) 42 percent had not seen their fathers in the previous year; (3) only 20 percent slept at their fathers' houses in a typical month; (4) only one in six saw their fathers once a week or more.

Gentlemen, it is time to tell it like it is: Our children are cherished by us, but when we lose custody of them, the biggest battle of our lives is only beginning. Visitation is tough, even under the best of circumstances, but an uncooperative or malicious ex-wife makes it almost unbearable. Nonetheless, it is our job to stay in touch with our children, no matter what the costs. They need us, we need them, and this culture is going to slide right down the tubes if we let angry mothers shut us out and shut us down.

Given all that, let this battle-scarred veteran of the visitation wars offer some suggestions for survival so you and your children can live and grow together:

1. *Be prepared for the psychological truth of visitation.* Especially at first, your children will be studying you to see if you still love them. And how do children scrutinize their noncustodial fathers? By testing their patience, by being combative and wary, by pushing the limits and daring their fathers to abandon them. Your role in all this? To endure the testing, to be patient, to set reasonable limits without letting your own tensions rule you and damage the relationship. I'm not saying all this is easy. But it is your job.

2. *The temptation to tell the kids how their mother is screwing with the visitation schedule will be great—but do not give in to it.* Your time with your children is limited and precious. The more you bitch and moan about their mother, the less credibility you will have with them. They know the two of you do not get along, so don't bore them with the details. Do not invite the image of your ex-wife into the room. Every time you do, the kids lose a little bit of you and are thrown back into the arena of divorce. Your children want to re-establish contact with *you.* Let them.

3. *Every time your ex-wife gets your attention and your anger by playing games with visitation, she has won the thing she wants. Do not give it to her.* The most effective antidote to attempted vengeance is a great big yawn. On visitation day, when you get to the house and the kids aren't there, when they seem to be afraid of you because of the stories she has fed them, when Lady Macbeth seems alive and well in your children's living room, your best tactic is to fold your arms, laugh and chant, "Boring, boring, boring." Humor deflates the meanest of intentions. And kids respond to it and are healed by it...as are fathers.

Hang in there, Dad. Your constant tenacity will be reaffirming proof of your love, and your children will thank you many times over. Through all your wonderful years together.

(1990)

The Wives Have It!_____

According to certain scholars, there is evidence that Albert Einstein's first wife was actually the genius. "My point is to say that the king had no clothes," Dr. Evan Harris Walker is quoted as saying about his research into the subject.

Einstein's first wife was named Mileva Einstein-Maric. She and Albert were married in 1904 and divorced 15 years later. Dr. Walker cites as evidence for his theory certain key phrases he gathered from correspondence between Einstein and Miss Maric in the years before Einstein published three important papers (including the one for which he won the Nobel Prize in physics in 1921).

Now, it is true that many traditional Einstein scholars scoff at Walker's investigations, but this is a blatantly feminist age in which many former kings are being stripped of their clothes (often in their very own offices and homes!). So I want to jump on Walker's feminist bandwagon in support of his theory (hey, I want to be popular with women, too, you know), and I want to go one step further and suggest that *every* male genius was actually shaped, molded and surpassed by his wife.

To prove my point, I have interviewed the wives of some famous men. Most of these women live in the Mothers, Wives and Daughters *Über Alles* feminist commune in Northern California.

"Albert? What a schmuck!" the former Mrs. Einstein said to me. She is an older woman now and she speaks vigorously but quietly. "He was impossible! He never wanted to work. He'd lie around, daydreaming, drinking beer, checking the Chicago Cubs box scores, calling his bookie. Oy vey! What could I do with him? I had these ideas about the universe, I tried to talk to him, but you know men— all they do is grunt. I'd scold him, he'd ignore me. I'd write his papers, he'd sign them, I'd send them off, he wouldn't even open the return mail unless it was from the lottery or Ed McMahon. Woody Allen called, wanted to do a movie about him, said he thought Albert was actually his natural father, presented a wonderful deal based on gross, not net, and Albert wouldn't talk with the boy. If it hadn't been for me...."

"If it hadn't been for me." That phrase resounded like an eerie echo in all my interviews with wives of famous men. Take the former Anne Hathaway, for example. She, too, is an older woman now, and she lives in the same feminist commune in California, but what she had to say about her playwright husband is amazing.

"Bill was a hopeless drunk," she reported in an Elizabethan accent. "He and Ben Jonson and Chris Marlowe used to go down to the Mermaid Tavern and drink all night. They never worked! I was shocked, absolutely shocked. 'Are you mad?' I would ask him. 'You're trying to make a living as a dramatist, the name Shakespeare finally has a little clout and can get top billing at the Globe, and yet you waste your time in bars and brothels, drinking and wenching, belching and throwing up. What am I to do with you?'"

"What *did* you do with him?" I asked.

"I wrote his plays, of course," she said to me with a sniff. "*Somebody* had to write them. If it hadn't been for me, nothing would have been produced. It was our family's only means of support, so I did it."

"You wrote *Hamlet* and *Macbeth* and *Othello?*" I asked.

"Oh, yes. All of them. Lady Macbeth was based on an absolute bitch of an actress who had her eyes on Willie."

"You're telling me that *The Tempest* and *Julius Caesar* and *Twelfth Night* were yours?"

"Yes," she said and sniffed again. "And when he died, what thanks did I get? He left me his 'second-best bed.' That was in his will. How typically, pitifully male of him, the ungrateful wretch."

But none of this can compare to my interview with the wife of Genghis Khan, supposedly the man who ruled over all and was ruled by none. His wife, Mitzi, lives in California, too, and what she has to say about him will curl your toes.

"When I met Genghis," Mitzi Khan said with some bitterness, "the guy couldn't ride a horse. As God is my witness, he would jump up on one side of the animal and then fall off on the other. What a *putz!* No ambition. No guts. He was afraid of everything when we started dating. He didn't like swords or razors, he was scared of fire, he hated loud noises, the very idea of violence made him nauseated. We're talking a serious case of momma's boy here. We're talking about an Oriental Alan Alda, the Phil Donahue of the Eastern world. Genghis the dingus, you know what I mean? If it hadn't been for me, you never would have heard of him."

"So you taught him to be ruthless and domineering and risk-taking?" I asked her.

"Nope," she said, sitting back.

"But he was all those things," I said.

She stuck her thumb toward her chest. "That was me," she said. "Genghis stayed at home. I did the real work. People thought it was him. But it was me."

"You?" I asked.

"You bet your bippie," she said. "I dressed up like him and people thought I was him. A little makeup, a false Fu Manchu mustache, a little cross-dressing, a few voice lessons—and bingo!—Mitzi Khan, emperor of the world." She stood and smiled.

I was stunned. "Wow!" I said. "I guess behind every famous man there's a more powerful woman."

"Honey," Mitzi Khan said to me, "if God had wanted men to rule the world, She would have given them courage and brains."

I agreed with her, as you knew I would.

(1990)

The Greek and Gretzky_____

I got a call from the Greek the other night. I hadn't heard from him for a couple of years—since he'd gotten married, as a matter of fact.

"Ace," he said, "we gotta talk. I mean *really* talk. I'm in trouble. Can you meet me at the restaurant tonight?"

"No problem," I said. The Greek's family, immigrants from Corfu, own a restaurant on Chicago's Halsted Street.

The Greek is slightly over 30 and slightly overweight. Today, he works as an executive for one of the biggest and best advertising firms in town. Growing up, he worked in the restaurant business with his mother and father and brothers. No matter how hard the Greek tries to be a Yuppie, there is always something a little out of sync with him. It is as if he hears at all times, somewhere in his inner ear, the surf on the beaches of Corfu, as if he will always be somewhat distracted from the workaholism of America.

Put it this way: The Greek is a rotund peg in a very square hole. He owns a BMW, but its fenders are dented and there is rust on the hood; he wears elegant suits, but they rumple as soon as he picks them up at the cleaner's; he tries to be smooth and controlled, but humor bubbles out of him like honey from a honeycomb.

"I keep having these dreams," he said as I walked into the

restaurant. He was pouring two glasses of *ouzo*. "They freak me out. I dream I'm Wayne Gretzky." He paused, as if I would understand.

"So what?" I shrugged.

"I think I'm being traded to Los Angeles. I've agreed with my wife that I'll go there. I cry at my press conference because I hate leaving Canada. It's the saddest day of my life."

"Greek, you brought me down here to tell me you dream about being Wayne Gretzky? I don't get it."

"Did you see Gretzky when he got married? Did you see that picture of him walking out of the church? He was winking, smiling, all relaxed, big thumbs-up for the crowd. It was terrible, really terrible."

"What was so terrible?" I asked. "It was a beautiful wedding. He was happy."

"You were at my wedding two years ago. Didn't I look like that?"

"Yeah. You looked really pleased."

"Exactly. I was fat, dumb and happy, right? I call it the Gretzky Syndrome now. I just figured it out. Look"—he pulled out a newspaper clipping—"see? Gretzky's smiling like a banshee."

"Agreed."

"But his wife—look at that picture of his wife. She looks grim to me, Ace, grim and determined."

"Maybe she's afraid she'll trip on her wedding gown," I said.

"That's a picture of a woman with a hidden agenda, Ace." The Greek pounded the table. "You can tell in that picture that she's got plans for Wayne. She's going to make him move to L.A."

"There's a debate about that," I said. "Pocklington says Gretzky asked to be traded. Gretzky agreed with that at first, then denied it."

"Three weeks, Ace. Three weeks and Gretzky caves in and agrees to leave Edmonton so his wife can be in Hollywood. She wins, he loses. It's as simple as that."

"That's harsh, Greek. You can't prove that."

"Maybe not, but it sure explains something to me. Us guys, we get married thinking that we're going to get laid forever. We marry for comfort. We can't see beyond the end of our dicks. But women? It's entirely different for them. They marry us to change us. A woman looks at a man the way a real-estate developer looks at a building. We're renovation projects to them. You say 'I do,' and right away, they are on your case—'Change this, change that, change your attitude, change your habits, yadda-yadda-yadda.' It's terrible."

"Yeah, you got something there, Greek," I said.

"Two years' renovation," he said, pointing to himself. "Two years and now I can't go to night games at Wrigley Field. I can't do the crossword puzzle in church, I have to presoak all the white loads before I do the wash, and if I want a night out with the guys, I have to file a flight plan. And the plants? You should see the plants. We have a sun porch that looks like Brazil. I will die in there one day. A new kind of insect that no one has ever seen before will bite me on the ass and I will die while I am watering the frigging plants on our sun porch. And I'm doing all of this to get laid! I don't get laid that often, anyway. Have I missed something, Ace? Do other guys have it better? Or is the Gretzky Syndrome universal? Tell me. Be honest. I can take it. Please. Before the insect gets me."

"OK, Greek. You've got it right. The Gretzky Syndrome exists. Guys get married. Then it hits. The honeymoon is over and the renovation begins. The bride becomes a wife/developer: 'I don't like your temper. I think you should learn some manners, I can't relate to you when you argue,' etc. So you have to learn how to subvert it. The Gretzky Syndrome can be overcome, but it takes practice."

"Tell me how!"

"You've got to be stubborn. You've got to claim your own territory. You start with socks. Dirty socks. You keep them where you've always kept them, even if it's in the freezer. You do not let her clean up your act completely. You fight to stay sloppy. And you say a pledge of allegiance every morning: 'On my honor as a man, I will not change everything for my wife, no matter what the pressure, even if she cuts my water off.' Every morning, you say that while you're holding Mr. Happy. Another thing: Talk with your buddies. Set up a Gretzky Syndrome Network. Compare notes with other married men. You'll see. Wives are out to change us the same way. Know what that is? *They want us to be very nice girls.* 'First we will have neatness and order and sweetness,' they are telling us, 'then we might have fun if you're very, very good.' That's their basic program. You have to fight it."

"But it sounds so lonely," the Greek whined.

"War is hell," I said, and the Greek laughed. Through his tears, that is.

(1988)